THE CRAFT GIN GUIDE

The Gin Distillery

David T. Smith and Ella Carr

Duncan Petersen

1st edition

123456789

Conceived, designed and produced by
Duncan Petersen Publishing Ltd,
Studio 6, 82 Silverthorne Road, Battersea, SW8 3HE

Sales representation and distribution in the UK and Ireland by
Octopus Publishing Group Ltd
Carmelite House, 50 Victoria Embankment, London EC4Y 0DZ

Copyright © Duncan Petersen Publishing Ltd 2019

Editor Eleanor Pyne
Contributors Ella Carr, Alexander Duncan, David T. Smith
Cover and layout design Nicky Collings
Maps Map Creation Ltd
Layout Eleanor Pyne
Photo credits Many of the photos were supplied by the bars and distilleries and
have been reproduced with their permission. See page 335 for other photo credits.
Front cover image: © Ballyvolane House Spirits Co.
Back cover images: © SMDSS/Shutterstock (cumin), © Diana Mower/
Shutterstock (elderflower), © Valentina Razumova/Shutterstock (juniper),
© Oliver Hoffmann/Shutterstock (cinnamon), © Sunghorn/Shutterstock
(cardamom), © Moving Moment/Shutterstock (cloves)
Editorial director Andrew Duncan

A CIP catalogue record for this book is available from the British Library

ISBN 978-0-9956803-5-7

DTP by Duncan Petersen Publishing Ltd
Printed in Bulgaria by Pulsio

Opening times were correct when we went to press but we recommend
checking the website or facebook page before visiting.

always been so popular. This introduction explains why it once went out of fashion, and of course tells the story of the gin renaissance of the past decade.

One the joys of this subject is picturing small gin makers in their tiny premises, many in kitchens, garages and sheds. We hope the many original photographs help bring this alive for you.

A brief history of gin

The word 'gin' derives from genever, Dutch for juniper. Variations of gin have been used in medicine as far back as 70 AD, when the first mention of a gin-like substance was recorded in an encyclopaedia of herbal medicine – a solution of juniper berries macerated in wine was recommended for chest ailments. Dutch physician Sylvius de Bouve is widely credited with creating the first batch of gin as we know it today, calling it genever, in the 1600s. However, genever probably existed as early as the 1500s.

Genever found its way to Britain from The Netherlands in the 17thC, during the Thirty Years' War. English soldiers had been supporting the Dutch revolt against the Catholic Philip of Spain and were given genever before battle to give them 'Dutch Courage.' It grew ever popular in Britain, largely due to William of Orange's heavy taxes and blockades on French wine and brandy. He introduced The Corn Laws (heavy taxes on imported food and grain), and tax breaks on spirits production in Britain, encouraging people to find a use for their surplus, subpar grain, and make their own spirits – genever became the logical choice as it's usually made with grain, not grape. Beer was also heavily taxed to fund the War of the Grand Alliance, making it about the same price as genever, so people wanted to try it.

Gin's notoriously bad reputation arose in the 1700s with the coronation of Queen Anne, who cancelled the 1638 charter giving The Worshipful Company of Distillers monopoly over spirit production

68. Gin Lane. Engraving by William Hogarth (3d state, 1751).

Hogarth's *Gin Lane.*

within a 21-mile radius of London. This meant they weren't able to regulate the quality of the spirits and hundreds of illegal distilleries opened. Genever appealed to the poor as, by this time, it was cheaper than beer and safer to drink than water, but that is not saying much. The produce of illegal distilleries was, by modern standards, toxic.

By the early 18thC 'genever' had been anglicized to 'gin', and half of the drinking establishments in London were bars or taverns, with more than ten million gallons of gin being produced. Over the decade following 1723, the death rate in London surpassed the birth rate, and gin played its part. People would add to gin substances like turpentine for a resinous, woody flavour, and sulphuric acid for a sweet and more intoxicating effect. Gin was blamed for low fertility rates, babies born with deformities, and mother's neglecting their children, earning it the name Mother's Ruin. One particular story about a mother strangling her child to death to sell her clothes for gin sparked outrage and pushed the government to make drastic changes. Following two unsuccessful acts, The Gin Act of 1736 was passed. This required distillers to hold a licence which cost £50 a year. It also allowed the public to buy a minimum of two gallons at a time, with a tax of £1 per gallon. The industry suffered and illegal production became difficult as informers were paid £5 to report them. Several more acts were implemented after this, which imposed higher taxes and removed licences from retailers so gin became scarce.

Selection criteria
We include bars/distilleries that offer at least one of the following:

- Customer experiences
- Local appeal
- A range of small-batch craft gins – for a definition see page 6

In the back section of the guide are other bars and distilleries that weren't right for the main section – see page 321

Gin today
On the 14th March 2009, Fairfax Hall and Sam Galsworthy launched Sipsmith, London's first traditional copper distillery since 1820, aiming to bring London Dry Gin back to its rightful birthplace. (See page 71 for a full review.) They have been credited with sparking a ginaissance, with the spirit gradually becoming one of the UK's most popular, second only to vodka. According to

The Independent, around 73 million bottles of gin were sold in 2018, with sales doubling between 2016 and 2018, and Waitrose spirit buyer, John Vine, claims it's the local and regional brands that are driving sales. With the rising popularity of craft spirits and beers, this doesn't come as much of a surprise – people want to know exactly where their products are coming from.

Some credit gin's success to the fact that it's quick and cheap to make – it doesn't need to be aged like whisky. While this may be true, there's another, rather more fascinating trend: the phenomena of millennials, and social media. Maybe it's just coincidence that Instagram was created around the same time the gin revolution took off, but could it be that Instagram had a hand in the spirit's success?

Millennials are, in marketing terms, a large target group. Nothing gets them saying 'yaas' more than a 'dank' Insta post – cue fire emojis. It's a versatile spirit – it must include juniper but, beyond that, distillers can experiment with different flavours. This has widened the market and made gins more Instagrammable. As we went to press, there had been almost six million Instagram posts with the 'gin' hashtag and almost all of them were of coloured or shimmery gins, gin cocktails, or G&Ts with bright flowers and fruit garnishes (top left).

And it's not just the spirit itself that has been given a makeover. As you'll see in this guide, a growing number of gin bars are making themselves Instagrammable (see HYDE Bar, page 307), tapping into the trend of flower walls (top right), and Shoreditch-style shabby-chic (see Martello Hall, page 80).

Gintourism is a great way to get to know a city. These are gin journeys you can follow in London, Edinburgh and Dublin.

Beefeater Gin Distillery to Mr Fogg's Gin Parlour

Begin with a tour of the Beefeater Gin Distillery – **see page 86** for more information. Tours run on the hour from 10 am to 5 pm – advanced booking required. 1 Leaving the distillery turn left, then left again on to Montford Place. 2 Continue down Kennington Road to Kennington Park. 3 Turn left and head down Kennington Park Road to Kennington tube station on your left. 4 Enter the station and take the Northern line northbound to Leicester Square. Leave using the 1 – National Galleries exit. 5 Crossing the road, turn left and continue on Charing Cross Road, turning left after Wyndham's Theatre. 6 Head straight down this road until you reach St Martin's Lane where you'll see Mr Fogg's Gin Parlour (opposite, bottom) straight ahead – **see page 74** for full review. Here, you can enjoy their afternoon 'G & Tea'. Sittings Fri-Sun 1 pm and 3.30 pm – advanced booking required.

Mr Fogg's Gin Parlour to The Distillery, Portobello Road

1 Retrace your steps back to Leicester Square tube station and take the Northern line northbound to Tottenham Court Road. 2 Change to the Central line, taking the westbound service to Notting Hill Gate where leave via the third exit (North Side – Portobello Road). 3 Turn right, then right again on to Pembridge Road where cross and continue straight, taking the first exit on the roundabout on to Kensington Park Road. 4 Cross the road and continue straight until you reach Chepstow Villas where turn right. 5 Continue on Chepstow Villas, heading straight on at the fork until you reach Portobello Road. 6 Turn left and continue on Portobello Road until you reach Blenheim Crescent. 7 Cross the road and The Distillery will be on the right – **see page 89** for review. Spend the afternoon enjoying G&Ts in GinTonica (open Tue 4 pm to 1 am and Wed-Sat 12 pm to 1 am), then move to The Resting Room (open Mon-Sat 11 am to 12 am and Sun 11 am to 11 pm), for gin cocktails and an early dinner.

The Distillery, Portobello Road to Martello Hall

1 Retrace your steps back to Notting Hill Gate tube station where take

the Central line eastbound to Liverpool Street. **2** Change here for the Overground service to London Fields. **3** Exit the station and cross the road, turning right on to Mentmore Terrace, then left down Fortescue Avenue. **4** Turn right when you reach Gransden Avenue, then left on to Lamb Lane. **5** Turn right at the fork on to Elizabeth Fry Road and continue straight, crossing Bayford Street before turning left, then right on to Bayford Mews. Martello Hall will be on your left (open Mon-Wed 10 am to 11 pm, Thu 10 am to 1 am, Fri-Sat 10 am to 3 am and Sun 12 pm to 12 am) – **see page 80** for review.

Summerhall Distillery to 56 North

Begin with a tour of the Summerhall Distillery (**see page 234** for more information – pictured opposite, bottom). Tours are held Thursday to Sunday, on the hour from 12 pm until 6 pm, and must be booked in advance. **1** Turn right out of the distillery and head up Hope Park Crescent. **2** Cross the main road (Hope Park Terrace) and head straight up Hope Park Crescent. **3** Continue as it becomes Buccleuch Street until you get to W Crosscauseway where turn right and 56 North will be on your left (open Mon-Sun 11 am to 1 am) – **see page 238** for review.

56 North to One Square

1 Retrace your steps back to Buccleuch Street, turning right on to Chapel Street. Head down Chapel Street, then turn right on to Crichton Street. **2** Take the first right between two Edinburgh University buildings then the first left. Follow the path to the end of the building and turn right then left at the university pharmacy. **3** Continue straight until you reach a T-junction, taking the right fork then follow the path to Lothian Street. **4** Turn left and continue as it becomes Teviot Place, then Lauriston Place. Head straight on until you reach Lauriston Street on the right by the Premier Inn. **5** Cross the road and head down Lauriston Street until you get to West Port where turn left and follow as it becomes Bread Street. **6** Continue until you get to Lothian Road where turn right and head straight on until you get to BrewDog bar. **7** Turn left in front of the bar and follow the path, making a slight right passed All Bar One. One Square will be on your left (open Mon-Fri 6.30 am to 1 am, and Sat-Sun 7 am To 1 am) – **see page 233** for review.

One Square to Heads and Tales

1 Retrace your steps back to Lothian Road and turn left. Continue straight until you come to a crossing where take the left turn on to Shandwick Place. **2** Turn left again to stay on Shandwick Place then continue until you reach Edinburgh gin Distillery/Heads and Tales bar on your left (Edinburgh Gin Distillery is open Mon-Sun 9.45 am to 4.45 pm, Heads and Tales bar is open Sun-Thu 5 pm to 1 am, Fri-Sat 5 pm to 3 am and Sun 5 pm to 1 am) – **see pages 228-230** for reviews.

Heads and Tales to The Jolly Botanist
1 Turn left out of Heads and Tales and head down Shandwick Place until you reach Antholl Crescent where turn left. 2 Follow Antholl Crescent to Coates Crescent where turn left and continue straight as it becomes Antholl Place. 3 When Devil's Scribe Tattoo parlour appears on your left, follow the road round to the left to the main road (Torpichen Street). 4 Cross the road and head straight down Torpichen Place until you reach Morrison Street. 5 Turn right and continue on Morrison Street until you reach The Jolly Botanist on your right (open Sun-Thu 10 am to 12 am and Fri-Sat 10 am to 1 am) – see **page 231** for review.

Celtic Whiskey Shop to Sams Bar

Begin at the Celtic Whiskey Shop on Dawson Street (open Mon-Wed 10.30 am to 8 pm, Thu 10.30 am to 9 pm, Fri-Sat 10.30 am to 8 pm and Sun 12.30 pm to 7 pm) – see page 323 for review. 1 After browsing their extensive selection of gins, leave the shop, turning left up Dawson Street. 2 Cross the road at Joshua Lane and continue straight until you reach Sams Bar on your left (open Sun-Wed 4 pm to 11.30 pm, Thu-Sat 4 pm to 2.30 am).

Sams Bar to JT Pim's

1 Turn left out of Sams Bar and head down Dawson Street until you get to Lemon Street. Turn left and continue straight until you reach Grafton Street. 2 Cross the road and turn right, then take the first left on to Johnson's Court. 3 Follow the road until you get to William Street S where cross and turn right, then immediately left down Castle Market. 4 Cross the road at Drury Street and continue straight down George's Street Arcade. 5 Turn right at South Great George's Street and continue straight, crossing the road to head down Exchequer Street. JT Pim's will come up on your right (Mon-Thu 12 pm to 11.30 pm, Fri-Sat 12 pm to 12.30 am and Sun 12 pm to 11 pm).

JT Pim's to The Bull and Castle

1 Turn right as you come out of JT Pim's and continue up South Great George's Street until you get to Dame Street where turn left. Head down Dame Street as it turns into Lord Edward Street. 2 Continue to T-junction opposite Christ Church Cathedral. 3 Turn left on to Christchurch Place and The Bull and Castle will come up on the left (open Mon-Tue 12 pm to 10 pm, Wed-Thu 12 pm to 10.30 pm, Fri-Sat 12 pm to 11 pm and Sun 12.30 pm to 10 pm).

The Bull and Castle to Street 66

1 Retrace your steps up Christchurch Place and head back down Lord Edward Street until you reach Parliament Street. 2 Turn left and continue straight until Street 66 (opposite, bottom) comes up on the left (Mon-Thu 12.30 pm to 12 am, Fri-Sat 12.30 pm to 2.30 am and Sun 12 pm to 12 am) – see page 313 for review.

Street 66 to The Gin Palace

1 Turn left out of Street 66 and continue up Parliament Street until you reach the waterfront, opposite Grattan Bridge. **2** Crossing the main road turn right, following the road to Millennium Bridge. **3** Cross the bridge then cross the road. **4** Turn right, heading down Ormond Quay Lower until you reach Liffey Street Lower where turn left. **5.** Follow the road to Middle Abbey Street where turn right and The Gin Palace Dublin will come up on your right (Sat-Thu 12 pm to 12 am, Fri 12 pm to 1 am).

Name of bar/distillery.

Region in which the bar/ distillery is located.

City, town or village and county, in which the bar/ distillery is located.

Type of establishment.

The botanicals used to make each distillery's main craft gin are listed, starting with juniper.

Postal address and other key information.

Review.

Opening hours as we went to press – check online.

Places of interest near the bar/distillery.

Newton House Gin

Yeovil, Somerset
Distillery, bar and shop

ESSENTIAL INFORMATION
Key botanicals (Newton House Gin):
   juniper, coriander seed, liquorice,
   almond, lemon peel, orange peel,
   grapefruit peel, bergamot, mint,
   blueberry, peach
Output: 200 bottles a week
Location: Newton House, Newton Sumaville,
   Yeovil, BA20 2RX
Telephone: 01935 471388
Email: jane@newtonhousegin.co.uk
Website: www.newtonhousegin.co.uk
Facebook: www.facebook.com/
   NewtonHouseGin
Instagram: @newtonhousegin
Twitter: @NewtonHouseGin

Opening hours:
Monday-Friday 0900-1700

Other reasons to go: Montacute,
Barrington Court, Lytes Cary and Stourhead
Gardens National Trust properties, and the
Jurassic Coast

*E*lla Carr writes: In 2007 Jane and Ro
Cannon (next page, bottom left) bou
the dilapidated Jacobean Newton House
in south Somerset, and embarked on a
major project of restoring it. Gin was th
next step: Newton House Gin (bottom le
was developed over a couple of years an
launched in Spring 2017, using spring w
from the estate and the house's 60 acres
gardens brimming with flowers and herb

The result is an elite gin, aimed at the
discerning gin drinker who knows a goo
London Dry when he or she tastes one
– it won a Gold Medal at the World Gin
Awards in 2018. It's made from English
distilled wheat spirit and 12 botanicals (r
page, top left), five of which are inspired
by plants grown in the walled garden, ar
blended with water from their own sprir
The taste is zesty, with an underlying
peppery spice, and the freshness of an
English garden coming through from the
peach, blueberries, mint and bergamot.

The recipe was first developed in a
10-litre copper still, Hermione, which wa
followed by the 60-litre Henrietta once th
recipe had been agreed. To keep up with
growing demand, the distillery was finall
moved from the Old Dairy in the main he
to the Carpenter's Workshop in the groun
They now have a new brood of stills – Un
Liberty and Hope – to keep up with dem

The label has a gold foil embossed
profile of Newton House and black-and-
gold lettering reminiscent of the jazz age
referencing Jane and Robin's twin passion
their new home and for jazz: before movin
Somerset they spent many a night at Ronr
Scott's, lubricated by classic gin cocktails.

In 2018 they started hosting their owr
Gin and Jazz evenings *á la* Ronnie Scott's

49

16

selected dates in The Bespoke Gin House –
formerly the Stable and Coach House, turned
Art Deco enclave. The evening involves
three bars: The Newton House Gin Bar for
G&Ts (right), The PeaCOCKTAILBar and
The Wine Counter, and a four-course dinner
cooked by a guest chef.

Fabulous interiors, food and live music
conspire to make these evenings very special
occasions, but more casual daytime Gin
Open Days are also held here, for which
they open their three bars and Gin Shop.
Light lunches and afternoon tea are on offer
and guests are free to roam the gardens and
grounds. Sign up to their mailing list to be
alerted to upcoming events and open days.

LOCATION MAPS

SOUTH-WEST
ENGLAND,
WALES,
WEST MIDLANDS.

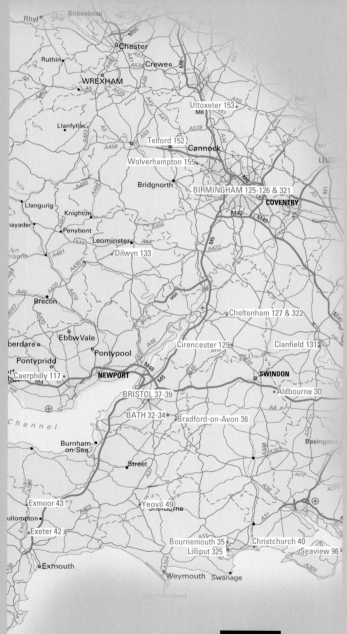

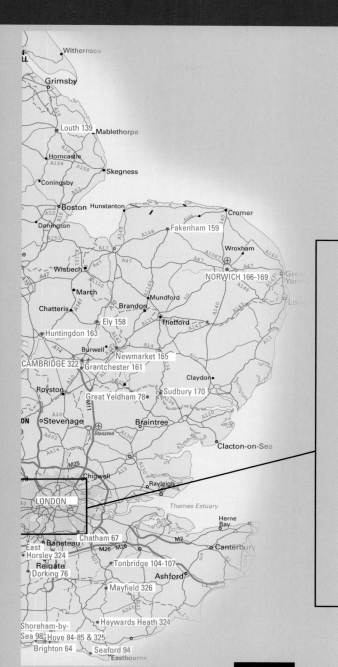

SOUTH-EAST ENGLAND, THE MIDLANDS, EAST ANGLIA, NORTHERN ENGLAND.

Montrose
Alyth • Forfar • Inverkeilor 248
Glamis 246
Arbroath
Carnoustie
DUNDEE 245
St. Andrews Bay
St Andrews 250
Fife Ness
• Leven • Isle of May
Kirkcaldy of Forth
Firth of
• North Berwick 240
EDINBURGH 227-239
Grantshouse
Penicuik Ayton
Lauder • Greenlaw
Peebles 216
• Galashiels Kelso 212
Ancrum 210 • Wooler
• Hawick
Alnwick 187
• Amble
Kielder Otterburn
Water
• Langholm
Morpeth 200
Longtown • Whitley Bay
Gretna Haltwhistle Newcastle upon Tyne 202-205
• Roker 206
Gateshead 196 SUNDERLAND
Consett • Durham 193-195
Alston •
Stanhope •
A689
Tees
Whitby
Brough
Stokesley
Colburn 191
• Northallerton
Ulverston 186 • Bedale 189
• Kettlewell
• Lancaster
Fleetwood
BLACKPOOL M55
Preston 181
Huddersfield M18
Ormskirk M6 Scunthorpe
WIGAN
LIVERPOOL 175-176 MANCHESTER 178
Spital 184 SHEFFIELD 183 Gainsborough
Knutsford • Wilmslow Worksop
Chester

SCOTLAND

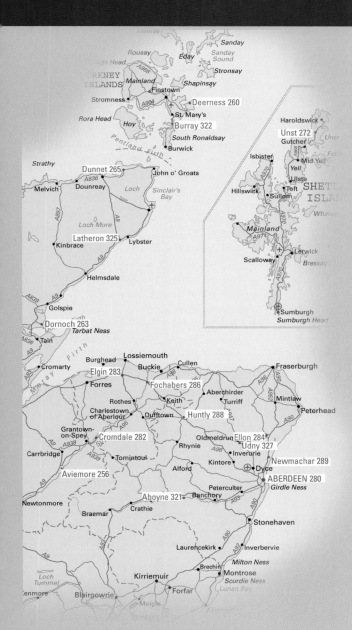

ORKNEY ISLANDS

Sanday
Rousay
Eday
Sanday Sound
Stronsay
Shapinsay
Mainland
Finstown
Deerness 260
Stromness
St. Mary's
Rora Head
Hoy
Burray 322
South Ronaldsay
Burwick

Haroldswick
Unst 272
Gutcher
Unst
Isbister
Mid Yell
Strathy
Dunnet 265
John o' Groats
Yell
Ulsta
SHETLAND ISLANDS
Melvich
Dounreay
Loch
Sinclair's Bay
Hillswick
Toft
Sullom
Whalsa
Loch More
Latheron 325
Lybster
Mainland
Lerwick
Kinbrace
Scalloway
Bressay
Helmsdale
Golspie
Dornoch 263
Tarbat Ness
Sumburgh
Sumburgh Head
Tain

Lossiemouth
Burghead
Buckie
Cullen
Fraserburgh
Cromarty
Elgin 283
Forres
Fochabers 286
Aberchirder
Mintlaw
Rothes
Keith
Turriff
Peterhead
Charlestown of Aberlour
Dufftown
Huntly 288
Grantown-on-Spey
Cromdale 282
Oldmeldrum
Ellon 284
Carrbridge
Rhynie
Udny 327
Tomintoul
Kintore
Inverurie
Newmachar 289
Aviemore 256
Alford
Dyce
Newtonmore
Peterculter
ABERDEEN 280
Girdle Ness
Aboyne 321
Banchory
Braemar
Crathie
Stonehaven
Laurencekirk
Inverbervie
Milton Ness
Loch Tummel
Brechin
Montrose
Scurdie Ness
Kirriemuir
Lunan Bay
Blairgowrie
Forfar

LOCATION MAPS

NORTHERN IRELAND
REPUBLIC OF IRELAND

GLOSSARY

bathtub method the botanicals are prepard by hand and slowly steeped in a neutral, bought-in grain spirit

genever the juniper-flavoured national spirit of Holland from which gin evolved. Also known as Dutch Gin, it's traditionally made with a grape-based spirit

head the first vapours to boil off the alcohol during distillation, containing volatile alcohols such as methanol

heart the 'middle' vapours to boil off during distillation, containing primarily ethanol, the most desirable compound of alcohol

tail the final vapours to boil off the alcohol during distillation, which have a bitter flavour

multi-shot method the botanicals are distilled individually so they stand out in their own right rather than thrown into a single distillation together

one-shot method all the botanicals are macerated in the neutral base spirit before they are heated

perfect serve the best combination of mixer, garnish and glassware to complement the spirit

rotary evaporation method botanicals are distilled with the base spirit in a vaccumed flask which rotates in a warm bath

vacuum (or cold) distillation method distilling in a vacuum. This creates a lower boiling point for the alcohol, so the botanicals aren't stewed

vapour infusion method botanicals are placed in a basket above the base spirit which infuses with the botanicals as it evaporates

REPORTING TO THE GUIDE

Please write and tell us about your experience of gin distilleries and bars whether good or bad, whether listed in this edition or not.

The address to write to us is:
Print editor, Duncan Petersen Publishing Ltd
Studio 6, 82 Silverthorne Road,
London,
SW8 3HE

Checklist
Please use a separate sheet of paper for each report; include your name, address and telephone number on each report.

Your reports will be received with particular pleasure if they are typed, and if they are organized under the following headings:

Name of establishment
Town or village it is in, or nearest
Full address, including postcode
The building and setting
Atmosphere, welcome and service

We assume that in writing you have no objection to your views being published unpaid, either verbatim or in an edited version. Names of major outside contributors are acknowledged, at the editor's discretion, in the guide.

Ramsbury Gin and Distillery

Aldbourne, Wiltshire
Distillery and shop

ESSENTIAL INFORMATION

Key botanicals (Ramsbury Gin): juniper, liquorice, cinnamon, dried lemon peel, dried orange peel, fresh quince

Output: 100,000 bottles a year

Location: Stock Lane, Aldbourne, Marlborough, SN8 2NN

Telephone: 01672 541407

Email: distillery@ramsbury.com

Website: www.ramsburyestates.co.uk

Facebook: www.facebook.com/RamsburyDistillery

Instagram: @ramsbury_distillery

Twitter: @Ramsburydistil

Opening hours:
Monday-Friday 0900-1700
Saturday 0900-1300

Other reasons to go: The Bell at Ramsbury, Liddington Castle, Aldbourne Heritage Centre, Wilts and Berks Canal, Coate Stone Circle

R amsbury is an interesting (and very old) Wiltshire settlement on the River Kennet, worth a visit in its own right, but to a gin head it's no competition for the Ramsbury Distillery (bottom left), up on the Downs 15 minutes from the village. It's in a marvellous location, with 360° of gently undulating chalk scenery rolling to the horizon – but more to the point, the fields you see surrounding the farm buildings are literally where the gin springs from.

Most distillers buy in ready-made grain spirit which is then re-distilled with botanicals to create a unique gin. Ramsbury is one of the few which makes its own basic spirit from home-grown wheat (opposite, bottom right) – they use Horatio which gives the spirit a smooth and slightly sweet flavour. The product (above and opposite top left and right) is therefore almost entirely local: even the juniper berries are foraged from the hedgerows, and of course the quinces that give the gin its unique fruity flavour are grown in the estate orchards.

The focus of this guide is strictly on genuine craft gin. We are wary of distilleries which make other products as well, and in the case of Ramsbury there are several other products to distract your attention – real ales, vodka, damson liqueur, and smoked meats. But because Ramsbury has such impeccable local credentials, the gin gets our vote.

You'll enjoy visiting the distillery housed

in modern farm buildings, plus a nicely fitted out shop. The estate covers around 20,000 acres of rolling woodland (below). Everything sold here is local and natural and even the waste gets ploughed back into the land – the water is drawn from a well on the site and all heat used in the distillation process is generated by using biofuel from the estate's own sustainable woodland.

Bath Botanical Gin Distillery and Herbal Apothecary

Bath, Somerset
Shop and tasting room

ESSENTIAL INFORMATION

Key botanicals (No.1 Gin): juniper, coriander, liquorice, star anise, lemon peel, Somerset lime flower

Output: 50 litres every two weeks

Location: 1A Prior Park Road, Widcombe, Bath, BA2 4NG

Telephone: 01225 635782

Email: mullettsue@gmail.com

Website: www.bathbotanics.co.uk

Facebook: www.facebook.com/BathBotanicalGinDistillery

Instagram: @bathbotanicalgindistillery

Twitter: @BathBotanics

Opening hours:
Wednesday-Saturday 1100-1730
Sunday 1200-1630

Other reasons to go: The Roman Baths, Bath Abbey, Pulteney Bridge

An intelligent twist (bottom left) on the gin microdistillery concept: Sue Mullet, who has an MSc in herbal medicine, distils not just regular gin but gin that will make you better. Alcohol extracts the essence of herbal remedies much better than water. Her ordinary gins are in clear bottles, and the herbal range in clay bottles. Taste the regular flavouring and medicinal extracts through a straw or taste the finished gins from a small glass. The Somerset lime flowers used in No.1 are hand foraged locally.

Alongside the regular gins she sells seasonal fruit gins and teas (left) grown on local biodynamic farms – which have an organic, holistic approach 'reliant on the ecological health of the farmland to grow crops in tandem with the astrological cycle.'

Then there are speciality gins such as Christmas Gin flavoured with cocoa, orange and cinnamon; or No.2 Grapefruit, infused with fresh pink grapefruit to make a bittersweet, zingy citrus gin.

This is a tasting and retail outlet only but the still is on display (right). As well as the gins, they sell kits for making your own botanical gin at home.

Bath Gin Distillery and Botanical Laboratory & The Canary Gin Bar

Bath, Somerset
Distillery and bar

ESSENTIAL INFORMATION

Key botanicals (Bath Gin): juniper, coriander, bitter orange, kaffir lime

Output: not disclosed

Location: 2-3 Queen Street, Bath, BA1 1HE

Telephone: 01225 462457

Email: info@thebathgincompany.com; bookings@thebathgincompany.co.uk

Website: www.thebathgincompany.co.uk

Facebook: www.facebook.com/BathDistillery

Instagram: @bathdistillery

Twitter: @BathDistillery

Opening hours:
The Canary Bar
Monday-Thursday 1700-0000
Friday 1600-0000
Saturday 1500-0000

Other reasons to go: The Roman Baths, Bath Abbey, The Jane Austen Centre

These premises used to house an art installation on the theme of blood and alcohol, and at street level some of the artwork still decorates the walls. Then in mid-2016 Peter Meacock and business partner Harry Brett turned it into Bath's first gin bar and distillery, so in one respect no change. This is quite a slick, cleverly promoted operation: they offer a range of 'Gin Austen' cocktails whose logo is a pastiche of the great author's face (right) with vivid red lips and one eye winking. As Jane Austen addicts know only too well, she lived in Bath for five years from 1801, but there are no records of whether she drank gin.

At street level is the Canary Bar; upstairs is the Distillers Bar and down in the basement, you'll find the distillery. This produces the core product, Bath Gin (left), which is "modern, fresh... floral, tangy, citrus and deep spice notes followed by mild sweetness... a gin that is at once warm, intelligent, soft and sophisticated... much like Jane Austen herself."

The other house gins on sale are variants on the basic product and include the popular hopped rhubarb gin, and more than 225 others from all over the world. Apart from his own concoctions, Peter is a fan of 209 – a Californian gin which packs a super-peppery punch.

Sub 13 Cocktail Bar

Bath, Somerset
Bar

ESSENTIAL INFORMATION
Location: 4 Edgar Buildings, George Street,
    Bath, BA1 2EE
Telephone: 01225 466667
Email: drinks@sub13.net
Website: www.sub13.net
Facebook: www.facebook.com/sub13bar
Instagram: @sub13bar
Twitter: @Sub13Bar

Opening hours:
Monday-Wednesday 1700-0000
Thursday 1700-0100
Friday 1700-0300
Saturday 1300-0300
Sunday 1700-2300

Other reasons to go: The Jane Austen
Centre, Museum of Bath Architecture, The
Roman Baths, Bath Abbey

Note what it says on the tin: gin is important here but not the only game in town – they do an ambitious range of cocktails using various spirits besides gin. However, in the large upstairs bar (top) they serve a sizeable range of around 80 gins from around the world. You can imagine it heaving at weekends – the space fits around 80 people but there's overspill room in the garden at the back. This is the biggest and pleasantest outdoor space attached to a bar in Bath – definitely Sub 13's strong point. The garden closes at 1 am, another good feature, and of course if you visit on a weekday the whole place is relatively relaxed.

Director Tim Whelehan told us that his current favourite is Cotswolds Gin (page 148). It's not put through the usual filtering process, which makes it slightly cloudy, and allows the botanical flavours to come through a touch more intensely, including a hint of lavender.

Sub 13 (originally a basement bar) is located on busy, thriving George Street in the city centre and you need to look out for the sign by the door (left), which is not especially conspicuous.

Conker Gin and Conker Spirit

Bournemouth, Dorset
Distillery

ESSENTIAL INFORMATION

Key botanicals (Conker Dorset Dry Gin):
   juniper, lime, elderberries, samphire, gorse
Output: not disclosed
Location: 16A Inverleigh Road,
   Bournemouth, BH6 5HA
Telephone: 01202 430384
Email: hello@conkerspirit.co.uk
Website: www.conkerspirit.co.uk
Facebook: www.facebook.com/
   ConkerSpirit
Instagram: @conkerspirit
Twitter: @ConkerSpirit

Opening hours:
Monday-Thursday 0800-1600
Friday 0800-1600

Other reasons to go: Bournemouth Parks,
Boscombe Chine Gardens

David T. Smith writes: Conker Spirit was founded in 2014 by Rupert Holloway, a chartered surveyor, as Dorset's first distillery but since then it's been joined by half a dozen others.

Conker Dorset Dry Gin (bottom left) was released in 2015 and is made using ten botanicals, including three that are locally sourced in Dorset: elderberries, samphire, and gorse flowers (above). There's also English coriander from Sussex in the gin, which is proofed down to bottling strength using spring water from the nearby New Forest.

The distillery's second release was a Cold Brew Coffee Liqueur, which was followed in 2018 by two limited edition gins: a port-cask aged gin and a navy strength gin. Conker Navy Strength Gin is a tweaked version of their original gin, without the gorse flowers, and £5 from each sale is donated to the RNLI.

In 2017, Conker Spirit partnered with local rum expert Peter Holland and That Boutique-y Gin Company to create Mojito Gin which has a molasses base, similar to rum, and botanical flavours including lime and fresh mint.

The distillery is located about 15 minutes walk from Pokesdown railway station and is open to visitors (book online) on at least one Thursday each month. The tours are conducted by Rupert who gives a talk on the entire gin production process, from botanicals to bottle, and guides you through a tasting of Conker's products. You'll leave with a full bottle of either the Dorset Dry Gin or Cold Brew Coffee Liqueur.

Widbrook Grange gin bar

Bradford-on-Avon, Wiltshire
Bar

ESSENTIAL INFORMATION

Location: Widbrook Grange, Bradford-on-Avon, BA15 1UH
Telephone: 01225 864750
Email: stay@widbrookgrange.co.uk
Website: www.widbrookgrange.co.uk/dining/ginbar
Facebook: www.facebook.com/widbrookgrange
Instagram: @widbrook.grange
Twitter: @widbrookgrange

Opening hours:
Monday-Sunday 1200-2230

Other reasons to go: Saxon Church of St Laurence, The Tithe Barn, Barton Grange Farm, Chapel of St Mary Tory, The Kennet and Avon Canal, Avoncliff

Widbrook Grange (below right) is a charming country hotel (for a review see www.charmingsmallhotels.co.uk) outside Bradford-on-Avon and close to Bath. Gin tourists visiting Bath's gin spots (see pages 32-34) could do a lot worse than take a drive out to the countryside for a session in this cosy bar (bottom left) with a choice of around 165 worldwide gins and 14 different tonics, maybe followed by lunch or dinner.

On our visit friendly Attila from Romania was manning the bar, ready to advise and to mix alcoholic and non-alcoholic cocktails. Jumping out from the pages of the menu were little-known names such as Blind Tiger, a refined Belgian gin; Granite Bavarian from Germany, filtered through granite; and Origin Arezzo, from Italy, a purist artisan gin using just one botanical, juniper sourced from a single estate.

If you can't decide what to choose, go for The Award Winner's Gin Flight, a selection of three award-winning gins chosen for you by the barman and served with different tonics and correct garnishes – £23.95 as we went to press.

There are three or four comfortable arm chairs in this cosy but quite dark den, plus the bar stools which are fashioned from old metal tractor seats. Widbrook Grange was once a model farm, and many of its quirky decorative artefacts are recycled from the farmyard.

Bristol Dry Gin Microdistillery and The Bristol Spirits Collective

Bristol
Distillery and tasting room

ESSENTIAL INFORMATION

Key botanicals (Bristol Dry Gin): juniper, coriander seed, cubeb, lemon peel, allspice, lime leaf, elderflower

Output: 6,000 bottles a year

Location: The Rummer, All Saints Lane, Bristol, BS1 1JH

Telephone: 01179 290111

Email: info@bristoldrygin.com

Website: www.bristoldrygin.com

Facebook: www.facebook.com/BristolDryGin

Instagram: @bristoldrygin

Twitter: @BristolDryGin

Opening hours:
The Distillery
Monday-Friday 1000-1700
Saturday-Sunday 1200-0000
Gin Tasting (booking required)
Friday from 1900
Saturday and Sunday from 1500

Other reasons to go: Covered market

What a great location for a microdistillery: it's in the heart of the bustling, quirky Bristol covered market (below middle), down some steps in the basement of The Rummer Hotel (bottom left). Owners David Blatch and Brett Hirt opened in January 2017 and at present produce 6,000 bottles a year.

Their range of three own-label gins are: Bristol Dry, 40%, the core product, a beautifully balanced classic dry gin – light and easy drinking; Docker's Strength, 55%, will kick your ass just as a Bristol docker would do should you be unwise enough to get into a fight; and Turbo Island Edition, a gasket-blowing 75%. Let the magic (pineapple, baby carrots, ginger, green tea and other botanicals) seduce you, but keep away from naked flames.

They also do a pink gin, a bilberry gin and a vodka.

The emphasis here is on retail sales and tasting with expert advice from David, Brett and friendly helpers. Fever-Tree and Franklin & Sons tonic water are their favoured mixers, the latter with less sugar than Fever-Tree. Distilling takes place behind a counter, and there's a big table around which six to eight people can gather and drink. Along a passage you reach a dining room which the hotel uses for special events and the distillery uses for tastings.

We think this is a very good microdistillery with its heart in the right place: they sell their Bristol Dry Gin at a competitive £27.

Hathor Gin and Psychopomp Microdistillery

Bristol
Distillery and taproom

ESSENTIAL INFORMATION
Key botanicals (Hathor Gin): juniper,
    coriander seed, cassia bark,
    pomegranate, heather, fig leaf
Output: 15,000 bottles a year
Location: 145 St Michael's Hill, Bristol,
    BS2 8DB
Telephone: 07511 934675
Email: info@microdistillery.co.uk
Website: www.microdistillery.co.uk
Facebook: www.facebook.com/
    microdistillery
Instagram: @microdistillery
Twitter: @PsychopompMD

Opening hours:
Tuesday-Friday 1200-2200

Other reasons to go: Bristol Museum and
Art Gallery, Cabot Tower, Bristol Cathedral

St Michael's Hill is quite a cool corner of Bristol, a student thoroughfare with a university department building at the bottom end. Shops are mostly scruffy, independent and quirky – take a look at Tiffins, the delicious fresh curry counter, Mocha Mocha (coffee) and Beerd (craft beer). Psychopomp Microdistillery is probably the most individual and interesting of them all. You need to look twice to spot it because the original shop sign (opposite, top left) still dominates – 'A. Jenkins Groceries – Provisions'.

Every religion has a psychopomp – a guiding spirit – and the admirable guiding spirit of this place, opened in 2016 by Danny Walker and Liam Hirt, is to concentrate on the liquid first and let the rest follow. They produce a modest 15,000 bottles year, there's no aggressive marketing, just a steady flow of sales to local outlets for whom the distillery makes customized gins.

Outside there are solid rough timber tables and benches where you can drink your G&T; inside there's a long table (below left) where you can also sample and drink. Behind a counter (opposite, bottom left) at the back is the still (opposite, top right) and along one wall a terrific display of produce. It's a taproom rather than a bar and the atmosphere is relaxed yet lively – as if the owners are enjoying a hobby as much as running a business.

Their house range of gins consists of Pinga, a limited edition, seasonal gin named after a female god in Inuit (Eskimo) mythology. She was a psychopomp, bringing souls of the newly dead to the underworld. Among the flavourings are bay leaves, bee pollen and chamomile. 'Hathor', another limited edition, was an

Egyptian goddess, also a psychopomp, flavoured with heather, pomegranate and fig leaf. Old Tom Gin is historic: during the 18thC crackdown on alcohol consumption, gin was dispensed from a lead tube on St Michael's Mount, above which was a plaque depicting a black cat. The original Old Tom Gin was sweetened with sugar or honey. The new distillery's version uses sweet botanicals, not sugar, among them liquorice root and white peony tea.

If you visit on Wednesday (Woden's Day) try a Wednesday Martini: six parts Woden, one part dry vermouth, stir over ice into a Martini glass and add grapefruit zest.

PSYCHOPOMP MICRO-DISTILLERY

WODEN — OUR SIGNATURE GIN FRESH GRAPEFRUIT & FENNEL

PINGA — SPRING SEASONAL 2018 BEE POLLEN CHAMOMILE & LEMON BALM

THE OX — BESPOKE RECIPE FOR THE STEAK RESTAURANT LEMON ZEST, BLACK TRUFFLE & THYME

GIN & TONIC 7.50   ABSINTHE 7.50

MARTINI 7.50   AQVAVIT & TONIC 7.50

NEGRONI 7.50   COFFEE DIGESTIF 5.00

Pothecary Blue Label Gin and Soapbox Spirits Ltd

Christchurch, Dorset
Distillery

ESSENTIAL INFORMATION
Key botanicals (Pothecary Blue Label Gin):
    juniper, lemon peel, black mulberry,
    lavender, lime flower
Output: 8,000-10,000 bottles a year
Location: 91 Stour Road, Christchurch,
    BH23 1JN
Telephone: 07534 804917
Email: info@pothecarygin.co.uk;
orders@pothecarygin.co.uk
Website: www.pothecarygin.co.uk
Facebook: www.facebook.com/
    PothecaryGin
Instagram: @pothecarygin
Twitter: @PothecaryGin

Opening hours: not open to the public

Methodical, thorough, perhaps even inspired: a fair summary of Martin Jennings's (opposite, bottom right) and business partner Lucas's approach. Both have a background in the wine and spirit and the hospitality industries and both did seven months' homework at trade events while waiting for HMRC to process their licence – plenty of time to work out what their niche would be.

They found that most of the gins they liked best were made in a multi-shot rather than the London Dry process. In multi-shot, the botanicals are distilled individually so they stand out in their own right rather than thrown into a single distillation together. The London Dry (or one-shot) process distils botanicals together and relies on angelica and orris root to 'fix' the flavours – stop them bleeding into each other, which in Martin's view means less clarity of the overall aroma and flavour.

Starting with around 90 botanicals, they set about a rigorous elimination process. With flavour, aroma and texture foremost in their heads, first they sacked about 50 because they were "one-dimensional" – these included coriander, angelica and orris root. Then they tasted the remaining 40, asking themselves which really were better than the rest, and got down to 25.

After that it became a question of personal preference, and which flavours they reckoned complemented each other best.

Martin's 27-year wine background made him keenest on the aromatics but he was also looking for an enjoyable taste on the palate and finally a clean aftertaste or finish that kept the drinker wanting more. Martin wanted a flavour that breaks through even if heavily diluted, but would also be good as

a sipping gin or as a Dry Martini. The last botanical knocked out was fennel because it overpowered the others. The final five are listed opposite under 'Key botanicals' and are the ingredients that make Pothecary Blue Label (top left) an award winner.

Soapbox also produces some limited edition gins. In June 2017, they released 982 bottles of Pothecary Gin Sicilian Blend (opposite, right-hand bottle), made with oranges, lemons, almonds and gentian root. In February 2018 they launched Pothecary Gin Thai Blend (opposite, left-hand bottle), using mango, pineapple, lime, coconut, coriander, turmeric root and ginger root to create a subtly spicy, yet fresh and fruity gin. Their most recent release, Pothecary Gin Trinity Blend (top right), is a reaction to the rise in what Martin describes as "gimmick-ridden so-called gins." Trinity's style represents a traditional gin recipe – there are only three botanicals: juniper, coriander seed and bergamot – but at the higher bottle strength of 49% it provides an intense and smooth flavour.

The gins sell through local and national wholesalers, independent retailers and farm shops. It's a shame that this interesting distillery does not sell over the counter, and that visits are by appointment only.

Crocketts

Exeter, Devon

Bar

ESSENTIAL INFORMATION

Location: 2 Upper Paul Street, Exeter, EX4 3NB

Telephone: 01392 332222

Email: info@crockettsbar.co.uk

Website: www.crockettsbar.co.uk

Facebook: www.facebook.com/ CrockettsDevon

Instagram: @crockettsexeter

Twitter: @CrockettsExeter

Opening hours:

Monday-Thursday 1700-2330

Friday 1600-0030

Saturday 1400-0030

Sunday 1700-2300

Other reasons to go: The RAM museum, Gandy Street, independent shops, eateries and bars

Ella Carr writes: This elegant gin bar (bottom left) can be found in the historic Gandy Street area of Exeter's bustling cultural quarter – rumoured to have been the inspiration for Diagon Alley in the *Harry Potter* books. Indeed, Crocketts' Grade II-listed building shares something of the faded grandeur of Grimmauld Place, with lovely antique chandeliers hanging from its 'Library' upstairs, and quirky curios adorning its two floors.

Having housed a clothes shop for many years, the building has gone back to its roots. It's located on the same spot where William Crockett, a wine and spirit merchant in the 1840s, sold his wares (he also happened to be Mayor of Exeter in 1823).

A bespoke handmade copper bar takes centre stage along the length of the cosy ground floor drinking area, behind which glisten a collection of 200 gins (and counting). Their speciality is artisan gins distilled across the South West – such as Exeter Gin, Salcombe (page 47), Curio, and Tarquin's (page 44). However, I was equally impressed with the rest of the collection, which holds both familiar and obscure names. Expect to see stalwarts such as Hendricks, Aviation Gin and Brooklyn Gin sitting alongside the weird and wonderful, such as gins that change colour, and even one distilled with collagen (and other anti-ageing botanicals). Taking pride of place at the centre of the back bar is their own mini gin still, named Billy.

The knowledgeable bartenders will guide you through the gins, and the bar regularly hosts gin talks and tastings from local distillers. If by chance you enter unsure of what you think about gin, we guarantee that you'll leave a convert.

Wicked Wolf Gin

Exmoor, Devon
Distillery

ESSENTIAL INFORMATION
Key botanicals (Wicked Wolf Exmoor Gin):
   juniper, coriander, cardamom, cubeb,
   grains of paradise, lemon peel, orange
   peel, kaffir lime leaf, hibiscus, lemongrass
Output: up to 23,400 bottles a year
Location: The Old Chapel Brendon Ltd, T/A
   Wicked Wolf, Brendon, Exmoor, EX35 6PT
Telephone: 01598 741357
Email: info@wickedwolfgin.com
Website: www.wickedwolfgin.com
Facebook: www.facebook.com/
   wickedwolfgin
Instagram: @wickedwolfgin
Twitter: @wickedwolfgin

Opening hours: not open to the public

Wicked Wolf's tagline, 'The spirit of Exmoor', is fair enough: it's distilled and blended on the banks of the East Lyn river, which rises on Exmoor. Co-founders and husband and wife Pat Patel and Julie Heap met at university in Falmouth and afterwards worked in London at design and branding agencies. Almost 20 years later, they moved back to the South West, aiming to set up a business that would allow them to work from home. They wanted to do something in the food and drink industry, and initially looked at opening a smokehouse but rejected the idea because of cost and fears there were already too many.

However, with the gin renaissance in full swing, and being fans of the spirit themselves, they decided to have a crack at craft gin. They knew their product (bottom left) had to be different, so opted for Asian flavours, including cardamom, kaffir lime leaves, lemongrass and hibiscus. Hibiscus gives the gin its sweet taste and is a replacement for liquorice, which is considered the marmite of botanicals – you either love it or hate it.

Like a number of other distilleries in this guide (see pages 40 and 161), Wicked Wolf's 11 botanicals are distilled separately. Each has a different boiling point, so distilling them separately prevents them from cooking and losing flavour at the same time as giving the distiller complete control over the strength of each component.

Wicked Wolf has completed an extension to house the distillery, which was initially in their garage. They intended to keep it small batch and were planning a limited edition to celebrate 150 years of the novel *Lorna Doone* – the distillery is based in the valley in which the story is set.

43

Tarquin's Cornish Gin and Southwestern Distillery

Padstow, Cornwall
Distillery

ESSENTIAL INFORMATION

Key botanicals (Tarquin's Cornish Gin):
 juniper, coriander seed, liquorice, green
 cardamom, cinnamon, bitter almond,
 lemon, orange, grapefruit, violet
Output: not disclosed
Location: 11 Higher Trevibban Farm, St
 Ervan, Padstow, PL27 7SH
Telephone: 01841 540121
Email: hello@southwesterndistillery.com
Website: www.tarquinsgin.com
Facebook: www.facebook.com/TarquinsGin
Instagram: @tarquinsgin
Twitter: @tarquinsgin

Opening hours:
Tours (booking required)
Thursday-Friday 1830-2000
**Saturday 1100-1230, 1400-1530 and
 1700-1930**
Sunday 1100-1230 and 1400-1530

**Other reasons to go: Prideaux Place,
Daymer Bay, National Lobster Hatchery, St
Enodoc Church**

*D*avid T. Smith writes: The first new gin distillery in Cornwall for more than 100 years, Southwestern Distillery is located on the outskirts of the hamlet of St Ervan, a stone's throw from the wild north Cornish coast and the Atlantic ocean beyond. The distillery was founded in 2012 by Tarquin Leadbetter, a classically trained chef who was working in an office in the City of London. Aged 23, he decided to start a new life making spirits.

Development began on both a Cornish gin (bottom left, middle bottle) and a Cornish pastis (an aniseed spirit, not to be confused with a Cornish pasty) using a 0.7-litre copper still from Portugal. Following the creation of the initial recipe, a second-hand 250-litre copper still was bought to enable commercial production. The distillery's first bottle of gin was sold in July 2013. The release of the pastis followed in the autumn of that year and was the first of its kind to be produced in the UK.

By 2016, Southwestern Distillery had released a second gin: bottled at navy strength (57%) and known as Seadog (left, second bottle from right). In the same year they also began to release limited edition gins, often focusing on local seasonal flavours or partnerships with local firms and individuals such as Sharps Brewery, the Eden Project, and celebrity chef Rick Stein.

In 2017, a new, third permanent release gin was launched: British Blackberry Gin (left, second bottle from left). Bottled at 38%, this is made by infusing blackberries into the original Tarquin's Gin and adding a little Cornish wildflower honey for sweetness.

Southwestern offers tours, including a history of the distillery, a talk on the production process, and tastings.

The Plymouth Gin Distillery

Plymouth, Devon
Distillery and bar

ESSENTIAL INFORMATION

Key botanicals (Plymouth Dry Gin): juniper, coriander seed, cardamom, lemon peel, orange peel

Output: 1,000,000+ bottles a year

Location: 60 Southside Street, Plymouth, PL1 2LQ

Telephone: 01752 665292

Email: info@plymouthdistillery.com

Website: www.plymouthgin.com

Facebook: www.facebook.com/homeofplymouthgin

Instagram: @homeofplymouthgin

Twitter: @RefectoryBar

Opening hours:
Monday-Saturday 1000-1700
Sunday 1100-1700

Other reasons to go: Smeaton's Tower, Bovisand Beach, Pennywell Farm, National Marine Aquarium, Plymouth Yacht Haven, The Mayflower Steps

David T. Smith writes: The Black Friars Distillery (bottom left), home to Plymouth Gin, is in The Barbican (next page, middle), the historic centre of the port of Plymouth. It's a great area to explore, with narrow alleys and lanes housing pubs, bars, and restaurants, as well as shops and stalls selling all sorts of vintage curios. A three-minute walk from the distillery is the famous dock from which the pilgrims set sail on the *Mayflower*, bound for the New World. Plymouth railway station is about 15 minutes on foot.

Black Friars can trace the history of distilling on this site back to 1793. Before that, legend has it that the location was home to a monastery of the Dominican Order, hence the name Black Friars.

A firm called Fox and Williamson started distilling on the site in 1793, which changed its name in the early 19thC to Coates & Company. Since then, the business had a number of owners; the present one is Chivas Brothers, who also own the Beefeater (page 86) and Monkey 47 gin brands.

Plymouth Gin Distillery is open for tours seven days a week except at Christmas and New Year. Currently three types of tour are available: Gin Distillery Tours are bookable on the day and include a tour of the site (next page, bottom right), a tasting of Plymouth Gin, and a free G&T or gin miniature; The Gin Connoisseur's Tour includes an in-depth blind tasting of gin; and The Master Distiller's Tour (also book in advance) during which you can make your own gin.

The first floor of the distillery is The Refectory Cocktail Lounge and an eaterie, the Tanner Brothers' Barbican Kitchen.

Plymouth Dry Gin (next page, top,

middle bottle – bottled at 41.2%) is technically a London Dry Gin made with seven botanicals. A stronger version, Plymouth Navy Strength Gin (top, left-hand bottle), is bottled at 57%. The distillery also makes a Sloe Gin (top, right-hand bottle) and has recently revived its Fruit Cup, a high-strength competitor to Pimms.

Plymouth Gin was one of the few gins that enjoyed geographical protection similar to champagne or Scotch whisky. However, it lost this status in 2014, since when it has relied just on its trademark 'Plymouth Gin.'

Salcombe Gin and Salcombe Distilling Co.

Salcombe, Devon
Distillery, bar, shop and gin school

ESSENTIAL INFORMATION

Key botanicals (Salcombe Gin 'Start Point'): juniper, coriander seed, liquorice, cardamom, cubeb, lemon peel, lime peel, red grapefruit peel, plus four secret ingredients

Output: not disclosed

Location: The Boathouse, 28 Island Street, Salcombe, TQ8 8DP

Telephone: 01548 288180

Email: ilovegin@salcombegin.com

Website: www.salcombegin.com

Facebook: www.facebook.com/SalcombeGin

Instagram: @salcombegin

Twitter: @SalcombeGin

Opening hours:
Distillery, bar, and shop
Seasonal opening hours – see website for up-to-date information

Other reasons to go: Overbeck's Museum Home and Gardens, Salcombe North Sands, Mill Bay

Salcombe Gin was launched in 2016 by friends Howard Davies and Angus Lugsdin, who met in Salcombe while they were young sailing instructors in 1995. Angus in particular was intrigued by the art of distilling, so when they returned to Salcombe some years later, they decided to start Salcombe Distilling Company.

They spent 18 months developing their gin recipe and building The Boathouse (which houses the distillery), so called because it happens to be on the site of the boat repair yard that belonged to the sailing club where they met. They wanted the gin to be citrus led to link it to the history of the port – in the 19thC citrus cargo ships, called the Salcombe Fruiters, would carry oranges and lemons to Britain from overseas. They invited friends to take part in blind tastings until they found the perfect blend which they Christened Salcombe Gin 'Start Point' (left).

Salcombe Distilling Co. uses the one-shot method (page 68). The still, named Provident (next page, top left), is filled with English grain spirit, the botanicals and Dartmoor water, which is naturally soft, making a smooth gin. They also add the tails of the previous run in which is concentrated the earthy flavour of angelica

– a key element. The process takes around nine hours and produces enough spirit to fill 600 70-cl bottles. More Dartmoor water is added to bring it down to 44%.

Their flagship gin, Salcombe Gin 'Start Point', is best served on its own with ice, with a premium tonic water and a slice of red grapefruit, or in a Dry Martini with a twist of grapefruit peel. They also recommend mixing 25 ml of the gin with 25 ml of St Germain Elderflower Liqueur, 20 ml of freshly squeezed red grapefruit juice, 70 ml of chilled soda water and red grapefruit peel to make a St Clair cocktail.

In 2018, Salcombe Distilling Co. launched their Voyager Series, limited edition gins made in collaboration with iconic winemakers and world renowned chefs. They also produce a cask-aged gin, Salcombe Gin 'Finisterre', in collaboration with Bodegas Tradición sherry house in Spain.

The distillery also has a bar (right and previous page, top) and hosts a Gin School (above right) where you develop and distil your own 70-cl bottle of gin and learn about the distillation process – see website for booking information.

Salcombe Distilling Co. is one of the few distilleries that can be reached by boat. In 2018 they set up a service for delivering gin to visiting yachts during the summer months.

Newton House Gin

Yeovil, Somerset
Distillery, bar and shop

ESSENTIAL INFORMATION

Key botanicals (Newton House Gin):
  juniper, coriander seed, liquorice,
  almond, lemon peel, orange peel,
  grapefruit peel, bergamot, mint,
  blueberry, peach
Output: 200 bottles a week
Location: Newton House, Newton Sumaville,
  Yeovil, BA20 2RX
Telephone: 01935 471388
Email: jane@newtonhousegin.co.uk
Website: www.newtonhousegin.co.uk
Facebook: www.facebook.com/
  NewtonHouseGin
Instagram: @newtonhousegin
Twitter: @NewtonHouseGin

Opening hours:
Monday-Friday 0900-1700

Other reasons to go: Montacute,
Barrington Court, Lytes Cary and Stourhead
Gardens National Trust properties, and the
Jurassic Coast

Ella Carr writes: In 2007 Jane and Robin Cannon (next page, bottom left) bought the dilapidated Jacobean Newton House in south Somerset, and embarked on a major project of restoring it. Gin was the next step: Newton House Gin (bottom left) was developed over a couple of years and launched in Spring 2017, using spring water from the estate and the house's 60 acres of gardens brimming with flowers and herbs.

The result is an elite gin, aimed at the discerning gin drinker who knows a good London Dry when he or she tastes one – it won a Gold Medal at the World Gin Awards in 2018. It's made from English distilled wheat spirit and 12 botanicals (next page, top left), five of which are inspired by plants grown in the walled garden, and blended with water from their own spring. The taste is zesty, with an underlying peppery spice, and the freshness of an English garden coming through from the peach, blueberries, mint and bergamot.

The recipe was first developed in a 10-litre copper still, Hermione, which was followed by the 60-litre Henrietta once the recipe had been agreed. To keep up with growing demand, the distillery was finally moved from the Old Dairy in the main house to the Carpenter's Workshop in the grounds. They now have a new brood of stills – Unity, Liberty and Hope – to keep up with demand.

The label has a gold foil embossed profile of Newton House and black-and-gold lettering reminiscent of the jazz age – referencing Jane and Robin's twin passions for their new home and for jazz: before moving to Somerset they spent many a night at Ronnie Scott's, lubricated by classic gin cocktails.

In 2018 they started hosting their own Gin and Jazz evenings *á la* Ronnie Scott's on

→

selected dates in The Bespoke Gin House –
formerly the Stable and Coach House, turned
Art Deco enclave. The evening involves
three bars: The Newton House Gin Bar for
G&Ts (right), The PeaCOCKTAILBar and
The Wine Counter, and a four-course dinner
cooked by a guest chef.

Fabulous interiors, food and live music
conspire to make these evenings very special
occasions, but more casual daytime Gin
Open Days are also held here, for which
they open their three bars and Gin Shop.
Light lunches and afternoon tea are on offer
and guests are free to roam the gardens and
grounds. Sign up to their mailing list to be
alerted to upcoming events and open days.

Silent Pool Gin and Distillery

Albury, Surrey
Distillery

ESSENTIAL INFORMATION

Key botanicals (Silent Pool Gin): juniper, coriander, grains of paradise, lime, bergamot, bitter orange, kaffir lime leaf, elderflower, lavender, chamomile, lime flower, rose petal, fresh and dried pear

Output: 350,000+ bottles a year

Location: Shere Road, Albury, GU5 9BW

Telephone: 01483 229136

Email: office@silentpooldistillers.com

Website: www.silentpooldistillers.com

Facebook: www.facebook.com/SilentPoolGin

Instagram: @silentpoolgin

Twitter: @SilentPoolGin

Opening hours:
Distillery
Monday-Friday 0900-1700
The Shop
Monday-Friday 0900-1700
Saturday 1000-1800
Sunday 1000-1700

Other reasons to go: Hatchlands Park

Silent Pool is located on the Duke of Northumberland's Albury Estate, on the banks of the spring-fed pool from which it draws its water – in theory as pure as it comes. When you visit the distillery you'll be taken straight to the pool to hear about the legend of the Silent Pool, before tasting the gin it inspired.

The distillery was established by Ian McCulloch and James Shelbourne, who set out to create hand-crafted, premium spirits that forged a direct link with the land. Business took off much faster than expected, and the present six-man team's output is 1,800 bottles a day, exporting to over 33 countries. This makes it one of the more serious operations in the guide, but they remain faithful to the craft distilling ethos by doing everything in house, and tasting every batch.

They describe their gin-making as 'intricately realized', reflected in the design of their signature bottle, which tells the story of their gin: copper – for the stills – set against a blue background that matches the deepest part of the pool.

Silent Pool (bottom left), the core product, is a juniper-led spirit with floral and citrus flavours, gentle enough to be sipped neat or on the rocks. Tom Hutchings – engineering student turned Distillery Manager – describes their recipe development as an art akin to layering a perfume: in this case, floral layers of lavender and chamomile, followed by citrus and kaffir lime, enhanced by local honey. Their 24 botanicals are selected by hand, and steeped for 24 hours before being diluted with water from the Silent Pool.

As we went to press Silent Pool was sold alongside Admiral Collingwood Navy Strength (57%), a vodka, gin cordials and an *eau de vie*, but the focus remains gin.

Twisted Nose Gin and Winchester Distillery

Alresford, Hampshire
Distillery

ESSENTIAL INFORMATION

Key botanicals (Twisted Nose Gin): juniper, coriander seed, liquorice root, cassia bark, grapefruit peel, fennel seed, lavender, watercress

Output: not disclosed

Location: Manor Factory, Old Alresford, SO24 9DH

Telephone: 01962 920290

Email: hi@winchesterdistillery.co.uk

Website: www.winchesterdistillery.co.uk

Facebook: www.facebook.com/WinchesterDistillery

Instagram: @winchester_distillery

Twitter: @WinchDistillery

Opening hours: tours by appointment only

Other reasons to go: local watercress beds, watercress festival (in May), The Watercress Line steam train, Hampshire countryside

An unusual location for a distillery: beside one of the commercial watercress beds in the Alresford and Winchester area, fed by the clear, pure chalk stream water that flows off the South Downs (Britain has 160 of the estimated 210 chalk streams in the world). Watercress thrives in chalk streams and watercress farms replicate the chalk stream habitat in large, shallow reservoirs with gravel beds, the chalk stream water diverted to flow through.

Paul Bowler runs Winchester Distillery at Manor Factory off the B3046 about a mile north of Alresford and distils his signature gin with, what else, watercress. The Latin name for watercress is *Nasturtium officinale*, derived from *nasus* meaning nose and *tortus* meaning twisted, referring to the effect of the peppery taste on the nasal passages. It makes an assertive, fresh G&T especially if served with Fever-Tree Elderflower tonic and a slice of pink grapefruit or, combined with vermouth, a stinger of a Dry Martini.

Paul makes six core products: Winchester Dry Gin (£37.95 – top right) uses 25 (secret) medieval botanicals; Twisted Nose Wasabi Vodka is distilled with seven botanicals and locally grown wasabi; as well as Twisted Nose Gin (left), Twisted Nose Oak Aged Gin, Hampshire Fine Dry Gin and Hampshire 'Gunpowder' Navy Strength Gin. They also do seasonal and experimental gins and all their spirits are currently produced in 200-litre batches.

Tours of the distillery can be booked on their website, involving a talk on the history and process of making gin, and a tutored tasting session.

Griffiths Brothers Gin and Distillery

Amersham, Buckinghamshire
Distillery and bar

ESSENTIAL INFORMATION

Key botanicals (Griffiths Brothers No.1 Gin): juniper, coriander seed, liquorice root, grains of paradise, cassia bark, lemon zest, orange zest, bay laurel, barberry, elderflower, orange blossom

Output: 20,000 bottles a year

Location: Unit 8, Penn Street Works, Amersham, HP7 0PX

Telephone: 01494 713955

Email: info@griffithsbrothers.com

Website: www.griffithsbrothers.com

Facebook: www.facebook.com/ GriffithsBrothersGin

Instagram: @griffithsbrothers

Twitter: @GriffithsGin

Opening hours:
Friday 1000-1600

Other reasons to go: Amersham Museum, Chiltern Society

*D*avid T. Smith writes: Located deep in the picturesque Chiltern Hills in the village of Penn Street, near Amersham, is Griffiths Brothers Distillery. The distillery was founded in 2016 by Alex Griffiths, who had previously worked in IT, and his brother Andrew, who works in finance.

Penn Street is a quintessential, small English village in an area of outstanding natural beauty; it has two pubs and is focused around the village common. The distillery is on the site of a 1930s aircraft factory where, during the Second World War, Mosquito fighter planes were manufactured.

The distillery opened for tours in 2019. These are hosted one day a week and include a welcome and departing G&T, an overview of botanicals and the vacuum distillation process (see below), and a tasting of the Griffiths Brothers range. The distillery also features a bar and plans to have "open bar nights" a few times a month where visitors can come and enjoy drinks and cocktails in a relaxed atmosphere.

The first gin produced by the distillery (2017) – Griffiths Brothers No.1 (left, middle bottle) – has a very classic flavour. It is distilled under reduced pressure in a glass still by vacuum distillation, which means that the spirit distills at a lower temperature and the botanicals are kept relatively cool, resulting in a different flavour than that produced by a copper pot still. Their second gin, Griffiths Brother No.2 (left, left-hand bottle), is bottled at a higher alcoholic strength and has greater focus on citrus and herbal flavours.

Unusually Griffiths Brothers recommend that their gins are served chilled and they even incorporate a heat sensitive indicator on their bottle labels so that consumers will know when it's at the ideal temperature for drinking.

Test Valley Gin and Wessex Spirits

Andover, Hampshire
Distillery and tasting room

ESSENTIAL INFORMATION

Key botanicals (Test Valley Gin): juniper, coriander seed, cassia bark, cubeb, basil, thyme

Output: 200 bottles a month

Location: 4 Dene Road, Andover, SP10 2AA

Telephone: 01264 710768

Email: info@wessexspirits.co.uk

Website: www.wessexspirits.co.uk

Facebook: www.facebook.com/ testvalleygin

Instagram: @testvalleygin

Twitter: @testvalleygin

Opening hours: tastings by appointment only – see website for booking information

Other reasons to go: Finkley Down Farm, Anton Lakes, Andover Museum, Army Flying Museum

When English teacher Kate Griffin's daughter was born with a cleft lip and palate in 2013, Kate stopped teaching as she needed frequent surgery. She had always loved gin and used to watch her mum make sloe gin so, with nothing to lose, she decided to make her own, opting for the London Dry style, making infusions in her grandad's kitchen. Test Valley Gin (above) was her first product, with batches of 36 bottles a week, and now production is up to 170 a week.

Kate uses local ingredients where possible – her mum grows some of the herbs in her garden. She also works with chocolatier Alexander Seaton from Salisbury, who sources the lemon verbena from local kitchen gardens used in her second product, Spire Gin (opposite, bottom right). He also helps to find hibiscus for her seasonal Summer Solstice Gin, in which she also uses local raspberries and redcurrants. The gin is not as sweet as you'd expect for a pink gin and is a great summer tipple when added to Prosecco.

The gins can be bought directly from the premises (left), online and through local shops and gin festivals. For £26 you can also sample the gins in one of her tasting sessions – there's room for six to ten visitors in her premises.

Kate thinks that people should drink gin however they want, but she prefers Test Valley Gin with Fever-Tree tonic and fresh

thyme. She recommends serving Spire Gin with a slice of grapefruit to emphasize its citrus flavours.

In October 2018, Kate launched Weyhill Fair Gin. Weyhill Fair was just up the road and she enjoyed the link to Thomas Hardy – Weyhill Fair was where *The Mayor of Casterbridge* Michael Henchard sold his wife.

Kate's latest release in summer 2019 was Resting Place Rum, a dark, spiced rum infused with Cornish sea salt. Future plans include a chilli vodka (there's a chilli farm just down the road).

Renegade Gin and Doghouse Distillery

Battersea, London
Distillery

ESSENTIAL INFORMATION

Key botanicals (Renegade Gin): juniper, coriander, cardamom, grains of paradise, bay leaf, sage, winter savory, plus seven secret ingredients

Output: not disclosed

Location: Unit L, London Stone Business Estate, Broughton Street, London, SW8 3QR

Telephone: 0207 622 9970

Email: rocknroll@doghousedistillery.com

Website: www.doghousedistillery.com

Facebook: www.facebook.com/doghousedistillery

Instagram: @doghousedistillery

Twitter: @doghousedistill

Opening hours: tours by appointment only. Open days run throughout the year – see website for details

Other reasons to go: Battersea Park, Battersea Park Children's Zoo, New Covent Garden Market

Ella Carr writes: Many craft gins thrive on a bit of rule-breaking, but the team (opposite, bottom right) at Doghouse Distillery have turned rebellion into a brand. Their signature gin, Renegade (bottom left), stands out on three counts: process, flavour and visual appeal.

For several years husband and wife team Braden and Katherine (opposite, middle) owned a successful craft beer pub in Australia, before Braden got interested in the creative distilling techniques coming out of the USA's west coast. In order to realize their new direction, in 2016 they moved back to England (Katherine is English), built a distillery and launched Renegade Gin from their Battersea premises the following year. They are one of only 15 distilleries in the UK (as we went to press) to produce gin entirely from scratch, from grain to bottle, and this claims to be the only one in London to do so. They mill, mash, ferment and rectify 100 per cent English wheat sourced from Norfolk to create a 96% vodka. This is sold as Baller vodka (opposite, top right), and also makes the base spirit of Renegade. If a distiller makes gin using bought-in grain spirit, they can produce their gin ready for bottling in 24 hours. Making one's own base spirit adds significant time and effort for Doghouse – about ten days to ensure there is enough for one batch of gin. But Braden feels it's worth it to have 100 per cent control over production, and to make a silky smooth spirit that leaves you wanting more.

While most gins are 'London Dry' or citrus-heavy, Renegade has an unusually herbaceous profile, with botanicals such as sage, bay leaf, cardamom and winter savory plus a hint of warmth from the grains of

paradise (sourced from West Africa) and, of course, plenty of juniper. The result is what Braden calls a middle palate 'sessionable' gin that can be drunk through the evening.

Doghouse's branding brings some overdue urban edge to craft gin. For Renegade they brought in London-based Italian tattoo artist Alo Loco to design the seedy sepia-and-grey bottle sleeve depicting scenes of old and new London. A reflection, Katherine tells us, of the gin's flavour profile, "a new age version of an old age spirit." For Baller Vodka they enlisted street artist Alex Lehours. The label depicts a cocky Jack Russell Terrier (the 'Baller') winning a game of poker against three intimidating Dobermans. In poker, a 'baller' plays for high stakes, so the label is a metaphor for Doghouse going up against the big dogs of the industry.

Doghouse have ambitious branding plans that involve bringing in street and tattoo artists to decorate the distillery. They also hold live performances and mini festivals throughout the year. With growth will also come new spirits – each one with their own individual branding, even their own music genre, to reflect their unique character, all tied back to the rebellious theme of the Doghouse.

Jensen's Gin and Bermondsey Distillery

Bermondsey, London
Distillery and tasting room

ESSENTIAL INFORMATION

Key botanicals (Jensen's Bermondsey Dry
   Gin): juniper, coriander seed, liquorice
   powder, cassia bark, almond powder,
   lemon peel, savory leaf

Output: 50,000 bottles a year

Location: 55 Stanworth Street, London,
   SE1 3NY

Telephone: 020 7237 1500

Email: info@jensensgin.com

Website: www.jensensgin.com

Facebook: www.facebook.com/jensensgin

Instagram: @jensensgin

Twitter: @JensensGin

Opening hours:
Saturday 1030-1800
Sunday 1100-1600

Other reasons to go: Druid Street Market,
HMS Belfast, Maltby Street Market, White
Cube Bermondsey, The Scoop, Fashion and
Textile Museum

Christian Jensen (opposite, top right) was in Tokyo working as a banking IT specialist when sitting in a bar one evening he had a moan at the bartender about how difficult it was to find a good gin in Japan. The barman pulled out a bottle of Gordon's from the 1960s. When they compared it with a more recent one, the difference was obvious. The barman told him he should make his own gin and when Christian got back to London he thought, why not?

He approached Charles Maxwell from Thames Distillers (one of only two distilleries in London at the time) with the vintage gin from Japan and asked him to recreate it. Charles produced around 30 distillations over the course of a year, and then they narrowed the choices down to what would become Jensen's Bermondsey Dry Gin (left, left-hand bottle).

Christian never intended to make a business out of gin, but because the rules of gin distilling were so tight, he couldn't simply buy the gin for his own use: he had to register with HMRC and set up a company. Charles told him he still couldn't just give him the gin, he needed to bottle and label it. In turn that meant he had to order – and buy – a minimum of 1,200 bottles. So he started taking the gin to bars, asking bartenders to taste it and use it in a Martini. One evening, in Bedales of Borough Market, he overheard a bartender saying there were no good gins. So he whipped out a bottle of Jensen's. Bedales

became his first customer.

Soon after, a friend told him that if he wanted to make money, he needed to make a second gin. After digging through archives, Christian found a recipe in a distiller's handbook from the 1840s. He gave it to Charles and Jensen's Old Tom Gin (bottom right, left-hand bottle) was born. Now the brand was established, Christian moved the distilling in house, founding Bermondsey Distillery under the railway arches (opposite, top right) in 2012.

The London Dry is citrus led and its smooth feel in the mouth means it's great as a sipping drink or in a Dry Martini. The Old Tom is more punchy as it has more juniper, spice and plenty of liquorice. Jensen's also produces seasonal gins: when we visited, they were working on a rhubarb-infused variety. This was to be a very limited edition, with only two barrels made by soaking rhubarb in a barrel of Bermondsey Dry Gin. Another limited edition is their honey-infused gin, made in collaboration with Bermondsey Street Bees.

For £20 you can do an after-hours tour of the distillery (above right), learning about distillation, the Jensen's brand and London's gin history. This is followed by a tutored tasting session and includes a G&T on arrival.

Two One Four

Bermondsey, London
Bar

ESSENTIAL INFORMATION

**Location: 214 Bermondsey Street, London,
SE1 3TQ (below Flour & Grape)**

Telephone: 020 7403 6875

Email: contact@two1four.com

Website: www.two1four.com

**Facebook: www.facebook.com/
two1fourbermondsey**

Instagram: @two1fourbermondsey

Twitter: @214Bermondsey

Opening hours:

Monday-Wednesday 1700-2300

Thursday 1700-0000

Friday-Saturday 1700-0130

Sunday Social 1600-2200

Other reasons to go: Druid Street Market

A dimly-lit basement (bottom left) with exposed brick walls offering 90 gins from all over the world, expertly served: a gin head's return to the womb.

It isn't immediately obvious from the street because it's the downstairs bar of the Flour & Grape, a ground-level pasta and wine restaurant, but once inside look left and you'll see a sign announcing Two One Four and steps to the basement.

Sam (from Sicily) was manning the bar. To kick off, he suggested his favourite gin, St George from California (below left, right-hand bottle), which is about as complex and one-off as they come, with a strong taste of peanuts. On the premises they make their own tonic water, Bermondsey Tonic Water, which has less sugar than regular slimline tonics and allowed the subtleties of St George to keep their head above the parapet.

Next, Sam recommended his most off-the-wall brand: Pink Pepper (left, left-hand bottle), a sweet-tasting French blend flavoured with aniseed and vanilla. Then for a complete contrast: a double Jensen's, which is very traditional, from nearby Bermondsey Distillery (page 58). Finally, time to throttle back with Sam's favourite gin cocktail made from Hendrick's, cucumber water and sparkling elderflower juice: as refreshing as a gin-based cocktail can be, setting us up for a sensible journey home by rail via nearby London Bridge station.

Bermondsey Street, off Tower Bridge Road, has been quite well regenerated, with some interesting shops including a great home-made pasta producer two doors down from Two One Four.

East London Liquor Company Gin and Distillery

Bow Wharf, London
Distillery and bar

ESSENTIAL INFORMATION

Key botanicals (London Dry Gin): juniper, coriander, cardamom, cubeb, lemon peel, grapefruit peel

Output: not disclosed

Location: Unit GF1, 221 Grove, London, E3 5SN

Telephone: 020 3011 0980

Email: distilling@eastlondonliquorcompany.com

Website: www.eastlondonliquorcompany.com

Facebook: www.facebook.com/EastLondonLiquorCompany

Instagram: @eastlondonliquorcompany

Twitter: DistillinginE3

Opening hours:
Distillery
Tuesday-Thursday 1700-2300
Friday 1700-0030
Saturday 1200-0000
Sunday 1200-2300

Other reasons to go: Mile End Park and Arts Pavilion, Ragged School Museum

Ella Carr writes: This is a serious operation with a staff of more than 30 as we went to press, a bar (bottom left), a restaurant and two bottle shops. Founded in 2014 in a converted glue factory, it's in the capital's old spirits district and can claim to be the first gin, vodka and whisky distillery to open there in over 100 years.

Vodka, whisky and rum are important here, but there is an emphasis on gin – they distil three. Besides London Dry (40% – right), there's Premium Batch No.1 Gin (45%) flavoured with Darjeeling tea, juniper, coriander seed, cassia bark, angelica, pink grapefruit and cubeb. The tea contributes to the clasically dry taste. Cubeb berries come from Indonesia and have long been used alongside juniper for their strong lavender and cracked black pepper flavour but these days are uncommon as a botanical – perhaps because they have to be used carefully. Besides being spicy and flowery, they can taste soapy – but not in this case.

Premium Batch No.2 Gin (47%) is made with juniper, coriander, orris root, angelica root, lemon peel, thyme, winter savory, fennel seed, sage, bay leaf and lavender – the flavours of a typical English herb garden. Terrific with a mixer, or in a punchy Martini or in a Negroni (one third gin, one third sweet vermouth and one third Campari).

Bookable tours run on Fridays and Saturdays, and tastings mid-week and one Saturday a month (also book in advance).

City of London Gin and Distillery

Bride Lane, London
Distillery, bar and gin school

ESSENTIAL INFORMATION

Key botanicals (City of London Dry Gin):
juniper, coriander seed, liquorice, lemon,
orange, pink grapefruit
Output: not disclosed
Location: 22-24 Bride Lane, London,
EC4Y 8DT
Telephone: 020 7936 3636
Email: enquiries@cityoflondondistillery.com
Website: www.cityoflondondistillery.com
Facebook: www.facebook.com/
cityoflondondistillery
Instagram:@cityoflondondistillery
Twitter: @COLDistillery

Opening hours:
Monday-Saturday 1600-2300

Other reasons to go: St Paul's Cathedral,
Millennium Bridge, Museum of London,
Charles Dickens Museum, Barbican Centre

The City of London Distillery opened in 2012 when owner Jonathan Clark decided to turn his cocktail bar on Bride Lane into a gin distillery. Jamie Baxter helped to install the stills (opposite, top left), which can be seen from the bar (opposite, bottom left) and lay the foundations for the signature gin recipe. The result: City of London Dry Gin (bottom left),which has a slightly higher dose of liquorice root and an emphasis on 'mouthfeel'. It works well in a G&T with a slice of fresh lemon or pink grapefruit (opposite, bottom right).

They also produce The Square Mile Gin (opposite, top right), named after the distillery's location in the City of London. This gin has a more herbal flavour because of a higher than usual amount of coriander. Try it in a Dry Martini. St Paul's Cathedral inspired the design of the dome-shaped bottle and as we went to press Christopher Wren was the latest gin to come out of the distillery, using five botanicals including juniper, coriander seed, liquorice root and orange.

City Of London holds a Distillery Tour and Gin Tasting experience where you are guided through the history of gin in London and learn about the distillery's gin making methods. This is followed by a gin tasting and includes a voucher for £5 off a bottle. Tours last about an hour and cost £25.

They also offer a Gin Lab Experience, where you can design and distil your own 70-cl bottle. This takes place on Wednesdays and Fridays at 2 pm and on Saturdays at 12 pm and 3 pm. For £125, you explore a range of botanicals and design and prepare a recipe of your own.

For £90, City Of London also holds what they call a Gin Competition lasting

for two and a half hours, where groups of ten to 18 people learn about distilling and then create their own bottle of gin based on their newfound knowledge. Blind tastings are then held to determine who has made the best gin.

All City Of London Distillery gins are available to buy from their online shop at prices ranging from £28 for the City of London Dry Gin to £35 for the Square Mile Gin. A Gin Taster selection is also available for £30 and includes 5-cl bottles of five of their main gins: London Dry, Christopher Wren, Old Tom, Sloe and Square Mile.

The Office

Brighton, East Sussex
Bar

ESSENTIAL INFORMATION
Location: 8-9 Sydney Street, Brighton,
  BN1 4EN
Telephone: 01273 609134
Email: enquiries@mypleasure.com
Website: www.pleisurepubs.co.uk
Facebook: www.facebook.com/
  OfficeBrighton
Instagram: @theofficebrighton

Opening hours:
Sunday-Wednesday 1200-2300
Thursday 1200-0000
Friday-Saturday 1200-0100

Other reasons to go: Brighton Pier,
British Airways i360 and shopping
in the Lanes

Ella Carr writes: There's a whiff of nostalgia about The Office (bottom left). Its bright, white-panelled interior – with enormous sash windows, bottle-green ceilings and chipped wooden furniture – reminded me of the old-fashioned waiting rooms in train stations. In fact a pub has been on this site since 1854, and instead of train times chalked up on the board you'll find a Gin Timeline running around its cornice, beginning at 1269 with the first major mention of juniper-based tonics in a Dutch publication.

If the decoration doesn't make you feel nostalgic, the prices certainly will. Starting at £3 for a shot of gin, and £6.95 for one of their craft gin cocktails, it's one of the rare gin bars catering to a student budget – perhaps unsurprising considering its Brighton location. Their gin count currently stands at 65, the most popular gins being McQueen's (page 243), Jinzu and of course Brighton Gin (page 325). They also stock genuine Dutch gin (above left). The friendly staff will happily guide you to your choice.

Punters flock here not only for the cheap tipple but for frequently held events such as Open Mic Wednesdays – I've also heard good things about their Thai menu, as well as a backyard that catches the afternoon sun – perfect for enjoying your G&T outdoors. The bar is a stone's throw from Brighton station on trendy North Laine, full of quirky cafés and hippy boutiques.

Canova Gin and Canova Hall

Brixton, London
Distillery and bar

ESSENTIAL INFORMATION

Key botanicals (Canova Gin): juniper coriander seed, liquorice root, lemon peel, bitter orange peel, goji berry, apple, pear, rosehip
Output: not disclosed
Location: 250 Ferndale Road, London, SW9 8BQ
Telephone: 020 7733 8356
Email: bookings@canovahall.com
Website: www.canovahall.com
Facebook: www.facebook.com/CanovaHall
Instagram: @canovahall
Twitter: @canovahall

Opening hours:
Monday-Thursday 0800-0000
Friday-Saturday 0800-2230
Sunday 0900-2230

Other reasons to go: Brixton Village, Brixton Academy, Hootananny music venue

The Albion and East group opened their second bar and microdistillery in September 2017 in the former worker's hall of Le Bon Marché – which was Britain's first department store. Their first one, Martello Hall, is on page 80. Canova Hall (bottom left) is over two floors, offering hot-desk facilities (including bottomless coffee for £10) and freshly made pizza from their wood-burning oven during the day, cocktails and dinner in the evening, and bottomless brunch on the weekends – for £25 you get brunch and unlimited drinks for two hours.

Canova Hall offers the same gin experiences as its sister bar – see Martello Hall for details – and brings the Hackney bar's warehouse glamour to Brixton, with exposed ceilings and plaster walls, a tiled bar and wooden benches (top). They make their own Canova Gin in their still, Grace, sited under the DJ booth, which they serve with Mediterranean tonic, Creme de Mure, blackberries and lemon. Martello Gin is also served here, alongside Jensen's Old Tom (page 58), East London Liquor Company Batch No.2 (page 61) and Aviation.

The gin is served on a cocktail trolley, which has various garnishes and tonics for you to make your own perfect serve. You can also 'Book a Bartender' who will mix cocktails at your table.

Half Hitch Gin

Camden, London
Distillery, bar and gin school

ESSENTIAL INFORMATION
Key botanicals (Half Hitch Gin): juniper,
    black tea, bergamot, wood, hay, pepper
Output: 15,000 bottles a year
Location: Unit 53, West Yard, Camden Lock
    Place, London, NW1 8AF
Telephone: 020 3096 3027
Email: enquiries@halfhitch.london
Website: www.halfhitch.london
Facebook: www.facebook.com/halfhitchgin
Instagram: @halfhitchgin
Twitter: @halfhitchgin

Opening hours:
Monday-Sunday 1100-1700

Other reasons to go: Camden Market, ZSL
London Zoo, The Regent's Park

Former Bacardi sales and marketing director Mark Holdsworth (bottom left) launched Half Hitch Gin (below) in September 2014. He chose Camden because of its gin history – in the late 1800s, distilleries were dotted over an area of 20 acres stretching from what is now the Lock to the Roundhouse Theatre.

Mark makes 'tinctures' (solutions of botanicals and alcohol) of wood and pepper, plus black tea and bergamot to make an Earl Grey flavour. These are added to the base gin (bought in from Langley Distillery in Birmingham), along with the rest of the botanicals, including a vacuum distillate (page 53) of hay. The result is a caramel-coloured gin with a sweet flavour and black tea aftertaste. Mark recommends serving the gin in a classic G&T or a Bronx cocktail with orange juice, plus both red and dry vermouths.

Production took place in the former warehouse vaults of Camden Lock until 2015 when Mark bought a site in Camden Market (left). He commissioned his own still and gradually brought production in-house. The new premises hosts a small tasting bar, plus a Gin School and Bespoke Gin-Making Experience, where you can bring ingredients to make your own recipe. You also receive two 100-ml bottles of gin to take away: one of your own creation and one of Half Hitch. The experience costs £60 and lasts between an hour and 90 minutes – visit their Facebook page for booking information.

Half Hitch? A type of knot used by sailors mooring their boats on Camden Lock.

Dockyard Gin and Copper Rivet Distillery

Chatham, Kent
Distillery and bar

ESSENTIAL INFORMATION

Key botanicals (Dockyard Gin): juniper, coriander seed, green cardamom, grains of paradise, lemon peel, orange peel, elderflower, plus two secret ingredients

Output: not disclosed

Location: Pump House No.5, Chatham Dockyard, Leviathan Way, Chatham, ME4 4LP

Telephone: 01634 931122

Email: enquiries@copperrivetdistillery.com

Website: www.copperrivetdistillery.com

Facebook: www.facebook.com/copperrivetdistillery

Instagram: @copperrivetdistillery

Opening hours:

Monday-Tuesday 1000-1700

Wednesday 1000-1800

Thursday 1000-1930

Friday-Saturday 1000-2200

Sunday 1200-1700

Other reasons to go: The Historic Dockyard

Ella Carr writes: Matthew Russell was visiting Upnor Castle with his young family when he spotted Pumphouse No.5 across from River Medway: a redbrick Victorian building in Chatham's historic dockyards (above) that had lain abandoned for decades, much to the despair of locals. He – along with his father, Bob, and his brother, Stephen (all pictured next page, top left) – had been looking for a site to house their new distillery, so he took a detour and discovered it was for sale. The ship-making history of the building and its location represented a fine tradition of local craftsmanship and industry, so what could be more fitting than turning it into a distillery that would support those same things? With 40 years of experience in the gin industry under his belt, Bob lost little time in launching Dockyard Gin (left and next page, top right) in 2016.

Copper Rivet can claim to be one of only 15 distilleries in the UK that make their own grain alcohol, growing and milling their grain in collaboration with local farmers. Grain alcohol is the basis of many spirits, re-distilled with botanicals (predominantly juniper) to make gin.

Rather than buy from Germany, Copper Rivet designs its own stills. Their first still, Joyce (next page, middle), was designed over five years by Master Distiller Abhi Banik who has taught distilling at Heriott-Watt University. The gin is made by infusing the spirits in a

single still (bottom right) using a one-shot process, which allows maceration to take place away from the still's heat source, consequently giving them the clearest flavours and maximum control.

The recipe for the gin itself was finally formulated after 40 tries, with nine botanicals comprising its backbone. These hit the palate in three waves: the first is citrus from the juniper, lemon peel and coriander seeds; the second is floral and sweet coming from the elderflower, cardamon and angelica root; and the third reinforces these flavours, providing a rounded feeling in the mouth from the grains, orange peel and orris root. The result is a smooth and easy gin: fresh, citrusy and moreish, with a peppery heat in the aftertaste. It's best drunk with tonic and grapefruit, whose bitterness perfectly offsets the natural sweetness (no sugar is added to the spirit: the sweetness comes from fermenting the wort for seven days. Wort is the liquid extracted from the grain 'mash' which is the starting point for making grain spirit).

Copper Rivet's Distillery Experience takes you on a tour of the remarkable listed building and the area's ship-making heritage. You learn about the history of Chatham's dockyard and distillation techniques, before taking part in a tasting, which includes Dockyard Gin, Vela Vodka, and their Damson Gin.

Chilgrove Gin and Chilgrove Spirits

Chichester, West Sussex
Distillery and gin school

ESSENTIAL INFORMATION

Key botanicals (Chilgrove Signature Edition Gin): juniper, coriander seed, liquorice root, grains of paradise, lime, orange, bitter orange, wild water mint, savory
Output: 50,000 bottles a year
Location: The Bakery, Watergate, Chichester, PO19 9RJ
Telephone: 02392 631808
Email: info@chilgrovespirits.com
Website: www.chilgrovespirits.com
Facebook: www.facebook.com/chilgrove
Instagram: @chilgrovespirits
Twitter: @ChilgroveGin

Opening hours: not open to the public

Other reasons to go: Fishbourne Roman Palace, Chichester Cathedral, Pallant House Gallery

Chilgrove Spirits claims to be the only distiller in the UK to make their gin from a 100 per cent grape-alcohol base as opposed to the more common cereal base (Foxhole Gin also has a grape-alcohol base – see page 324). The operation is run by Christopher Beaumont-Hutchings and his wife Celia (bottom left and next page, bottom right) who grew up in Holland – the home of gin. Traditionally, genever (Dutch gin) was made using alcohol distilled from wine, but because the Little Ice Age (14th to 19th centuries) caused a wine shortage in Europe, many distillers turned to a cereal base. Given Celia's Dutch heritage and their own taste preferences, it made sense to revive the grape base. In grape spirit, botanicals act differently – the grape emphasises the floral flavours in the gin – so they spent a few months of trial and error to find the right balance of flavours to complement the spirit, with the help of Charles Maxwell at Thames Distillery.

Chilgrove recommends adding two shots of its Signature Edition Gin (left) to tonic water, with plenty of ice and a sprig of fresh English mint. It also works well in a gin fizz cocktail: mix equal measures of the gin, fresh pink grapefruit juice and fresh lemon juice and top up with English sparkling wine (or Champagne or Prosecco if you prefer), adding a twist of orange peel to garnish.

They also produce Chilgrove Bluewater Edition Gin (next page, top left), a London Dry which is bottled at 46% and takes inspiration from the relationship between Australia and England by incorporating native botanicals from both countries: finger limes, lemon myrtle, riberry and Davidson plum from Australia and mint, savory, angelica and coriander from England. These botanicals

are illustrated on the sides of the bottle and are distilled with the grape-alcohol base plus water from the South Downs. The blue neck of the bottle is a reference to Captain James Cook (the first European to map the coastline of New Zealand and land on Australia's east coast at Botany Bay) and his first voyage on the *HM Bark Endeavour*. The name Bluewater refers to deep water (ocean) sailing.

They also make Chilgrove Bramble Edition Gin (right), which includes all the botanicals of the London Dry plus English blackberries, which are infused in the spirit to create a deep, ruby red colour. They recommend serving 50 ml of the Bramble Edition with 100 ml of light tonic, plenty of ice and a frozen blackberry and slices of apple to garnish.

The Chilgrove Gin School (top right) is held at The White Horse in Chilgrove. You get a brief history of gin while sipping a Chilgrove G&T, followed by a talk on how the company operates. But the main event is the interactive cocktail making masterclass, typically involving four or five different serves.

Contact info@chilgrovespirits.com to book. The masterclasses can be held on any day of the week and at alternative venues by arrangement. They can be tailored for groups of two to a hundred people and can be combined as a package with dinner and accommodation at The White Horse.

Sipsmith Gin and Distillery

Chiswick, London
Distillery

ESSENTIAL INFORMATION

Key botanicals (London Dry Gin): juniper, coriander seed, liquorice, cassia bark, cinnamon, ground almond, lemon peel, orange peel

Output: not disclosed

Location: The Distillery, 83 Cranbrook Road, London, W4 2LJ

Telephone: 020 8747 0753

Email: tours@sipsmith.com

Website: www.sipsmith.com

Facebook: www.facebook.com/sipsmith

Instagram: @sipsmith

Twitter: @sipsmith

Opening hours: evening tours by appointment only

Other reasons to go: Chiswick House and Gardens, Hogarth's House

Ella Carr writes: In 2009 childhood friends Fairfax and Sam were the first craft distillers to obtain a distilling licence for nearly 200 years, helping to kickstart the craft gin renaissance. They've grown into a mainstream distiller, but their philosophy is still to produce gin the old-fashioned way, and make it good enough to be sipped neat.

They sold their flats to buy their first still, ironically named Prudence. Today they distil down the road in Chiswick in Prudence plus two shiny new stills named Constance and Verity. They produce in a year what the big dogs do in a week, but they still manage to export to 150 countries worldwide.

Another reason for including Sipsmith in the guide's main section is their week-night tours. These begin with a refreshing gin cocktail, before hearing about the history of gin and Sipsmith itself, followed by a tasting session of four of their gins. First up is their classic London Dry Gin – a very traditional recipe of ten botanicals plucked straight from the 18thC by their Master Distiller (and resident drinks historian) Jared Brown. This is followed by Lemon Drizzle: not overly sweet despite its name, it's essentially their London Dry with a kick of citrus achieved from fresh grilled lemon peel, lemon verbena and lots of coriander. Next comes a gin from their Sipping Society (see below). When I visited, this was Strawberries and Cream with a genuine aroma of strawberry cheesecake morphing into a fruity-fresh finish. But it was their Sloe Gin that did it for me, bursting with ripe cherry flavour.

I left the evening feeling a little giddy, and tempted to join their Sipping Society: pay a subscription of £180 a year to receive a different sample gin every other month.

Stovell's Gin and Distillery

Chobham, Surrey
Distillery and restaurant

ESSENTIAL INFORMATION

Key botanicals (Batch 11 Gin): juniper, liquorice, lemon balm, Alexander's seed, wild fennel, meadowsweet, nettle, sweet flag, bilberry, hawthorn berry, wild rosehip, rose petal, elderflower, chamomile, lovage, woodruff, oak moss, honey

Output: not disclosed

Location: 125 Windsor Road, Chobham, GU24 8QS

Telephone: 01276 858000

Email: enquiries@stovells.com

Website: www.stovells.com

Facebook: www.facebook.com/stovells

Instagram: @stovells_chobham

Opening hours:
Monday-Sunday 1200-1530 & 1800-2230

Other reasons to go: Chobham Common, Thorpe Park, Windsor Great Park, Virginia Water Lake

Fernando Stovell (chef/director) and Geyan Surendran (distiller/mixologist), between them winners of six awards, have been cooking and serving cocktails using ingredients foraged in the local Surrey countryside since 2013. They both enjoyed gin, so the natural next step was to make their own.

They use the finest base spirit from grain grown on organic farms and go the extra mile to prepare the botanicals for maximum natural flavour. Juniper berries are cracked by hand. Woody stems and tough seeds are ground into a coarse powder using a special grinder which keeps them cool. Some botanicals, for example fennel and angelica seeds, are toasted, some left as they are.

Next the botanicals are separated into flavour families and steeped in spirit. The resulting infusions are then strained and distilled using a rotary evaporator (opposite, top right and bottom) which allows the boiling point of alcohol to remain low. The botanicals never stew or burn, their flavours stay lively.

These flavoured spirits are then blended back into the base spirit. Locally made honey is added. This resulting concoction is very strong – 92% – so it's diluted down to 40% using filtered water. The gin is now ready, but they let it rest for a few weeks to encourage the flavours to coalesce and to stabilize. Then it's hand bottled.

The same energy and care goes into assembling the botanicals. All are from within the UK unless there's an ethical reason for going elsewhere. For example, the juniper berries are foraged wild in Croatia where the warm climate makes them extra plump. (In the UK, juniper bushes are in decline.) None of the

botanicals used have ever been cultivated and, unusually, Stovell's contains no citrus, no cumin and no orris root. The flavourings change all the time so the botanicals listed opposite, top left, were unique to Batch 11 (above), in production when we visited.

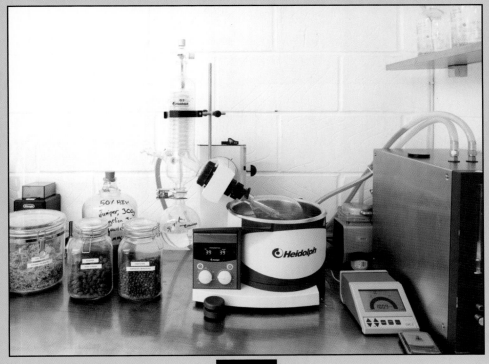

Mr Fogg's Gin Parlour

Covent Garden, London
Bar

ESSENTIAL INFORMATION
Location: 1 New Row, London, WC2N 4EA
Telephone: 020 7581 3992
Email: ginparlour@mr-foggs.com
Website:
www.mr-foggs.com/mr-foggs-gin-parlour
Facebook: www.facebook.com/
  MrFoggsGinParlour
Instagram: @mrfoggsgb
Twitter: @MrFoggsGB

Opening hours:
Monday-Thursday 1600-0000
Friday 1600-0030
Saturday-Sunday 1300-2330

Other reasons to go: Theatreland

Ella Carr writes: Mr Fogg's Tavern (bottom left) is set in the re-imagined home of Phileas Fogg – protagonist of *Around the World in Eighty Days* – and adorned with artefacts and heirlooms from his travels (opposite, top left). Above it is Mr Fogg's Gin Parlour (with its own entrance on New Row – opposite, top right), a salon straight out of the *Belle Epoque*. It might whiff of gimmick, but we think they've pulled it off splendidly.

A narrow staircase around the side of the tavern leads you up to the boudoir-esque gin bar (opposite, bottom left) – low-ceilinged and intimate, with tinkling piano music in the background – fulsomely decorated with tassels, swags and upholstered French furniture (opposite, middle). Corseted, full-skirted hostesses lead you to your seat and advise on the gins available (200 and counting), and bring over bottles for you to nose before trying.

On my visit, gin-o-phile Giovanni suggested some of his favourites, such as KI NO BI, the unique rice-based gin produced out of Kyoto's first distillery. He also talked me through their new cocktail menu, especially designed to reel in gin-skeptics. The small red booklet, enclosed in the drawers of Victorian music boxes found on each table, has cocktails inspired by the travels of Phileas' aunt and landlady, Gerty. For example, the African-inspired Under a Baobab Tree, flavoured with tamarind

syrup, a rooibos-date reduction and turmeric foam.

I settled back with a Pink Pepper Gin & Tonic on Giovanni's recommendation, fragrantly garnished with pink peppercorns, dried orange and a sprig of lavender. The perfect 'gateway' gin (in line with Giovanni's mission to educate the masses), it has floral tones and hints of quince, finishing off with a kick of pink pepper.

Gutsy Monkey Winter Gin and The Gin Kitchen

Dorking, Surrey
Distillery, bar and shop

ESSENTIAL INFORMATION

Key botanicals (Gutsy Monkey Winter Gin):
   juniper, black pepper, cumin, allspice,
   thyme, ginger

Output: 11,000 bottles a year

Location: Punchbowl Lane, Dorking,
   RH5 4DX

Telephone: 01306 889598

Email: fabulous@gin.kitchen

Website: www.gin.kitchen

Facebook: www.facebook.com/
   theginkitchen

Instagram: @theginkitchen

Twitter: @theginkitchen

Opening hours:
Monday-Friday 1000-1700

Other reasons to go: Box Hill, Denbies
Hillside, Leith Hill, Dorking Museum and
Heritage Centre

Kate (opposite, bottom right, left-hand side), co-founder, was in her car on the way to the airport to catch a flight to Paris when she heard a radio item about the craft gin craze. A light bulb went on in her head and she knew there and then that she would give up her job with a multinational company to distil craft gin with her friend Helen from work. Before catching the plane she rang Helen to tell her the news. Helen: "I'm just going into a meeting". Kate: "The meeting doesn't matter any more, we're going to make gin."

Kate began researching gin-making techniques on her phone, and couldn't concentrate on work because her head was full of flavour extraction and designing her own still. Back from Paris, she went to Waitrose to buy all the gins they had in stock in order to work out how to differentiate her own flavours.

In 2016 she and Helen launched The Gin Kitchen (left) in a coal shed at the back of The Spotted Dog pub in Dorking, distilling twice a week to make about 60 bottles. Now they distil Monday to Friday producing about 60 bottles a day.

We tried their first gin, Gutsy Monkey Winter Gin (top right), neat on the rocks and hugely enjoyed the warm glow as it hit the stomach. Their second gin to be launched, Dancing Dragontail Summer Gin (opposite, top right), flavoured with pink grapefruit zest, cardamom and cassia bark is a fresh, summery spirit set off nicely by their own tonic water (opposite, top left). Alongside a range of exclusive gins for the likes of The Vineking, Fortnum & Mason and Lingfield

Park Estate, the latest creation as we went to press was Blushing Monkey Pink Gin, a fruity and sweet tipple which, thanks to macerated black grapes, turns to the colour of candyfloss when mixed with tonic.

As the business expanded, so did their team and premises – in late 2017 they moved into a barn on the outskirts of Dorking's town centre with a den for tippling their Eternal Absinthe. You can taste gins on the spot and buy direct at the distillery bar and shop (bottom left), where you can also buy bottles and accessories. The gins can also be found in a range of independent retailers and larger stores such as Majestic and Fortnum & Mason.

Dr J's Gin and English Spirit Distillery

Great Yeldham, Essex

Distillery

ESSENTIAL INFORMATION

Key botanicals (Dr J's Gin): juniper, coriander, citrus zest, macadamia nut

Output: not disclosed

Location: The Black Barn, Great Yeldham Hall, Church Road, Great Yeldham, CO9 4PT

Telephone: 01787 237896

Email: sales@englishspiritdistillery.com

Website: www.englishspirit.uk

Facebook: www.facebook.com/englishspirituk

Instagram: @englishspirituk

Twitter: @englishspirituk

Opening hours:
Monday-Friday 0900-1700

Other reasons to go: Colne Valley Railway, Ridgewell Airfield Commemorative Museum, Roman Villa

Former Oxford biochemist Dr John Walters owned and sold several businesses, including a pharmaceutical company, and was looking for a new challenge. He'd heard on the radio that *eau de vie* couldn't be made in England and set about proving them wrong. When he succeeded, he decided to go into the spirits business himself, as he was convinced that commercially produced spirits were not up to scratch. Digging about in HMRC regulations, he found that stills up to four litres in size could be bought for personal use, if you register. In 2011, he received his permit, becoming one of the first small batch distillers to open in the UK for over 200 years.

He started making brandy, using the grapes that grew on the side of his house. He compared it to a supermarket cognac and decided his tasted better, so branched out into other spirits, experimenting with an elderberry *eau de vie* and a vodka. Distilled from East Anglia sugar beet, the vodka is re-distilled as the base spirit for Dr J's Gin (left). John uses five different types of coriander to make his gin, which he macerates in the base spirit with the rest of the botanicals, adding them at different stages before distilling them together. The undiluted gin is then cut to 45% with purified water in a separate still. John wanted to make a gin that could be drunk neat but for a perfect serve he recommends mixing it with a quality tonic, crushed ice and a couple of salted capers.

He also produces Plum, Rhubarb, Lemon, Lavender and Raspberry Gin Liqueurs, and makes gin under contract for several drinks companies. Future plans include a visitors' centre with a shop and café.

58 Gin and Distillery

Hackney, London
Distillery and gin school

ESSENTIAL INFORMATION

Key botanicals (58 Gin): juniper, coriander
seed, cubeb, lemon, pink grapefruit,
bergamot, vanilla

Output: not disclosed

Location: 329 Acton Mews, London, E8 4EF

Telephone: N/A

Email: hello@58gin.com

Website: www.58gin.com

Facebook: www.facebook.com/58Gin

Instagram: @58gin

Twitter: @58Gin

Opening hours: visits by appointment only

Other reasons to go: London Fields Lido,
Victoria Miro art gallery, Hackney City Farm

When Australian diving instructor Mark Marmont moved to London in 2007, he needed to find a new career – diving in the Thames didn't appeal. Living near an experimental cocktail bar, The Bar With No Name at 69 Colebrooke Row, he tried various gin-based cocktails and, inspired by the mixologist's ability to balance flavours, decided to learn about distilling gin. After a couple of years experimenting, he finally landed on a recipe he liked based on cocktail recipes from the 1930s prohibition era. The result, 58 Gin, was named after his house, 58 Colebrooke Row. He steeps the botanicals in a wheat-based spirit in a 650-litre copper still overnight. The product is then distilled for around eight hours before it's cut with water to 43%. The head and tail are eliminated, removing any sharp flavours, for a crisp final taste with a soft finish. Try it in a classic G&T or a Martini to enjoy its citrus flavour.

58 Gin also produces seasonal gins such as Distilled Sloe Gin, Navy Strength Gin, and Apple and Hibiscus Gin. They can be bought from the online shop as well as various shops around London, including Fortnum & Mason, Jones of Brockley and The London Gin Club (page 100).

The distillery (left) runs a Gin School featuring a Make Your Own Gin Class where you create your own recipe to bottle, seal and label. This is followed by a tasting session including four gin cocktails, nibbles and a brief history of gin in East London. It takes between two and three hours and costs £120 per person.

Contact ginschool@58gin.com to book.

Martello Gin and Martello Hall

Hackney, London
Distillery and bar

ESSENTIAL INFORMATION

Key botanicals (Martello Gin): juniper, coriander seed, cardamom pod, lemon peel, grapefruit peel, allspice berry, bay leaf, lemon thyme, lavender, chamomile flower

Output: not disclosed

Location: 137 Mare Street, London, E8 3RH

Telephone: 020 3889 6173

Email: bookings@martellohall.com

Website: www.martellohall.com

Facebook: www.facebook.com/MartelloHall

Instagram: @martellohall

Twitter: @MartelloHall

Opening hours:
Monday-Wednesday 1000-2300
Thursday 1000-0100
Friday-Saturday 1000-0300
Sunday 1200-0000
Bank holidays 1200-0300

Other reasons to go: London Fields, Stoke Newington High Street

Operated by the Albion and East group, Hackney's Martello Hall (bottom left) is a bar (above) and restaurant occupying three floors. Everything on the menus is made from scratch, including their own gin. Head distiller Jack produces Martello Gin (left) in their still, Nicola, and recommends serving it with Fever-Tree tonic, lemon and lime zest, orange, mint and plenty of ice. The gin can also be found in sister bars Cattivo and Canova Hall (page 65), both in Brixton.

For £40, Martello Hall offers a Gin Cocktail Masterclass where you get a welcome Prosecco before you mix three gin cocktails. The class lasts an hour and a half and includes a farewell limoncello. They also host a Gin Blending Masterclass where, for £80, you create your own recipe with the help of head distiller Jack. This masterclass lasts around two hours and includes four different G&Ts and a 400-ml bottle of your gin to take away.

Albion and East's mission is to create spaces for the 'millennial working generation' so Martello Hall is a hot-desk café by day and a cocktail bar-cum-pizza joint by night.

BANQUET HALL

Sacred Gin and Sacred Spirits Company

Highgate, London
Distillery

ESSENTIAL INFORMATION

Key botanicals (Sacred Gin): juniper, coriander, liquorice, cardamom, cinnamon, lemon, lime, orange, pink grapefruit, nutmeg, frankincense

Output: 70,000 bottles a year

Location: N/A

Telephone: 020 7263 8293

Email: info@sacredgin.com

Website: www.sacredgin.com

Facebook: www.facebook.com/ SacredSpiritsCompany

Instagram: @sacredgin

Twitter: @SacredGin

Opening hours: not open to the public

Ian Hart founded Sacred Spirits in 2008 with his wife Hilary at their house in Highgate. As a child, he was intrigued by the process of distilling and when he was old enough, a G&T became his drink of choice. He'd often thought about creating his own London Dry and liked the idea of "producing what is traditionally a London product, actually in London."

Ian has a degree in Natural Sciences, and worked for many years in finance. Then came the crash of 2008, work got scarce and Ian was drawn back to his scientific roots. He experimented with extracting water from below-par vintages to create a better quality wine, then turned to gin.

Ian believes he is the first to use the vacuum distillation method (page 53) to make gin, rather than the traditional pot still. The vacuum creates a lower boiling point: the botanicals aren't 'cooked', but their essence gently drawn out. Ian designed the stills (left) himself, giving him complete control over the production process and allowing him to adapt the equipment to suit each distillation.

Each of the botanicals used in Sacred Gin (next page, top left, middle bottle) is macerated in English wheat spirit for four to six weeks to allow for optimum extraction. The distillates are then distilled separately, to allow for experimentation with different flavour combinations, before blending them for the gin. One of the more unusual botanicals used in their signature London Dry is *Boswellia sacra* (Latin for Frankincense), which inspired the name

Sacred Gin. Ian and Hilary believe it gives the gin a fresh, resinous flavour.

Ian likes Sacred Gin in a Dry Martini, made with Sacred English Dry Vermouth and Hilary recommends serving the gin in a Gimlet with Rose's Lime Cordial.

In the early days, Ian and Hilary would take their gins into the local pub for the regulars to taste. The 23rd recipe was their lucky number – everyone knew this was the winner. The pub's landlord agreed to sell the spirit behind the bar, a nice incentive to produce the first 2,500 bottles.

Encouraged by the success of Sacred Gin, Ian also created Sacred Organic Gin plus seven additional gins, each of which focuses on a key botanical: Juniper, Coriander, Cardamom (right, middle bottle), Pink Grapefruit, Orris, Old Tom (top left, left-hand bottle) and Christmas Pudding. He also produces Sloe Gin (top left, right-hand bottle), Organic Vodka, London Dry Vodka, three vermouths, a Negroni, a whisky liqueur and Peated English Whisky. Their products can be bought from the online shop.

Sacred Spirits is currently based at Ian and Hilary's home in Highgate but as we went to press they were looking for a new premises where they will host tastings and distillery tours – check the website for updates.

Holborn Dining Room

Holborn, London
Bar

ESSENTIAL INFORMATION
Location: 252 High Holborn, London,
   WC1V 7EN
Telephone: 020 3747 8633
Email: info@holborndiningroom.com
Website: www.holborndiningroom.com
Instagram: @holborndiningroom
Twitter: @HolbornDining

Opening hours:
Monday-Friday 0700-2230
Saturday 0730-2230
Sunday and bank holidays 0730-2200

Other reasons to go: The Courtauld Gallery

Ella Carr writes: Located under the arches of Rosewood London, the Holborn Dining Room – marble-clad and high-ceilinged, with dusky mirrored surfaces – does justice to its stately exterior. Its copper-topped bar (bottom left) gleams with garnishes and botanicals laid out on silver trays (below left), with aromatic bitters in glass vials. With more than 500 gins and 15 tonics to choose from, this is the largest collection in London, so making a decision is a challenge. Fortunately, a fetching bartender called Andrea, dressed in tartan livery and speaking with a thick Italian accent, was on hand to guide me through their 'Gin Bible' – which is divided into chapters: Citrus, Floral, Herbal, Spice and Vintage.

Highlights from my tasting session included Dà Mhìle Seaweed Gin (page 120), Copperhead, and Citadelle No Mistake Old Tom Gin – the last a Caribbean-inspired, cask-aged gin from the esteemed French brand, flavoured headily with liquorice, cinnamon and caramelised brown sugar for a surprisingly fresh taste. This is best tried neat or on the rocks. True connoisseurs might want to sample their 'Vintage' list, but will have to line their pockets accordingly: the 1950s tipple comes to around £40 per 50 ml. Their lowliest G&T starts at £13 – here, sophistication doesn't come cheap.

For cocktails, Andrea recommends The Alchemist – a summery take on the Negroni, with the addition of limoncello foam; and Prudence, 'for the ladies' – a fruity pineapple and nutmeg concoction with a Sloe Gin base.

There's a stunning Edwardian courtyard for drinking outside in the summer – often enlivened by a gin-themed installation.

The Gin Tub

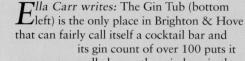

Hove, East Sussex

Bar

ESSENTIAL INFORMATION
Location: 16 Church Road, Hove, BN3 2FL
Telephone: 01273 772194
Email: info@thegintub.co.uk
Website: www.thegintub.co.uk
Facebook: www.facebook.com/
   thegintub
Instagram: @thegintub
Twitter: @thegintub

Opening hours:
Monday-Wednesday 1700-2300
Thursday 1600-late
Friday-Saturday 1300-late
Sunday 1600-late

Other reasons to go: Brighton Pier, shopping
in the Lanes, the British Airways i360

Ella Carr writes: The Gin Tub (bottom left) is the only place in Brighton & Hove that can fairly call itself a cocktail bar and its gin count of over 100 puts it well above other gin bars in the area. While its more ramshackle neighbours have opted for a minimalist approach to serving, The Gin Tub takes its cue from cosmopolitan gin bars: G&Ts are served in goblets on a bed of crushed ice, with generous garnishes such as petals and rosemary sprigs. There's also a host of gin-themed events, from Afternoon G&T to gin cocktail classes and gin tastings.

Whether to your taste or not, the surreal interior is certainly different. Grey ruched material on the ceiling gives the impression of a stormy sky, while tables are adorned with vintage lamps and telephones from which you order your drinks. One Dali-esque feature includes a ceiling light made from half a still, with tentacular tubes protruding bulbs.

Cosy corners and sultry lighting makes this a good date spot. Head to the intimate Mezzanine level to share a charcuterie board, followed by a gin tasting session or a 'gin slider'. If the date goes well, a casual evening drink can easily bleed into a night out, as the bar stays lively until 2 am on weekends.

The Old Albion

Hove, East Sussex
Bar

ESSENTIAL INFORMATION
Location: 110 Church Road, Hove, BN3 2EB
Telephone: 01273 772929
Email: hello@oldalbion.pub
Website: www.oldalbion.pub
Facebook: www.facebook.com/oldalbionpub
Instagram: @oldalbionpub
Twitter: @oldalbionpub

Opening hours:
Sunday-Thursday 1200-0000
Friday-Saturday 1200-0100

Other reasons to go: Brighton Pier, the
Royal Pavilion, shopping in the Lanes

Ella Carr writes: Despite calling itself a 'gin palace', The Old Albion (bottom left) feels more like a pub than a palace-era bar. A charmingly ramshackle one at that, with bunting (below right) and fairy lights hanging haphazardly across its ceiling and bizarre curios dotted about – including an old rocking horse. Located in Hove, Brighton's quieter neighbour, it's a proper locals place with plenty of cosy corners to settle into. There's also a large back room for watching TV sports, and a pleasant patio for enjoying the sunshine.

Lest people forget its gin focus, a large antique still is perched in the corner with four barrels hanging above it, and a glass table displaying their gins. When it comes to serving gin, The Old Albion have a no nonsense attitude. There's no cocktail menu (although there are gin-infused herbal teas). Instead, the 60 gins are chalked up on a board and served as shots or in G&Ts. Their floral selection of gins – such as Rhubarb and Elderflower – are particularly popular.

Another reason to come here is their food menu, full of robust dishes such as crispy Korean chicken burgers and juicy steaks.

The Beefeater Gin Distillery

Kennington, London
Distillery

ESSENTIAL INFORMATION

Key botanicals (Burrough Reserve Special Edition Gin): juniper, coriander, liquorice, lemon peel, orange peel, almond

Output: not disclosed

Location: 20 Montford Place, London, SE11 5DE

Telephone: 020 7587 0034

Email: info@beefeaterdistillery.com

Website: www.beefeaterdistillery.com

Facebook: www.facebook.com/Beefeater-Distillery

Instagram: @beefeatergin

Twitter: @BeefeaterGin_US

Opening hours:
Monday-Saturday 1000-1830

Other reasons to go: Kennington Park, Imperial War Museum, London Aquarium

Ella Carr writes: A titan of the British gin industry for at least a hundred years, with an output of 60 million bottles a year, Beefeater isn't 'craft' or 'small batch'. Within this operation, however, Beefeater have produced two craft gins known as Burrough Reserve Special Editions. They are worthy of this guide's attention – so I paid a visit to find out more.

My tour of Beefeater kicked off with an interactive walk through gin history (opposite, middle and bottom), beginning with its introduction to Britain in 1689, through to the 18thC Gin Craze and right up to Prohibition in the roaring 20s. After, I joined Ryan for a look around the distillery, where I had the chance to handle Beefeater's ten core botanicals before seeing their stills in action. But it was one still that caught my special attention. Dwarfed in size by the others but with a remarkable history attached to it, Still Number 12 was used by James Burrough to formulate the original recipe of their London Dry Gin (bottom left, left-hand bottle). After decades of inaction it has now been fired up once more to distil the two Burrough Reserve Special Editions, formulated by Beefeater's Master Distiller, Desmond Payne.

With 50 years' distilling experience and an MBE, Desmond had already been recognised for his inventiveness after using tea as a botanical in Beefeater 24 (left, second bottle from left), before he came up with the idea in 2014 for the first barrel-chested gin to complement a cheeseboard. He travelled to Bordeaux to purchase cask barrels that previously stored the aromatised wine, Jean de Lillet, in which he aged distilled Beefeater London Dry Gin for four to six weeks. For the Second Edition, this

ageing process was combined between Jean de Lillet and Lupiac barrels – Lupiac being a sweeter dessert wine from the same region.

If I had misgivings about pairing gin with cheese, they were quickly laid to rest by my tasting session (top right). The oakiness that comes through from the barrel-ageing creates a characterful gin that can hold its own with the cheese, whilst being light enough not to swamp its subtle flavour. The First Edition, paired with Comté, is a rich juniper-led gin with oak spice and hints of liquorice; the Second Edition – paired with a Gruyère – has a richer, sweeter kick of vanilla spice coming from the Lupiac, reminiscent of a fortified wine. Jean de Lillet has been discontinued, so they're both limited edition in the truest sense, but Desmond constantly has his ear to the ground, picking up new ideas and flavours.

Beefeater, which was founded in 1831 by industrialist James Burrough, is a worthy pit stop for anyone with an interest in the history of British gin. Unlike its competitors such as Tanqueray and Gordons, it claims to be the only major brand true to its London identity – produced from start to finish in their Kennington distillery using Burrough's original recipe and the same copper-pot method. This huge operation is overseen by a tight-knit family of 20 workers.

Mary-Le-Bone Gin and
The Mary-Le-Bone Hotel

Marylebone, London
Distillery and bar

ESSENTIAL INFORMATION

Key botanicals (Mary-Le-Bone Original
London Dry Gin): juniper, coriander,
liquorice, cassia bark, lemon, orange,
grapefruit, cloves, lime flower,
chamomile, lemon balm

Output: 36,000 bottles a year

Location: 108 Brasserie, The Mary-Le-Bone
Hotel, 47 Welbeck Street, London, W1G 8DN

Telephone: 020 7486 6600

Email: info@marylebonegin.com

Website: www.marylebonegin.com

Facebook: www.facebook.com/
marylebonegin

Instagram: @marylebonegin

Twitter: @marylebonegin

Opening hours:
108 Brasserie
Monday-Sunday 0700-2230

Other reasons to go: Baker Street

From the founder of Whitley Neill Gin (page 176) comes Mary-Le-Bone Gin (bottom left). At a strength of 50.2%, it's a bold spirit. Johnny wanted to create a gin using botanicals inspired by the Marylebone Pleasure Gardens that were at the height of their popularity during the Georgian period, and which he had known in his childhood.

The gin is made at two separate locations: the version sold in retailers is made on a larger scale at The City of London Distillery, using 180- and 500-litre copper pot stills and the multi-shot method (page 40). The other location is 108 Bar & Brasserie at The Mary-Le-Bone Hotel (top), where it's distilled on a 50-litre copper pot still using the one-shot method (page 68). As we went to press, Johnny was planning to change all production to the one-shot method. The gin can only be found in the hotel bar, or in various bars and restaurants nearby.

Mary-Le-Bone Gin is a robust London Dry Gin, slightly more floral and full of sweet citrus. Try serving it with premium tonic water and garnish with grapefruit – which brings out the chamomile and lime flower flavours.

Portobello Road Gin, The Distillery and GinTonica gin bar

Notting Hill, London
Distillery, bar and gin school

ESSENTIAL INFORMATION

Key botanicals (Portobello Road Gin): juniper, coriander seed, liquorice root, cassia bark, lemon peel, orange peel, nutmeg

Output: 50,000-1 million bottles a year

Location: 186 Portobello Road, London, W11 1LA

Telephone: 020 3034 2233

Email: info@the-distillery.london

Website: www.the-distillery.london

Facebook: www.facebook.com/DistilleryLDN

Instagram: @distilleryldn

Twitter: @DistilleryLDN

Opening hours:
The Resting Room
Monday-Saturday 1100-0000
Sunday 1100-2300
GinTonica
Tuesday 1600-0100
Wednesday-Saturday 1200-0100

Other reasons to go: Portobello Road

*E*lla Carr writes: The Distillery used to be housed at the Portobello Star pub a few doors down, before migrating to its current palatial residence on the corner of Portobello and Talbot Roads in 2016 (bottom left). It's part of a four-story gin Mecca: a distillery in the basement, two bars, and on the top floor three bedrooms. A place of pilgrimage, no less, for gin fanatics, as well as for drop-in gin dilettantes who find themselves bar-crawling up the iconic Portobello Road.

At the heart of The Distillery is its internationally renowned Portobello Road Gin (next page, top right), whose basic spirit is now produced at Thames Distillery in Clapham after it outgrew its 30-litre still at Portobello Road. It then goes to Portobello Road to be re-distilled with botanicals. However, several gins are made here, providing the perfect base for different gin cocktails: the Smokey Gin for the Negroni; King Theodore of Corsica Gin for The King Theodore Sour; while the distinctive Butter Gin – made with English salted butter – is the dream partner for sweet vermouth cocktails. Their classic Old Tom Gin is distilled by Jake Burger (resident Master Distiller and Gin Historian) using 18thC techniques, before being aged in an old sherry barrel.

On the ground floor, five of these re-coppered barrels can be seen suspended above the bar in The Resting Room (next page, bottom right), which serves whisky, tequila, bourbon, and of course gin. The spirits are drawn direct from the barrels, where they have slowly acquired character from the wood. No two drinks are the same because the ageing process is constant. The atmosphere is suffused with blues music

→

and olde worlde charm, but it's the upstairs GinTonica bar (above) that I think gives The Distillery its edge. Unique among London gin bars it pays homage to Spain, which is the world's largest consumer of gin and spiritual home of the spirit. The style is *modernista*, with an open kitchen serving tapas and a brass corner bar with a glittering array of spirits, including a hundred gins from around the world.

And, as in Spain, they serve the gin in a Copa da Balón 21-oz glass goblet that was developed by chefs in the Basque region to keep their gin cool. I recommend Portobello Road Gin Plus: their home brew pimped with grapefruit liqueur, grapefruit marmalade and hop bitter, served with Nordic Mist Blue tonic water and garnished with a grapefruit slice.

Other spirits and wines are available for non-gin drinkers, but gin is unquestionably the star of the show. Not only does it have the distinction of being the world's first gin hotel, but located in the depths of The Distillery is The Ginstitute, led by Jake and his team of Ginstructors. Join their gin tutorial and soak up a gin history session, learn how to nose botanicals and distillates, and finally create your own blend (£120).

The Old Bakery Gin Distillery

Palmers Green, London
Distillery and pop-up bar

ESSENTIAL INFORMATION

Key botanicals (Old Bakery Gin): juniper, plus three secret ingredients

Output: 300 bottles a week

Location: The Old Grain Store, 4 Pymmes Mews, London, N13 4PF

Telephone: 020 8829 8241

Email: hello@oldbakerygin.com

Website: www.oldbakerygin.com

Facebook: www.facebook.com/oldbakerygin

Instagram: @oldbakerygin

Twitter: @OldBakeryGin

Opening hours:
Distillery
Monday-Friday 0900-1700
Pop-up bar last Saturday of every month 1600-2300

Other reasons to go: Broomfield Park, Trent Park, Go Ape

Old Bakery's website uses the tagline 'illegal London recipe'. A pedant might argue that all gin was illegal at the time this bakery was functioning as a gin distillery in the 19thC, but it's not an entirely bogus claim. In 2013 Ian Puddick (next page, top left), a former management consultant who had invested in some run-down properties in Palmers Green, ran into legal problems when he had to remove a 140-foot chimney from one of the properties – The Old Bakery. As a result of a land registration mix up, the chimney was actually the property of the neighbouring building and during his legal research to identify where this problem had first arisen, he discovered that The Old Bakery and The Old Grain Store attached to it were used to make gin, illegally, more than a hundred years ago. He decided to restore the building to its former use, even rescuing the yellow sign on the side of the bakery (below left) and using it as a label.

Ian wanted his botanicals to be as close to those used in the original recipe as possible. The original recipe used stinging nettles, but after many attempts, he decided to go without – the taste was awful however he tried to bring them in.

As we went to press, the distillery (next page, bottom right) was using bottled water while they were waiting for commercial water mains to be installed in the building. The gin is made on site by Ian's dad, Ron, a former soldier. He macerates the four botanicals for nine hours before distilling them with the water and base spirit. The result is a classic, citrus-led London Dry Gin, which is great to sip at room temperature. Ian also recommends serving Old Bakery Gin (next page, middle, left-hand bottle) with Merchant's Heart Floral Aromatics

tonic, a slice of pink grapefruit, fresh basil and plenty of ice.

They also produce Old Bakery Gin Baker's Strength (right, right-hand bottle) at 57.3%, plus a couple of limited edition gins: Old Bakery Gin Baker's Pepper Edition, limited to 1,000 bottles, and made with the same botanicals as the original but with the addition of black pepper. Old Bakery recommends serving this with thinly sliced fresh strawberries and a floral tonic.

The gins can be bought from the Old Bakery's online shop, priced from £38 for a 50-cl bottle of the Original Gin to £42 for a 50-cl bottle of Baker's Strength Gin. They also sell a 20-cl bottle of the Original for £17 and for £50 you can buy an Old Bakery Gin Wooded Gift Set, including a handmade wooden box with a 600-ml Copa glass engraved with the Old Bakery Gin logo and a 50-cl bottle of the Original Gin.

Old Bakery Gin can also be bought from various shops around London, including Harrods, Fortnum & Mason and Harvey Nichols, as well as from The Juniper Club's online shop.

In 2019, Old Bakery opened the Enfield Gin Palace Pop Up Bar at the distillery. As we went to press, this was held on the last Saturday of every month between February and December from 4 pm to 11 pm.

Fort Gin and The Portsmouth Distillery

Portsmouth, Hampshire
Distillery

ESSENTIAL INFORMATION
Key botanicals (Fort Gin): juniper, elderflower, gorse flower, sea radish
Output: not disclosed
Location: Coastguard Casemate, Fort Cumberland, Fort Cumberland Road, Southsea, Hants, PO4 9LD
Telephone: 02392 733339
Email: info@theportsmouthdistillery.com
Website: www.theportsmouthdistillery.com
Facebook: www.facebook.com/ PortsmouthDistillery
Instagram: @portsmouthdistillery
Twitter: @pompeystill

Opening hours:
Monday-Friday 1100-1400 or by appointment

Other reasons to go: Spinnaker Tower, Hawk Conservancy Trust, The Great Hall

David T. Smith writes: Portsmouth's connection with the Royal Navy goes back to the time of Henry VIII. Given the equally long association between the navy and gin, it is perhaps surprising that only in 2018 did the first modern gin distillery open in the city.

The city is full of historic interest, from Henry VIII's Southsea Castle to The Historic Dockyard, which houses the wreck of the *Mary Rose* as well as the restored *HMS Warrior* and Admiral Nelson's flagship *HMS Victory*. All are a must to visit in combination with the distillery.

Portsmouth Distillery was started by three friends, two of whom – Vince Noyce and Giles Collighan – are ex-naval officers. The third member of the team, Dich Oatley, has a background in the spirits industry.

The distillery is in the vaulted casemates of Fort Cumberland, which is in Eastney at the SE tip of Portsmouth. The pentagonal Georgian fort was built to prevent invasion forces from landing in Langstone Harbour to attack the dockyard overland. The fort is currently owned by Historic England and a limited number of tours of the distillery are available throughout the year. See the website for details.

In 2018, the distillery released Fort Gin (left), which is made using a combination of classic gin botanicals and three that are found within the walls of the fort: elderflower, gorse flower, and sea radish. The distillery also makes a 1968 White Rum, which is distilled from scratch using evaporated cane juice, and Cinnabar, a spiced rum.

Pure Sussex Gin and Harley House Distillery

Seaford, East Sussex

Distillery

ESSENTIAL INFORMATION

Key botanicals (Pure Sussex Gin): juniper, coriander, cardamom, cinnamon, cubeb, lemon, grapefruit, ginger, vanilla, honeysuckle flower, frankincense

Output: 1,500 bottles a year

Location: Sutton Road, Seaford, BN25 4QH

Telephone: 01323 491998

Email: info@harleyhousedistillery.co.uk

Website: www.harleyhousedistillery.co.uk

Facebook: www.facebook.com/ harleyhousedistillery

Instagram: @harleyhousedistillery

Twitter: @harleyhousegin

Opening hours: not open to the public

Adam Cowley and co-founder Heidi launched their signature gin, Pure Sussex Gin (bottom left, right-hand bottle), in autumn 2017. Adam describes it as the spirit of Sussex because he carries out the entire distilling process in the East Sussex town of Seaford. The base spirit is made by Adam with water sourced from an aquifer in the South Downs National Park. The water has been naturally filtered through layers of chalk in the South Downs and is then brought to the surface, tested and filtered before it is used in the production of the spirit. Most distillers buy in their base spirit because making it from scratch is so time-consuming – it takes between five and seven days for Adam to produce his base spirit. The spirit is distilled with 15 botanicals, including wild honeysuckle and coriander which are grown in the South Downs, and is great as a cocktail gin, a sipping gin, or a classic gin and tonic.

For a classic G&T, Adam and Heidi recommend mixing a measure of Pure Sussex Gin with plenty of ice and a few slices of grapefruit zest, topped up with a premium tonic. This also works well when mixed with apple juice, a dash of lime juice, fresh mint and slices of lime to create a Sussex Mojito. For a winter warmer, mix 250 ml of Pure Sussex Gin with 500 ml of red wine, 1 dessert spoon of honey, thin slices of lemon and orange, a tin of pineapple, cloves, cinnamon and a pinch of ground nutmeg to make a Sussex Hot Gin Punch. Simmer the mixture for 45 minutes and allow to cool for a further ten.

Harley House also produces Sussex Blue Gin (left, middle bottle), which was inspired by the local Adonis Blue Butterfly (opposite, bottom right). One of the botanicals, the

butterfly pea flower, is a medicinal flower from Asia where it's used to lower blood pressure and increase libido. The flower is a natural pH indicator, giving the spirit a blue tint when it's neutral and changing to a candy pink when an acidic mixer is added. Or try Sussex Blue with grenadine and lime cordial, blueberries, raspberries and a sprig of rosemary to create The Gatsby cocktail.

The Seven Sisters Cliffs are part of the chalk South Downs from which Harley House gets purified water for its gins (see opposite page).

Their third signature gin is Harley House Sussex Sloe Gin, made with Pure Sussex Gin and locally sourced sloes. In May 2019, they also released Honey and Hibiscus Gin (opposite, bottom left, left-hand bottle) and Rhubarb and Ginger Gin Liqueur.

The gins can be bought from the Harley House online shop, where a 70-cl bottle of Pure Sussex Gin costs £37.50, a 50-cl bottle of Sussex Blue Gin £35, and Sloe Gin £30. You could also buy a miniature gift pack, which includes all five gins in 5-cl bottles for £15.

Mermaid Gin and Isle of Wight Distillery

Seaview, Isle of Wight
Distillery, bar and shop

ESSENTIAL INFORMATION

Key botanicals (Mermaid Gin): juniper, coriander, liquorice root, grains of paradise, lemon zest, elderflower, Boadicea hop, rock samphire

Output: 100,000+ bottles a year

Location: The Mermaid Bar at the Wishing Well, Pondwell Hill, Seaview, PO33 1PX

Telephone: 01983 613653

Email: office@isleofwightdistillery.com

Website: www.isleofwightdistillery.com

Facebook: www.facebook.com/mermaidgin; www.facebook.com/iowdistillery

Instagram: @isleofwightdistillery

Twitter: @iowdistillery

Opening hours:
Visitors' Centre
Monday-Sunday 1100-2300

Other reasons to go: No Man's Land Fort, Priory Bay, Seagrove Bay

David T. Smith writes: Isle of Wight Distillery, the island's only distillery, is in the small village of Pondwell on the outskirts of the island's largest town, Ryde, housed in an old public house known as The Wishing Well. Ryde is quite easy to reach from the mainland: catamarans, car ferries, or hovercrafts leave from Portsmouth and Southampton.

The distillery was founded in 2014 by close friends Conrad Gauntlett and Xavier Baker. Before working together in the distillery, Conrad had been in wine-making and Xavier had been a brewer.

In 2015, the distillery released their first product, Mermaid Gin (above right), a well-rounded gin with a bright citrus taste and a pleasant freshness. The same year, it partnered with the nearby Portsmouth Historic Dockyard and the Royal Navy Museum to create a Navy Strength version known as HMS Victory Gin, a nod to the Navy's love of the juniper spirit. Shortly after, HMS Victory Aged Gin was launched, aged in ex-wine barrels, each of which also included a stave made from wood from the *HMS Victory*. This began maturing in May 2016, with versions released after six months, 12 months, three years, and five years.

The distillery is open for talks and tastings throughout the week – there's no access to the stills (above middle) but you can see them from the bar (left). There's a

Left: at the Isle of Wight's western tip are the iconic chain of chalk rocks known as The Needles. A great spot to visit if you are already on the island seeing this distillery. Bottom left and below: a selection of Mermaid Gin botanicals.

shop selling the distillery's spirits and other local products.

In addition to the gins, Isle of Wight Distillery also produces a Sea Salt Vodka, a Navy Rum and a single malt whisky.

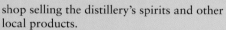

Slake Sussex Dry Gin and Slake Spirits

Shoreham-by-Sea, West Sussex
Distillery

ESSENTIAL INFORMATION

Key botanicals (Sussex Dry Gin): juniper, coriander, cardamom, cassia bark, lemon balm, lemon verbena, fennel

Output: 2,000 bottles a year

Location: 14 Feversham Close, Shoreham-by-Sea, BN43 5HD

Telephone: 01273 457765

Email: info@slakespirits.com

Website: www.slakespirits.com

Facebook: www.facebook.com/SlakeSpirits

Instagram: @slakespirits

Twitter: @SlakeSpirits

Opening hours:
Monday-Saturday 1000-1800
Sunday 1000-1600

Other reasons to go: Shoreham Harbour, Friends of Shoreham Fort, Bramber Castle

Another blue-chip small-batch gin maker who deserves a medal for almost monastic dedication to the calling and for charting his own course. Dr Thomas Martin-Wells (opposite, bottom right, second from left), usually called Tom, founded his distillery in 2015 on Shoreham beach in what he describes as "laboratory meets forager's den, which was once a run-down old wood workshop belonging to my grandad."

He produces "fine sipping gin, distilled at the crossroads of science and nature. By capturing the Sussex *terroir* – a term used by French winemakers to describe the essence of the local land – our gin is a passionate reflection of where and how it's made."

Tom's core product, Sussex Dry Gin (below left), is designed to be smooth and well balanced, equally good served neat or over ice but also bold enough to mix. He pushes the boundaries, using locally foraged ingredients you may never have heard of let alone tasted and is obsessed by flavour, aiming to take you to places on your palette you did not imagine existed. An obsessive level of detail is maintained throughout the production process, which takes place in-house under the watchful eye of Tom. He distils in batches of 50 bottles, which are carefully blended, bottled, numbered, inspected and finished by hand.

Sussex Dry Gin is a classic London Dry, but made Tom's way. It's juniper and citrus led, but without a citrus fruit in sight. Instead, he grows lemon balm and lemon verbena to give it a crisp, clean citrus-herbaceous flavour that marries with the more traditional London Dry Gin botanicals. Then there's a depth of warming spice, which gives way to a clean herbaceous citrus on the finish.

He also makes Hedgerow Gin (above, left-hand bottle), a unique seasonal sipping gin, using hand-foraged hedgerow fruits and flowers plus traditional spices (juniper, coriander, cassia, cardamom, fennel, liquorice, lemon grass, elder, rowan and rose) with a soft, almost sweet, floral finish. This complex recipe delivers across the full taste spectrum, a lively balance of fruit, floral, herbs and spice.

A third product, Roman Garden Gin, was first made for Fishbourne Roman Palace's 50th anniversary. The recipe was created using only botanicals known to and used by the Romans and includes herbs grown in the palace's gardens and some foraged locally. These include Alexanders, which the Romans introduced to Britain and is now very common along the South Coast, and mugwort, which may sound like something out of Harry Potter but was historically used instead of hops to flavour beer. The gin tastes dry and compact with juniper, citrus and spice at the fore, giving way to a herbaceous and slightly bitter finish.

Tom says: "I'm driven by a curiosity to understand the natural world and work harmoniously with it." Less driven mortals can slake their curiosity by trying his gin.

From left to right: local MP Tim Loughton, Slake Spirits founder Thomas Martin-Wells, Masterchef 2018 winner Kenny Tutt and his wife Lucy at an event in the House of Commons to raise awareness for Sussex produce.

The London Gin Club

Soho, London

Bar

ESSENTIAL INFORMATION
Location: 22 Great Chapel Street, London,
  W1F 8FR
Telephone: 020 749 42488
Email: thelondonginclub@gmail.com
Website: www.thelondonginclub.com
Facebook: www.facebook.com/
  The-London-Gin-Club
Instagram: @londonginclub
Twitter: @LondonGinClub

Opening hours:
Tuesday-Friday 1600-2300
Saturday 1300-2300

Other reasons to go:
Soho, The British Museum,
shopping on Oxford Street

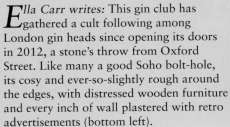

Ella Carr writes: This gin club has gathered a cult following among London gin heads since opening its doors in 2012, a stone's throw from Oxford Street. Like many a good Soho bolt-hole, its cosy and ever-so-slightly rough around the edges, with distressed wooden furniture and every inch of wall plastered with retro advertisements (bottom left).

Their current gin count stands at an amazing 400, but their jovial team of ginsperts are forever on a quest to source exciting new brands from around the world, as well as from small-batch producers and microdistilleries. Inevitably, there are some eccentric options in the mix – such as Caviar and Truffle gins – but as a rule they favour quality over gimmick. The same purist philosophy filters down to how they serve the spirit. Their G&T, for example, is serious business: served in a Copa glass with ice that they freeze and crack themselves, individually paired with garnishes and tonic.

There's a seasonal cocktail list with a British slant to it (summer cocktails include the Rhubarb and Ginger Collins and the Cucumber Celery Gimlet). More exciting, however, is their Classic Cocktails menu, listed in a timeline that starts with the first ever gin cocktail (the 1714 Mary Rockett's Gin Punch) before steamrolling through the Victorian age and roaring 20s right up to 1930 (the Hanky Panky). Each cocktail is served true to its original recipe, meaning you can merrily drink your way through gin history. Alternatively, you can go to one of their gin tasting sessions: at £27 for four G&Ts it's good value, and a great introduction to the world of craft gins.

Belgium and Blues

Southampton, Hampshire
Bar

ESSENTIAL INFORMATION
Location: 184 Above Bar St, Southampton,
  SO14 7DW
Telephone: 023 8022 5411
Email: jack@belgiumandblues.co.uk
Website: www.belgiumandblues.co.uk
Facebook: www.facebook.com/
  BelgiumandBlues
Instagram: @belgiumandblues
Twitter: @BelgiumandBlues

Opening hours:
Gin Bar
Monday-Tuesday 1200-2300
Wednesday-Thursday 1700-2300
Friday-Saturday 1200-0000
Sunday 1200-1700

Other reasons to go: SeaCity
Museum, Tudor House and
Garden, Southampton Common,
Guildhall Square

Southampton's only gin bar (opened 2016) is in a useful central location on the city's main street known as Above Bar. They offer 40 craft gins in a dedicated gin bar (bottom left) at street level. Downstairs is a big, dimly lit basement bar (below left) and brasserie where they serve craft beers, with an emphasis on interesting Belgian ones, which explains the name. Blues music plays in the background.

Belgium produces not just beer but good gin, and you will find examples (above right) in the gin bar. It's long and thin, a bit dark, with black chairs, dark green panelling, duck egg green walls and high Kentish-style tables. Friendly manager Jack has sought out several local gins including Mermaid from the Isle of Wight (page 96) or Pothecary from Christchurch (page 40), and he is also keen on Boudier Saffron from France – a deep golden colour and tasting strongly of saffron – "decadent and buttery". But his favourite is Black Pepper – "a seriously spicy hit".

He and his co-owners want to promote a "healthy, happy enjoyable way of drinking in Soton." Clients respond from across the spectrum of social types and ages. There is additional seating on chairs outside on the broad pavement, or in an upstairs bar.

Willow Tree Gin and Willow Tree Distilling

Stanbridge, Bedfordshire
Distillery

ESSENTIAL INFORMATION

Key botanicals (Willow Tree Gin): juniper, coriander, cassia bark, cubeb, lemon peel, lemon thyme, Thai basil, plus five secret ingredients

Output: not disclosed

Location: Stanbridge, Leighton Buzzard

Telephone: 07826 518601

Email: hello@willowtreedistilling.co.uk

Website: www.willowtreedistilling.co.uk

Facebook: www.facebook.com/ willowtreegin

Instagram: @willowtreegin

Twitter: @willowtreegin

Opening hours: not open to the public

Other reasons to go: Mead Open Farm, Ascott House, Woburn Safari Park

Willow Tree Distilling was established in 2016 and, as we went to press, was Bedfordshire's only distillery.

Founder and director Mary Vincent had always been interested in experimenting with food and drink having been exposed to African and Indian flavours at a young age – her parents lived in Nigeria for ten years before she was born. These flavours became the guiding force in building her gin recipe. She grew up on the farm where the distillery (top) is based, so she naturally became conscious of sustainable living and now grows some of the herbs used in Willow Tree Gin (left).

Some of the botanicals are smoked (using wood from the farm) before they are distilled with the rest of the botanicals for six to eight hours. Mary recommends serving Willow Tree Gin with a quality tonic, a thin lemon slice, a bruised kaffir lime leaf and plenty of crushed ice. For a winter warmer, try mixing the gin with warm apple juice and cinnamon to make Willow Tree's Hot Gin Toddy.

The gin can be bought from the online shop, plus various shops, bars and restaurants around Bedfordshire. Fifty pence from the sale of every 50-cl bottle goes towards planting new trees in the Forest of Marston Vale.

The distillery also offers a mobile Willow Tree Gin Pop Up Bar bookable for events.

The Good Life Gin Company and No.97 gin bar

Surbiton, London
Bar and restaurant

ESSENTIAL INFORMATION

Key botanicals (The Good Life Gin): juniper, coriander, cardamom, lemon peel, grapefruit, pink peppercorn, Earl Grey tea leaf

Output: 1,500 bottles a year

Location: 97 Maple Road, London, KT6 4AW

Telephone: 020 34119797

Email: hello@thegoodlifeginco.co.uk

Website: www.thegoodlifeginco.co.uk

Instagram: @thegoodlifecompany

Opening hours:
Tuesday-Friday 1200-0000
Saturday 1000-0000
Sunday 1000-1430

Other reasons to go: Bushy Park, Richmond Park, Hampton Court Park

Sam and Alex Berry opened their gin-themed Surbiton restaurant, No.97, in 2016. With Sam's background in bar tending and his love of gin, it was inevitable that he would want to create his own to add to the restaurant's collection of more than 150. Licensing restrictions led him to team up with Union Distillers' Mark Gamble (page 140) who offered to make the gin in his Leicestershire distillery while they worked on securing their licence. The result is The Good Life Gin, which takes its name from the 1960s TV series based on a couple in the London suburb of Surbiton who opt out of the rat race. It is produced in batches of 100 bottles.

Naturally, The Good Life (bottom left) is the star gin at the gin bar in the restaurant, which they style 'Surbiton's hidden gin bar' and where the Berrys also run Gin and Cocktail Masterclasses. You will taste five gins and two G&Ts, the experience lasts one and a half hours and costs £35 per person.

In 2018, as a result of No.97's success, Sam and Alex opened another restaurant in Teddington – One One Four, and a third restaurant in April 2019 – Cento Uno a Pizzeria, next to No.97.

Try serving The Good Life in a Negroni with Campari, Cocchi Torino and Italicus liqueur or, for a juniper take on the Espresso Martini, add it to Mr Black Coffee Liqueur, Chimney Fire Kenyan Coffee and Creme de Banane.

Future plans include bringing the distilling in-house and also creating Navy and Sloe gins, but Sam and Alex insist that the restaurants come first for the time being. As we went to press, The Good Life had a pop-up bar in the Historical Royal Palace Food Festival in the summer.

Anno Gin and Anno Distillers

Tonbridge, Kent
Distillery and tasting room

ESSENTIAL INFORMATION

Key botanicals (Anno Kent Dry Gin): juniper, lavender, chamomile, hop, samphire

Output: 46,000 bottles a year

Location: Unit 4, Crest Industrial Estate, Pattenden Lane, Marden, Tonbridge, TN12 9QJ

Telephone: 01622 833278

Email: info@annodistillers.co.uk

Website: www.annodistillers.co.uk

Facebook: www.facebook.com/AnnoDistillers

Instagram: @annodistillers

Twitter: @annodistillers

Opening hours:
Monday-Friday 0900-1700

Other reasons to go: Tonbridge Castle, Haysden Country Park, The Hop Farm, All Saint's Church (Tudeley)

Anno's subtitle is 'The spirit of alchemy' and although this is a nice promotional tag, we wondered if it's quite right for this reliable, well established craft gin – one of the first on the market, in the early days of the craft gin craze? Medieval alchemists were on a quest to convert base metal into gold, impossible of course, and were often considered to be charlatans. Nothing could be less true of Andy and Norman (opposite, bottom right), founders of Anno in 2011. They both have PhDs in science subjects; both have worked for Glaxo before going out on their own and their hallmark is consistent quality.

Their core gin, Kent Dry (bottom left, middle bottle), launched in 2013, is a smooth, complex, floral gin, good for sipping and mixing and can claim to be 'the taste of Kent' – hops (opposite, middle) are of course a very Kentish crop, but so is samphire, which grows on the coastal saltmarshes and gives a sweet, grassy dimension to the flavour. The gin has earned an impressive list of awards.

Andy and Norman bring something extra to the gin tours hosted at the distillery most Saturdays. In a unit on an industrial estate, this may not be as attractive a location as others in the guide, but their approach is especially strong when it comes to educating the palate. Upstairs is a comfortable air-conditioned room with space for 24 visitors and after a tour of the distilling area on the ground floor you sit down to a blind tasting of five different

gins each in a glass. Two are mainstream commercial brands, two craft gins and one is Anno. You will try them neat, with water and with tonic and then write down which you think is which. People are often surprised at how bad they are at this, and go away determined to hone their palates. Andy and Norman also test their clients with 'extreme gins' that are so experimentally flavoured they might not be gins at all. One such experiment was with coconut – all 24 on the tour failed to recognize it.

Anno's other spirits are sloe gin (top, left-hand bottle), an elderflower and vodka spirit (top, second bottle from left), a 60% gin (top, middle bottle) and a cranberry gin (top, right-hand bottle) available October to December.

Anno? Nothing to do with *Anno Domini*, just an amalgamation of ANdy and NOrman.

Greensand Ridge Gin and Distillery

Tonbridge, Kent
Distillery and gin school

ESSENTIAL INFORMATION

Key botanicals (Greensand Ridge London Dry): juniper, poppy seed, hawthorn berry, rosehip, bay laurel, gorse, oak moss, honey

Output: 12,000 bottles a year

Location: Box 588, Shipbourne Road, Shipbourne, TN9 9NT

Telephone: 07971 164688

Email: info@greensanddistillery.com

Website: www.greensanddistillery.com

Facebook: www.facebook.com/GreensandRidge

Instagram: @greensand_ridge

Twitter: @GSRdistillery

Opening hours:
The Gin Experience (by appointment only)

Other reasons to go: beautiful countryside and walks along the Greensand Way to fabulous pubs

Ella Carr writes: There's much in a name when it comes to Greensand Ridge Gin (right), called after the hills that surround the Weald of Kent. Will Edge, who grew up in the area, has gone the extra mile to distil a sense of place into his gin by sourcing ingredients from the Weald's orchards, nutteries and hedgerows. Even the bottle design, with its mellow greens and blues, and sunburst gold writing, is inspired by the area's rolling hills.

The name also reflects their sustainable ethos – not just a marketing buzz word in this case but the lifeblood of the brand, feeding into every bit of Will's gin-making process. For the energy-intensive process of distillation they use 100 per cent renewable power; no chemicals are used to clean their stills (opposite, bottom right), and they recycle or reuse almost all their materials; waste fills one bin bag every eight weeks. Will even works with local farmers to turn their excess crop into brandies and *eaux-de-vies*.

Within a crowded market sustainability is definitely Greensand's differentiator at the moment, but Will is just as concerned with flavour – spending hours at a time in his distillery eking out the most of his botanicals (opposite, middle). These include eight local ingredients – bay laurel, poppy seeds, oak moss, hawthorn berries, cobnuts, rosehips, honey and gorse – reinforced by more traditional botanicals such as juniper, coriander, cardamom and cassia bark. The result is a

well-balanced London Dry Gin with a hint of nuttiness, which Will recommends serving with a bay leaf and a few bruised juniper berries. They also produce seasonal gins.

Inspired by the growing number of entrepreneurial distillers in the gin renaissance, Will – who has a background in IT and finance – finally packed up his corporate job in 2016 to turn his 15-year hobby of making alcohol into a career, first doing a Masters in Brewing and Distilling at Heriott-Watt. The evocative nature of gin made it a natural spirit of choice for Will, although he is also making an *eau de vie* (called Raspberry Ghost – top) from Kentish raspberries, brandies from apples and plums, and a golden rum.

This microdistillery is a charming place to visit, sitting just below the Greensand Ridge in the village of Shipbourne, in a former Victorian coaching house – with an enchanting courtyard and sweeping views across the Weald. The Greensand Ridge Gin Experience takes place in its tutorial area (opposite, bottom left) and provides insight into the complexity of the distillation process. Guests are introduced to the history of gin and to the nature of botanicals, before allowing them to distil their own gin from a selection of 40 botanicals.

Graveney Gin

Tooting, London
Bar and tasting room

ESSENTIAL INFORMATION
Key botanicals (Graveney Gin): juniper,
   orange, pink grapefruit, baobab, goji berry
Output: 2,100 bottles a year
Location: Unit 22a Tooting Market, 21-23
   Tooting High Street, London, SW17 0SN
Telephone: 07398 531795
Email: contact@graveneygin.com
Website: www.graveneygin.co.uk
Facebook: www.facebook.com/graveneygin
Instagram: @graveney_gin
Twitter: @graveneygin

Opening hours:
Tooting Market Bar
Tuesday-Wednesday 1200-1800
Thursday 1200-2300
Friday-Saturday 1200-2330
Sunday 1200-1800

Other reasons to go: Tooting Common

Victoria Christie has loved gin almost as long as she can remember. As a girl, she lapped up her mum's enjoyment of a G&T in the African heat of Malawi, where her father was working. When old enough to drink, it had to be gin, and in bars she would always keep her eyes open for new and interesting gins to try. A visit to the Ginstitute in London's Portobello Road (page 89) finally made her decide that she would produce her own. Her mission would be to honour and protect the tradition of gin with a 45% spirit: it had to have teeth. Her recipe is made of mostly traditional ingredients, plus a few botanicals from her favourite gins. All of the botanicals are certified organic.

First she made the gin at home – the operation was completely self-funded until she was approached by Tootopia, an annual three-day food, drink and entertainment festival held in Tooting, South London. She worked every night after her day job in a bank to produce 200 bottles of Graveney Gin, which launched at Tootopia in September 2015. It was such a hit that Tooting Market offered her a unit (left), and with some crowdfunding, she turned it into a tasting room and bar (opposite, bottom and top right) with an on site distillery. Later she moved the distillery to Merton Abbey Mills, a business and retail centre in South London. You can buy the gin from Cut & Cured, a shop in Merton Abbey Mills. She still makes all the gin herself using the one-shot method (page 68). Two 30-litre copper stills produce 30 bottles per batch on a daily basis.

Try Graveney Gin (opposite, middle) with a Mediterranean tonic and a large slice of pink grapefruit to emphasise the sourness

of the baobab (above), a nod to Victoria's South African heritage. For a cocktail, try serving 60 ml of the gin with 30 ml of fresh lemon juice, 15 ml of sugar syrup and 15 ml of Crème de Mure liqueur.

You can buy direct from the website or you can pay by subscription, receiving a bottle at a discounted price each month. Graveney is also sold in various bars around South-West London.

Ten per cent of Graveney's profits go to Gearing up for Gorillas, which protects rare mountain gorillas in the Congo and educates the rangers that care for them. A new gin under development as we went to press will support St George's Hospital, Tooting.

Silverback Mountain Strength Gin and Gorilla Spirits Co.

Upton Grey, Hampshire
Distillery, bar and gin school

ESSENTIAL INFORMATION

Key botanicals (Silverback Mountain Strength Gin): juniper, coriander, orange, calamus root, lemongrass, acacia blossom

Output: not disclosed

Location: The Workshop, Manor Farm Yard, Upton Grey Road, Upton Grey, RG25 2RQ

Telephone: 01420 446175

Email: info@gorillaspirits.co.uk

Website: www. gorillaspirits.co.uk

Facebook: www.facebook.com/gorillaspirits

Instagram: @gorillaspirits

Twitter: @gorillaspirits

Opening hours: visits by appointment only

Other reasons to go: Milestones Museum, The Vyne Tudor house, Basing House, Eastrop Park

Andy Daniels founded Gorilla Spirits Co. in 2014 with the aim of creating an ethical business that produces quality spirits and liqueurs – which is why £1 from every bottle of gin goes to the Gorilla Organization who work on the conservation of mountain gorillas in the wild. The distillery was originally located in Four Marks near Alton but moved to a larger premises in Upton Grey, Hampshire in summer 2018, allowing them to open a new visitors' centre, including a ten-station Gin School and a copper-topped bar (opposite, bottom right).

Their signature product, Silverback Mountain Strength Gin (bottom left), is a London Dry bottled at a strength of 46%. Among the more unusual botanicals are calamus root and acacia blossom: up to the 1960s, the former has been used to treat digestive disorders, but now it's used in food and drink to give a warm, spicy flavour. Acacia blossom is used both for its sweetness and its link to the gorilla – acacia forms part of the ape's diet. Silverback is often served with Peter Spanton's No.9 Cardamom Tonic, but Andy also recommends serving it with Fever-Tree Mediterranean tonic, plenty of ice and a twist of orange peel.

Andy also produces Silverback Old Tom Gin (opposite top, second bottle from right), made with the same botanicals as the Mountain Strength Gin but with 50% more botanical content. It's sweetened with a touch of sugar and bottled at the slightly lower strength of 43%. Try mixing Old Tom with lemon juice, sugar and soda water to make a Tom Collins cocktail.

Gorilla Spirits offers distillery tours where for £25 you get a history of the

brand and the work they do to support the Gorilla Organization. They talk you through each of their spirits, the botanicals used and the distillation process before the tour of the distillery and production areas. The tour ends with a tasting of the full Gorilla Spirits range and a signature G&T. Tours are held Wednesday to Sunday at 12 pm and 3 pm.

For £45, they hold a Cocktail Masterclass on the last Saturday of each month, or on other days according to demand, from 6.30 pm. The masterclasses are run by award-winning mixologist Spike van de Merwe who teaches you how to make cocktails using the Gorilla Spirits Co. range.

They also hold a Gin School from Wednesday to Saturday at 2 pm, led by either Andy or Gin School Manager Kirsty Peet, who guide you through the gin making process. You then make your own recipe which you taste in a G&T before it's bottled for you to take home. The Gin School costs £125 per person, or £175 for two when sharing a still and bottle. Distillery experiences can be booked through the Gorilla Spirits Co. website.

Mother's Ruin Gin and Bar

Walthamstow, London
Distillery and bar

ESSENTIAL INFORMATION

Key botanicals (Mother's Ruin Old Tom Gin): juniper, coriander, bay leaf, nutmeg, vanilla pod, orange peel, lemon peel, demerara sugar

Output: 1,200-1,800 bottles a year

Location: Unit 18, Ravenswood Industrial Estate, Shernall Street, London, E17 9QH

Telephone: 07905 484711

Email: beckywynngriffiths@yahoo.co.uk

Website: www.mothersruin.net

Facebook: www.facebook.com/MothersRuinE17

Instagram: @mothersruine17

Twitter: @MothersRuinE17

Opening hours:
Friday 1800-0000
Saturday 1200-0000
Sunday 1400-2000

Other reasons to go: God's Own Junkyard gallery, William Morris Gallery

Based in a First World War munitions factory, Mother's Ruin (bottom left) was founded by Becky Griffiths in July 2014 after she decided to expand her business making fruit liqueurs and gins.

She stocks over 80 different gins, including her own Old Tom Gin (below left), distilled in small copper pot stills named Naomi (20 litres) and Cecilia (60 litres). She grinds the botanicals by hand and then steeps them in a base spirit for 12 hours.

For her fruit liqueurs, which include Damson and Sloe gins, she steeps the botanicals (many of which are homegrown or sourced from East London or Essex) in the base spirit for at least a year before distillation takes place. Other fruit liqueurs she produces include a bitter orange rum, rhubarb vodka, raspberry vodka and cassis. She also produces limited edition, seasonal gins – check the website for new releases.

Other brands Becky serves include Gin Mare, Poetic License Northern Dry (page 206), Bobby's Scheidam, Bloom Gin and Nordes. As we went to press, her tipple of choice was Zeer Oude Five-year-old Genever which she says makes a great gin-based Old Fashioned due to its whisky-like flavour.

Every month, Mother's Ruin hosts a range of events including a spoken word night, alternative bingo, and a number of pop-up kitchens – see the website for upcoming events.

Campfire Gin and
The Puddingstone Distillery

Wilstone, Hertfordshire
Distillery and shop

ESSENTIAL INFORMATION

Key botanicals (Campfire Gin): juniper, coriander, orange peel, grapefruit peel, roasted hazelnut, golden berry, lavender, rooibos

Output: 7,000 bottles a year

Location: Unit 1, Artisan Workshops, P E Mead & Sons Farm Shop, Lower Icknield Way, Tring, HP23 4NT

Telephone: 01442 502033

Email: hello@puddingstonedistillery.com

Website: puddingstonedistillery.com

Facebook: www.facebook.com/puddingstonedistillery

Instagram: @campfiregin

Twitter: @PuddingstoneGin

Opening hours:
Friday-Saturday 0930-1700

Other reasons to go: Ivinghoe Beacon, Natural History Museum at Tring, College Lake, National Trust (Ashridge Estate)

David T. Smith writes: Located in the picturesque Chiltern Hills on the border of Hertfordshire and Buckinghamshire, Puddingstone Distillery (bottom left), home of Campfire Gin (right), was launched in 2016 by husband and wife team, Kate and Ben Marston.

Their interest in gin was rekindled during a six-hour delay to a wrist operation, when Kate bought some books on flavour and gin to help pass the time. Inspired by what they had read, two weeks later they decided to found Hertfordshire's first gin distillery.

Kate runs a design consultancy, applying her expertise to the branding of Campfire Gin. Ben had been in product design, copywriting, illustration and photography, before spending eight years brewing and marketing at Tring Brewery.

The name Puddingstone comes from the rare Hertfordshire puddingstone, a naturally occurring conglomerate of sediment and flint pebbles that resembles the raisins and fruit in a plum pudding.

The distillery is located on the outskirts of Tring on the site of a farm shop, alongside a number of other regional producers, including one that sells local rapeseed oil and an artisan patisserie.

On entering the distillery, visitors are greeted by a gleaming copper-topped bar (next page, bottom right), with all manner of stills and equipment visible behind it. The wood-lined room (next page, top left)

has a cosy feel – reminiscent of a log-cabin – that instantly makes visitors feel at home.

Puddingstone also has a shop where gin, vermouth and cocktail accessories are sold and where they host a series of different tastings and masterclasses throughout the year. Pre-book for evening tours.

There are four main styles in the Campfire Gin range: the original London Dry, which is fruity and spicy with a zip of orange; the bolder and more piney Navy Strength (right); the mellow Cask Aged (top right), which is rested in ex-bourbon American oak casks for 22 days; and a sweet, spicy Old Tom. Unusually, the gins are made using a variety of production techniques, including pot and vapour distillation (page 254) as well as the bathtub method (page 168), also known as compounding, allowing visitors a greater breadth of understanding of gin making.

In addition to the core range, the distillery has released a number of gins in collaboration with local partners, including Summer Edition Gin which uses Himalayan Balsam and another using local juniper. It also has annual releases of PUD PUD Gin, a seasonal gin made with locally made Christmas puddings.

Star of Bombay Gin and Bombay Sapphire Distillery

Winchester, Hampshire
Distillery, bar, shop and gin school

ESSENTIAL INFORMATION

Key botanicals (Star of Bombay Gin): juniper, coriander seed, liquorice, cassia bark, grains of paradise, cubeb, lemon peel, bergamot peel, almond, ambrette seed, berries

Output: not disclosed

Location: Laverstoke Mill, London Road, Whitchurch, RG28 7NR

Telephone: 01256 890090

Email: hello@bombaysapphire.com

Website: www.distillery.bombaysapphire.com

Facebook: www.facebook.com/BombayDistillery

Instagram: @homeofbombay

Twitter: @homeofbombay

Opening hours:
April to October
Monday-Sunday 1000-2000 (last admission 1800)
November to March
1100-1800 (last admission 1600)

Other reasons to go: Whitchurch Silk Mill, Finkley Down Farm

David T. Smith writes: Located alongside the beautiful River Test in rural Hampshire, Laverstoke Mill has a long and interesting history and is currently the home of Star of Bombay Gin (next page, top left), the craft gin counterpart of the familiar, globally recognized Bombay gins – see below.

The site was home to Laverstoke Manor from the 10thC and two mills were recorded as being based there in the Domesday Book. There was a paper mill on the site for 300 years, making use of the local water supply and, in 1719, the mill was the exclusive supplier of paper for banknotes for the Bank of England.

Star of Bombay Gin was released on the 1st of April 2015 and was developed by a team of distilling, botanical and gin cocktail experts, including distillery ambassador Sam Carter, and master of botanicals Ivano Tonutti. Master Distiller Dr Anne Brock oversees four stills, including two Dakin stills (next page, middle), one dating from 1831 which is the original still used by Mary Dakin, a pioneer of the vapour infusion method of gin production (page 254). The other is a replica of the 1836 model, which was built in 2014. Both stills were moved down from Warrington following a refurbishment in 2014.

From early 2019, cold-distilled Oxley Gin was also made on the site. The whole distillation system for this gin is airtight and operates under reduced pressure as air is pumped out of the still. As a result, the distillation process can take place at -5°C rather than the more typical 78-80°C used in hot distillation. This lower temperature brings out delicate, bright flavours such as grapefruit and cocoa, which can taste stewed if heated.

$\longrightarrow$

Perhaps the jewel in the crown of Laverstoke are the two glasshouses designed by Thomas Heatherwick (previous page, bottom left), heated using the waste energy from the stills. In each glasshouse grow examples of the botanicals used to make the Bombay gins, in two different climate zones: Mediterranean and tropical. After visiting the glasshouses and seeing the botanicals in their natural state, guests move to the Botanical Dry Room to explore the aromas that each botanical gives to the gin.

In addition to the Dakin stillhouse, the site boasts a range of attractions: there is a glassware gallery featuring a number of glass creations from famous designers, as well as a bar serving bespoke gin cocktails and a gift shop.

A range of experiences are available at the distillery, including self-guided tours, gin cocktail masterclasses (right), and a tailored, in-depth experience for gin connoisseurs – see the website for booking information.

In addition to Star of Bombay, the following gins are made at the distillery: Bombay Dry, Bombay Sapphire, and Bombay Sapphire English Estate Limited Edition.

Eccentric Gin Distillery

Caerphilly
Distillery

ESSENTIAL INFORMATION
Key botanicals (Madame Geneva): juniper, coriander, lemon peel, orange peel, grapefruit, meadowsweet, sunflower
Output: 4,000-5,000 bottles a year
Location: Unit D, Pontygwindy Industrial Estate, Pontygwindy Road, Caerphilly, CF83 3HU
Telephone: 07814 166983
Email: rob@eccentricgin.com
Website: www.eccentricgin.co.uk
Facebook: www.facebook.com/
   EccentricGin
Instagram: @eccentricginco
Twitter: @EccentricGin

Opening hours:
Monday-Friday 0800-1530
You can also collect the gin by arrangement on weekends

Other reasons to go: Caerphilly Castle, Llancaiach Fawr, Brecon Mountain Railway

The Eccentric Gin Distillery was built in 2014 in the cellar of a pub, The Wheatsheaf Rooms in Llantrisant. Their signature gin, Madame Geneva (bottom left, second bottle from left), is a genever-style gin made with locally sourced marchalan, Welsh for 'wild sunflower', which gives the gin a subtle sweetness and bitterness. They recommend serving a double shot of the gin with a slice of orange and a dash of tonic to taste. For a cocktail, serve the gin in a Martini: add 60 ml of Madame Geneva to 10 ml of dry vermouth, a dash of orange bitters with a lemon twist and sprig of rosemary to garnish.

Eccentric Gin also produces an Old Tom-style gin (bottom left, left-hand bottle), ironically named Young Tom. The spirit is twice distilled with Celt Experience Ogham Willow Beer and then barrel aged and vapour infused (page 254) with fennel, wild sunflower root and star anise. It then rests for six weeks to allow the flavours to develop. Their newest addition is Limbeck Gin (below left, right-hand bottle), made with blue ginger, citrus, tarragon and bitter orange. The botanicals are rested in old Burgundy French oak casks, which give the gin a smooth texture and a subtle peach colour.

All the gins can be bought from various shops around Wales and the online shop. At £30 is Cardiff Dry Gin (left, middle bottle) which, at its inception, was a new style of gin using fennel as one of its key botanicals, plus rosemary, sorrel, liquorice, lemongrass and verbena – great as an aperitif. The gin was chosen by a cross section of people from South Wales who carried out multiple tastings to come up with the final flavour.

Dyfi Gin and Distillery

Dyfi, Machynlleth
Distillery

ESSENTIAL INFORMATION
Key botanicals (Dyfi Original Gin): juniper,
    bog-myrtle, pine shoot
Output: 10,000 bottles a year
Location: Corris Craft Centre, Machynlleth,
    SY20 9RF
Telephone: 01654 761551
Email: danny@dyfidistillery.com
Website: www.dyfidistilery.com
Facebook: www.facebook.com/
    DyfiDistillery
Instagram: @dyfidistillery
Twitter: @DyfiDistillery

Opening hours:
Easter to end of October
Monday-Sunday 1000-1700
For other opening times, check the website

Other reasons to go: Cader Idris, Southern
Snowdonia, Ospreys, kites, dolphins

The wild beauty of Dyfi Valley would seem more at home in New Zealand than Wales's west coast. As well as being the country's only UNESCO World Biosphere Reserve, it boasts some of the cleanest water, darkest skies and lowest population counts in Europe. So beautiful, in fact, that when Pete Cameron came here 35 years ago to study biology and botany, he decided never to leave. Meanwhile, his brother Danny (both pictured bottom left) was gaining expertise in the world of spirits and wine (earning himself the title Commander of the Order of Prince Henry, awarded for his services to Portuguese wine), so when they decided to go into business together in 2015, opening up a gin distillery was the natural step – pooling their shared experience in foraging and professional tasting.

Their ambition was to produce an artisan gin that expressed the beauty of the Dyfi area. Mission accomplished as far as we're concerned: a sip of their Pollination Gin (above right) is an almost synaesthetic experience. It's crafted from 29 botanicals, 20 of which are foraged from the valley – the taste conjuring up freshly-cut herbs and wildflower. As a G&T it's best served at a ratio of 1:3, garnished with basil or lemon verbena leaves, bruised juniper berries and a twist of unwaxed lemon peel. Hibernation (opposite, middle) – their gin inspired by the wild fruit harvest – is spicy and fruity, with

hints of blackberry and praline, making it a great sipping gin or base for a Negroni.

They make just three gins – Original, Pollination and Hibernation – produced through the distilling season (each bottle is hand signed and lot numbered). This means they are true to source and sustainable. Their distillation process is run by a green energy supply, part of which is located less than a mile away. The stills are small and custom-built, and in the case of Hibernation a rare White Port cask is used for barrel-ageing.

The distillery (top left and bottom right) is open to visitors every day between Easter and the end of October, and on a few dates in winter. While not offering formal tours, there is a warm welcome from the family, and the opportunity to taste all the gins produced and chat about how things are done, or just browse the information boards.

Dà Mhìle Gin and Distillery

Llandysul, Ceredigion
Distillery, tasting room and shop

ESSENTIAL INFORMATION
Key botanicals (Dà Mhìle Botanical Gin):
   juniper, coriander, cardamom, citrus,
   fennel, sage, star anise, peppermint,
   chamomile, dandelion, elderflower,
   gorse, rose petal, white clover
Output: 4,000 bottles a year
Location: Glynhynod Farm, Llandysul,
   SA44 5JY
Telephone: 01239 851998
Email: hi@damhile.co.uk
Website: www.damhile.co.uk
Facebook: www.facebook.com/DaMhile
Instagram: @damhiledistillery
Twitter: @DaMhile

Opening hours:
Monday-Friday 1000-1700

**Other reasons to go: National Wool
Museum, Skanda Vale, West Wales Museum
of Childhood, Coed Y Foel Woodland Trust**

John Savage-Onstwedder came to Wales from Holland in 1981 with a passion for organic farming. He settled at Glynhynod Farm in Ceredigion intending to make artisan cheese using raw milk and local produce. Then in 1992 he branched out to spirits, commissioning the Springbank Distillery in Campbeltown to produce the world's first organic whisky. In 1999 Dà Mhìle (pronounced da-vee-lay), Gaelic for 2,000, was released to celebrate the new millennium.

John carried on mainly with cheese until in 2006 he applied for a distiller's licence, one of the first for a 350-litre still in the UK. The distillery was opened in 2012 on John's farm, run by his oldest son, John-James, who trained at Kilchoman Distillery in Scotland, and head distiller Mike Melrose.

Dà Mhìle Botanical Gin was the distillery's second release, after its Orange 33 liqueur, and is made in a still powered by a wood-fired steam boiler. The process is slow, taking five to eight hours, but Mike believes it allows for optimum flavour extraction. He recommends serving the gin with a quality tonic and mint.

Their second gin was Dà Mhìle Organic Seaweed Gin (left), launched on the 1st March 2014 to celebrate St David's Day, designed to complement seafood and inspired by a seaweed cheese. It's distilled with seaweed hand picked from the Celtic coast, infused with garden herbs for three weeks and triple filtered before bottling. The result, a savoury gin with a light green hue, works well in a Dirty Martini.

Tours run from March to October on Wednesdays and Fridays – advanced booking is recommended. See the website for details. They also have a shop and tasting room, open Monday to Friday from 10 am to 5 pm.

Cygnet Gin, Distillery and Juniper Place

Swansea
Distillery, bar and restaurant

ESSENTIAL INFORMATION

Key botanicals (Cygnet Gin): juniper, coriander seed, liquorice root, cardamom seed, almond, lemon peel, lime peel, orange peel, pink grapefruit peel, chamomile

Output: 10,000+ bottles a year

Location: 1 York Street, Swansea, SA1 3LZ

Telephone: 01792 464111

Email: sales@cygnet-distillery.co.uk

Website: www.cygnet-distillery.co.uk

Facebook: www.facebook.com/cygnetdistillery

Instagram: @cygnet_gin

Twitter: @CygnetDistille1

Opening hours:
Monday-Sunday 1000-2200

Other reasons to go: National Waterfront Museum, Swansea Bay, Mumbles Pier, Oystermouth Castle

Cygnet Gin (next page, top left) was launched in March 2018, but its history goes back as far as the 19thC, when local Swansea men Peter Wakely and William Lee were brought together by their efforts to cure cholera. Wakely knew about the power of spring water and herbs to ward off infection and Lee knew about distilling. Together they worked on infusing their ingredients to create what they hoped would be an effective antidote to the dreaded disease.

Unfortunately, they both died of cholera in the process, but their spirit lives on: Dai Wakely is the descendant of Peter and he created Cygnet Gin with co-founder David Bellis, using a recipe based on his forebear's. Dai, the Master Distiller, was in the hospitality and drinks trade for 15 years, learning mixology along the way. He developed Cygnet Gin alongside Burleighs Gin distiller, Jamie Baxter (page 142), using Welsh spring water. Cygnet claims to be the first microdistillery in South Wales to create, bottle and sell its own gin on the premises.

The distillery offers gin experiences for all budgets. The free Distillery Tour lasts 30 minutes and includes a meet and greet in the Juniper Place restaurant (left) after which you will be taken through to the distillery. Here, you learn about the history of Cygnet, its distilling and bottling process and how it gets to the shelf.

For £37, you can take part in a two-hour Cygnet Masterclass, which starts with the Distillery Tour. You are then escorted back to Juniper Place where you can enjoy a meal from the Light Bites and Bar Menu with a view of the 300-litre still (next page, bottom right). This is followed by a guided gin tasting with Dai where you try

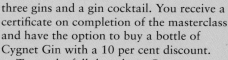

three gins and a gin cocktail. You receive a certificate on completion of the masterclass and have the option to buy a bottle of Cygnet Gin with a 10 per cent discount.

To get the full three-hour Cygnet Experience, you pay £55 for a guided tour, a two-course lunch, dinner or afternoon tea in Juniper Place, followed by a gin tasting. You then 'get to know' the botanicals used in Cygnet Gin and learn how to make a perfect serve cocktail from scratch. You then have the option to buy a bottle of Cygnet Gin at a 20 per cent discount.

Shining Cliff Gin and White Peak Distillery

Ambergate, Derbyshire

Distillery and shop

ESSENTIAL INFORMATION

Key botanicals (Shining Cliff Floral Gin): juniper, coriander, liquorice, lemon, orange, elderberry, bilberry, bay, rosehip, lime tree leaf, lime flower, Derbyshire mayflower

Output: 10,000 bottles a year

Location: Derwent Wire Works, Matlock Road, Ambergate, DE56 2HE

Telephone: 01773 856918

Email: info@whitepeakdistillery.co.uk

Website: www.whitepeakdistillery.co.uk

Facebook: www.facebook.com/whitepeakdistillery

Instagram: @whitepeakdistillery

Twitter: @whitepeakwhisky

Opening hours:
Distillery
Tuesday-Friday 1100-1700
Saturday 1100-1600
Tours (booking required)
Thursday 1500
Friday 1100 and 1500
Saturday 1100

Other reasons to go: Cromford Canal, The Heights of Abraham

White Peak claims to be the first full-scale craft distillery in the Peak District and takes much inspiration from its Derbyshire surroundings. Local folklore says in the late 17thC, the ancient woodlands of Shining Cliff (from which White Peak's gin takes its name) were home to Luke and Betty Kenny and their eight children. They were charcoal burners who travelled from Nottingham each winter for work and the favourite location for their movable hut was the 2,000 year old yew tree that features on the Shining Cliff Gin bottle (next page, top left). The label (bottom left) also carries the tagline 'Rock-a-Bye Baby', referring to the lullaby Betty sang to her babies as they slept in the boughs of the yew tree while she worked.

The gin is distilled with botanicals which White Peak say are inspired by the Shining Cliff woods, including rosehip, bilberry, elderflower, lime flower, and mayflower. In fact, the botanicals are bought in commercially, with the exception of mayflower, which is foraged once a year. They use the vapour infusion distillation method (page 254) to capture these delicate flavours. Co-founders Max and Claire recommend sipping the gin neat, or mixing with a premium tonic and garnishing with a slice of fresh orange peel or pink grapefruit.

They also produce three other small batch gins in their Shining Cliff range – Citrus (next page, bottom left, right-hand bottle), Spiced, and Bakewell Pud (next page, bottom left, left-hand bottle). The latter takes inspiration from the nearby town of Bakewell and incorporates English cherries, almonds and raspberries to imitate the classic Bakewell Pudding. The botanicals give the gin a natural pink hue. As the

flavours are complex in their own right, Max and Claire suggest simply serving with a premium tonic over ice and raspberries.

White Peak offers distillery tours and tastings, reasonably priced at £5 for under 18s and £12 for adults. The tours are largely about whisky production, but they do offer a chance to see the gin still, Betty, and to take part in a guided tasting of the gins. Tours run in groups of up to 16 people and last for approximately 90 minutes. As we went to press, the tours were held on Thursdays and Fridays but Max and Claire were hoping to increase this to four days a week in-keeping with their operational hours.

The Shining Cliff Gin range is available to buy on their website, or from their Distillery Shop (above right), where they also sell maps of the locality, hot and cold drinks and cakes.

40 St Paul's

Birmingham, West Midlands
Bar

ESSENTIAL INFORMATION
Location: 40 Cox Street, Birmingham, B3 1RD
Telephone: 07340 037639
Email: info@40stpauls.co.uk
Website: www.40stpauls.co.uk
Facebook: www.facebook.com/40StPauls
Instagram: @40stpauls
Twitter: @40StPauls

Opening hours:
Tuesday-Friday 1700-2300
Saturday 1500-2300

Other reasons to go: Cadbury World, Bullring
and Grand Central, National Sea Life Centre,
Birmingham Museum and Art Gallery

A table service only bar serving 140 gins, each with their own garnish. The idea, according to owner Amanjot Singh Johal, was to give Birmingham a bar that serves gin properly.

They also offer gin tastings with prices starting at £32.50 per person. The tastings last three hours and include a tutorial on the history of the gin, and a tutored tasting of ten different gins exploring the breadth of flavours now commonly available.

There's no distillery here but the bar infuses its own seasonal gins. The spring edition, Under the Blossom, includes rose, hibiscus and cherry blossom. Eton Mess (bottom left, left-hand bottle) is the gin of choice for summer, with classic botanicals of strawberry, raspberry and cream distillate. The autumn edition, Rainy Orchard, is oak aged for three days with apple, maple and acorn. The winter warmer is a Salted Caramel Hot Chocolate – not a gin, but made using the bar's homemade salted caramel syrup.

You could also try the Gin, Cheese & Chocolate experience: for £25 you get five gins to pair with award-winning cheeses and hand-made chocolate truffles. This lasts two hours and is open to a minimum group of eight.

As we went to press you could also buy a Christmas Hamper for £35, including a copy of the 40 St Paul's gin menu, gin glasses, a bottle of Hockley Tonic (left, right-hand bottle) and metal straws.

Future plans include the release of a Reserve Selection of 20 of the most rare and exclusive gins they've been able to get their hands on, with a tutored tasting and a membership card with rewards including t-shirts, badges and other merchandise.

The Canal House

Birmingham, West Midlands
Bar

The Canal House (bottom left) is one of the newer brands conceived by The New World Trading Company, the creators of The Smuggler's Cove bar in Liverpool and The Botanist bar and restaurant chain. The nautical theme of these bars permeates the Canal House, but it also celebrates the legacy of James Brindley – the notable 18thC canal engineer – a theme carried over from the building's former life as a 'James Brindley' pub in the 1980s.

The pub's 135 seats span two floors: on the ground floor is The Engine Room, dimly lit with wood-panelled walls and rewired gas lighting. Upstairs, The Residency's alcoves showcase the re-imagined rooms of James Brindley's residence. There are three private dining rooms: The Study and The Brew Room which each seat up to eight people, and The Office which can cater for up to 14. There is also a beer garden which overlooks the canal – a summer hotspot to enjoy a refreshing G&T.

The recipe for their own gin, Secret Gin, was created on the premises and it was initially distilled on site, but due to the unprecedented popularity of the gin, it's now distilled by Drinks of Manchester Ltd, the makers of Manchester Gin. Secret Gin is sold exclusively through the New World Trading Company bars and restaurants, alongside other gins mentioned in this guide including Poetic License (page 206), Silent Pool (page 51) and Forest Gin (page 177).

The Canal House offers a Gin Discovery Masterclass where you learn about the history of the spirit and then taste a range of gins, learning to identify the flavours and botanicals in each. The class costs £25 per person, for a minimum of six people, and lasts for approximately 90 minutes.

Sibling Gin and Distillery

Cheltenham, Gloucestershire
Distillery and shop

ESSENTIAL INFORMATION
Key botanicals (Sibling Original Gin):
   juniper, coriander, liquorice, cardamom,
   cubeb, orange, lemon, blueberry, vanilla
Output: 70,000 bottles a year
Location: Coxhorne Farm, London Road,
   Cheltenham, GL52 6UY
Telephone: 07875 163655; 07882 125969
Email: info@siblingdistillery.com
Website: www.siblingdistillery.com
Facebook: www.facebook.com/SiblingGin
Instagram: @siblingdistillery
Twitter: @SiblingGin

Opening hours:
Brewery shop
Monday-Friday 0930-1730
Saturday 0900-1300

Other reasons to go: The Wilson history
archive, Pittville Park, Cheltenham Town Hall

The four siblings who run this operation, Felix, Clarice, Cicely and Digby Elliott-Berry, have the drinks industry in their blood – their parents run Battledown Brewery next door to the distillery. They chose to make gin in 2013 for its versatility, and for the creative fun that comes with using natural botanicals. After a rigorous trial and error period, Sibling Original Gin (bottom left) was launched in 2014.

Sibling creates its own base spirit, starting with a pure cane sugar which is mashed with a canoe paddle. Then, it's heated, chilled and fermented with yeast for around ten days before being added to the pot still for a further four days to strip out the alcohol. It's then transferred to the column still for distillation to create the neutral spirit before turning it into gin. They weigh, peel and chop the blueberries (next page, middle), oranges and lemons by hand before adding them to the still to vapour infuse (page 254) the gin. The glass and stainless steel still is more sustainable than copper and allows clarity for a more precise distillation. To retain the freshness of the botanicals, the vapour basket is replenished throughout the distillation, with a new load of botanicals being added for every 17.5 litres of gin produced. After distillation, the product is cut down to a strength of 42%.

Sibling recommends serving the Original Gin with Fever-Tree Naturally Light tonic, a small slice of orange or a twist of orange peel or blueberries.

They also produce seasonal gins: Sibling Spring Edition (next page, top, left-hand bottle) is infused with lemon zest and rosemary which they recommend mixing with tonic, a slice of lemon and plenty of ice.

→

The Summer Edition (above, second bottle from left) is an infusion of strawberries and black pepper, and is best served with tonic, strawberry slices, fresh basil and ice. The Autumn Edition (above, second bottle from right) uses apples, blackberries and cardamom and works well with tonic, a couple of blackberries and ice. The Winter Edition (above, right-hand bottle) is made with cranberries and clementine peel, and is best served with ginger ale, orange peel and ice. The seasonal editions are made from fresh and predominantly local ingredients where possible.

The gins can be bought directly from the online shop and the adjacent brewery shop, costing £40 each for a 70-cl bottle, including delivery.

Sibling offers distillery tours, including seasonal tastings and a history of gin, followed by a pub quiz. The tour lasts around two hours and costs £25 per person. It also entitles you to a 15 per cent discount in their brewery shop. Visit their website for dates and bookings.

Garden Swift Dry Gin and Capreolus Distillery

Cirencester, Gloucestershire
Distillery

ESSENTIAL INFORMATION
Key botanicals (Garden Swift Dry Gin):
    juniper, blood orange zest, rowan
    berry, lime flower, hops, mullein flower,
    wormwood, plus 27 secret ingredients
Output: 13,000 bottles a year
Location: The Mount, Park View, Stratton,
    Cirencester, GL7 2JG
Telephone: 01285 644477
Email: barney@capreolusdistillery.co.uk
Website: www.capreolusdistillery.co.uk
Facebook: www.facebook.com/
    CapreolusDistillery
Instagram: @capreolusdistil
Twitter: @CapreolusDistil

Opening hours: not open to the public

Barney Wilczak (bottom left) founded the Capreolus Distillery in 2014, its main product *eaux de vie*. Having grown up surrounded by the countryside and wildlife of the Cotswolds (above), he loved natural history, becoming a conservation photographer. He wanted to capture the local botanicals at their peak of ripeness and his research into *eaux de vie* made him think about different ways botanicals could be used, and if gin's versatility could be harnessed for the purpose.

Barney crushes the spices, berries and herbs (next page, top right and bottom) by hand and steeps them in a bought-in neutral grain spirit for 40 hours before transferring them to a 120-litre copper still (next page, top left), heated by a bain-marie. The rest of the botanicals, including the blood orange zest, flowers and leaves, are vapour infused (page 254) in a basket at the top of the still. An additional bag is needed for the vapour infusion because of the large number of botanicals

involved. Each run takes seven hours and produces 270 bottles. He doesn't chill filter the gin because he believes this strips the aroma, flavour and texture, so the result is a cloudy spirit when the mixer is added. Barney recommends serving Garden Swift Dry Gin (previous page, bottom right) with a quality tonic and an orange slice, or in a Negroni.

Capreolus? It's the Latin name for roe deer, often spotted on Barney's foraging expeditions.

The Gin Pantry at The Cotswold Plough

Clanfield, Oxfordshire
Bar

ESSENTIAL INFORMATION
Location: Bourton Road, Clanfield, OX18 2RB
Telephone: 01367 810222
Email: gin@ginpantry.co.uk
Website: www.thecotswoldplough.co.uk
**Facebook: www.facebook.com/
   theginpantry**
Instagram: @thecotswoldginpantry
Twitter: @theginpantry

Opening hours:
Monday-Thursday 1100-2230
Friday-Saturday 1100-2300
Sunday 1200-2200

**Other reasons to go: Butser Ancient Farm,
Hollybank Woods History**

Ella Carr writes: Worth a detour. The Cotswold Plough Hotel (bottom left) is a beautiful 16thC local stone building west of Oxford – gables, mullioned windows, oak floors and beams – quaint and sophisticated.

Owner Martin Agius originally stocked ten well-chosen gins in the hotel bar. When he saw the interest they generated he started building a collection, which now stands at more than 450 brands in a dedicated room known as The Gin Pantry (next page, bottom right). Instead of ordering over the bar, customers are encouraged to browse the Pantry's shelves (next page, top left) in their own time, taking off tops and sniffing before ordering what appeals most. Only two bottles have ever been stolen. He thinks that gin should be emphatically juniper led, so although the Pantry has a shelf of fruit gins, there's a sign saying 'Drink these if you want, but they're not gin.' Expert bar tenders will personalize your order with the best tonic and garnish, then encourage you to experiment with different brands. Don't forget the Alka Selzer.

Before arrival, visitors are challenged to check whether their favourite gin is in the Pantry. If not, they're asked to bring a bottle and ask the Pantry's tasting panel to approve it. If it passes, you donate the bottle to the Pantry in return for a free three-course lunch or dinner in the hotel restaurant.

The tasting panel, led by Martin and calling themselves The Gin Connoisseurs, hold gin experiences where you can taste, learn and blend your own bottle (next page, middle and bottom left) – see the website to buy gift vouchers for these events online.

Centre stage in the Pantry is Martin's own bespoke collection of 18 gins – Gin

→

in a Tin. The flask-shaped metal tin is wittily designed as if intended for olive oil. You can buy the gins from the website (www.gininatin.co.uk) individually or on subscription – a newsletter describes new editions and seasonal variations.

Martin started offering this service in 2010, even before craft gin took off, so he can claim to be a founding father of the microdistillery bandwagon. He's known locally as The Gin Man and savvily describes gin as "the only spirit which spans age and gender from 18 to 80 years, 50-50 male and female."

Sly Gin and Haven Distillery

Dilwyn, Herefordshire
Distillery

ESSENTIAL INFORMATION
Key botanicals (Sly Gin): juniper, coriander
    seed, cassia bark, citrus peel, bay, apple,
    mint, rosemary, lemon thyme, lavender
Output: 7,000-10,000 bottles a year
Location: Tump Ash Farm, Dilwyn, HR4 8JF
Telephone: 01544 319335
Email: duncanfox@havendistillery.co.uk
Website: www.havendistillery.co.uk
Facebook: www.facebook.com/
    HavenDistillery
Instagram: @haven_distillery
Twitter: @HavenDistillery

Opening hours: visits by appointment only

Other reasons to go: Herefordshire
Raceway, Monkland Cheese Dairy, National
Trust's Croft Castle and Parkland

Deep in sleepy north Herefordshire, in the tiny hamlet of Haven, is the 5 by 4 m shed where Duncan Fox and his wife Alex have made Sly Gin (bottom left and next page, top right) since 2016. He was a software engineer with an interest in chemistry which he bought to bear on his distilling, and Alex always had a love of herbs: for many years she ran a herb nursery and garden open to the public.

These are authentic small-batch craft gin makers. After months of experimenting, helped by gin-loving friends, they arrived at the recipe. Most of the botanicals are picked by hand from their garden (next page, middle) in summer and dried to ensure batch consistency throughout the year. The spices are ground by hand in a pestle and mortar.

They combine hot vapour-infused (page 254) juniper with cold distilled botanicals (page 280). The cold distillation (next page, top middle) prevents the more delicate flavours of the citrus and the home-grown botanicals from being 'cooked' – so the flavours remain bright. It's diluted to 43% with naturally pure Malvern Holywell Water. "We wanted our gin to be proofed with the purest water that came out of the ground and there it was just a short drive away".

The bottle tops are waxed using wax melted in a slow cooker. Batches are no more than 100 bottles.

Their main gin is the classic London dry (left, left-hand bottle), with a full, rich spruce-like juniper flavour combined with complex herb and spice elements. It's exceptionally smooth – sippable but also great with a mixer. Serve with ice or with tonic, a wedge of citrus and a sprig of lemon thyme.

The Lemon Verbena Gin (left, right-hand

bottle) combines soft, rounded juniper with a natural 'sherbet lemon' zest. It almost fizzes on the tongue and is especially good with tonic, fresh strawberries or a segment of orange. It also makes a snappy Martini.

The Pink Grapefruit Gin (previous page, bottom left, middle bottle) is a blast of grapefruit, orange and lemon with a hint of vanilla and black pepper. Great in sparkling wine or with tonic and a pink grapefruit slice, it also makes a wicked Negroni.

Haven is open to visitors by appointment for buying bottles and a quick look around – it's too small for a tour – you can see it all from the doorway. There's no bar, but gin is drunk regularly in the couple's kitchen.

Warner's Gin and Distillery

Harrington, Northamptonshire
Distillery

ESSENTIAL INFORMATION

Key botanicals (Harrington Dry Gin):
   juniper, coriander seed, cardamom,
   cinnamon, black pepper, lemon peel,
   orange peel, nutmeg, elderflower

Output: not disclosed

Location: Falls Farm, 34 High Street,
   Harrington, NN6 9NU

Telephone: 01536 710623

Email: info@warnersdistillery.com

Website: www.warnersdistillery.com

Facebook: www.facebook.com/WarnersGin

Instagram: @warnersgin

Twitter: @warnersgin

**Opening hours: tours by appointment only –
   see website for booking information**

**Other reasons to go: West Lodge Rural
Centre, Kelmarsh Hall, Cottesbrooke Hall
& Gardens**

David T. Smith writes: Located in the tiny village of Harrington, set in the picturesque Northamptonshire countryside, Warner's was founded by husband and wife team Tom and Tina Warner. The duo had initially looked at distilling botanicals to create essential oils, but quickly saw the potential in creating spirits and, in particular, gin.

The first offering, Harrington Dry Gin (bottom left, middle bottle), was released in December 2012. It is a classic London dry gin, and substituting 'London' for the name of the village is a reminder to the team to focus on where the gin is made as well as *how* it is made.

The distillery itself (next page, top left) is located in a 200-year-old barn on Falls Farm, which had previously been used to house livestock. A medieval manor once stood on the land owned by the Knights Hospitaliter of Saint John of Jerusalem until the early 16thC.

After that, there were a number of different owners who rebuilt the manor house and created gardens, along with terraces which can still be seen today. At the foot of the remaining terraces is a natural spring, where they get the water for their gin.

In addition to the classic dry gin, the distillery has also released a series of fruit gins. In 2014, they released what is widely recognised as the original Rhubarb Gin (left, third bottle from left), which helped to blaze a trail for many of the other fruit and pink-coloured gins that are so popular in the market today.

In 2016, Tom and Tina converted his late mother's kitchen garden into a botanical garden (next page, bottom right) packed full of all sorts of classic gin botanicals, as

well as some that are not so common. The garden is both an attraction for visitors, who can see botanicals in their natural state before distillation, but also provides inspiration for the distillers when they are coming up with new recipe ideas. It's also home to Warner's 2018 award-winning Chelsea Flower Show artisan garden.

The garden also inspired the launch of a new range of botanical gins, which was – in turn – inspired by the love and dedication of Tom's mother, a keen gardener. The first in the range was Melissa Gin, now called Lemon Balm Gin (previous page, second bottle from right), made using lemon balm, lemon thyme and lemon verbena harvested by hand from one of the gardens at Falls Farm. These botanicals are distilled within an hour of being harvested. The second was Honeybee Gin (previous page, third bottle from right), which uses local honey and a dollop of nectar from Warner's own apiary at Falls Farm (top right).

Fifthspire Gin, Greywood Distillery and The Spirit Works

Lichfield, Staffordshire
Distillery and bar

ESSENTIAL INFORMATION
Key botanicals (Fifthspire Gin): juniper, coriander seed, liquorice root, cassia bark, lemon, lime, orange peel, grapefruit, almond, pink peppercorn
Output: 5,000-10,000 bottles a year
Location: The Spirit Works, Swan Road, Lichfield, WS13 6QZ
Telephone: 01543 301758
Email: rory@fifthspire.co.uk; tom@fifthspire.co.uk
Website: www.fifthspire.co.uk
Facebook: www.facebook.com/thespiritworkslichfield
Instagram: @thespiritworkslichfield
Twitter: @thespiritworks

Opening hours:
Tuesday-Thursday 1700-2230
Friday-Sunday 1400-2230

Other reasons to go: Lichfield Cathedral, Samuel Johnson Birthplace Museum, Coventry Canal

Greywood Distillery was formed in 2015 by best friends Rory McKerell and Tom Lindsey, who wanted to break away from their engineering backgrounds and work for themselves. They had a shared love of spirits and had done several camping trips in Scotland where they visited whisky distilleries, but it was a trip to Spain that sparked their interest in gin. The gin renaissance had been flourishing there for some time and with home-based microdistilleries – such as Sacred Spirits (page 81) – succeeding in Britain, they decided to give it a shot.

Tom turned his spare room into a microdistillery and the duo spent about a year getting the right recipe. Fifth Spire Gin (next page, top left) was launched at Lichfield Gin Festival in November 2016 and named after the view from the distillery – a three-spired cathedral in the distance and two spires between there and Tom's house. They wanted to make a simple London Dry, citrus-led gin avoiding what they describe as unnecessary frills.

They have two stills: one contains the lemon, lime and grapefruit which has a run time of four hours so the citrus doesn't cook. The rest of the botanicals are placed in the other still, on a low heat for a longer run of seven hours. The spirits are then blended together with more wheat spirit (bought in from Langley Distillery in Birmingham) before being cut with Elmhurst spring water to 47%. The gin has a slightly higher than normal bottle strength to keep it 'stable', as the oils from the citrus can make it go cloudy when cold. Rory and Tom recommend serving the gin with Franklin & Sons tonic and a wedge of pink grapefruit (next page, middle), or dried

→

bitter orange peel. It also works well in a Dry Martini.

The gins can be bought from Rory and Tom's bar, The Spirit Works (bottom right and previous page, bottom left) on Swan Road in Lichfield, which they describe as a premium spirits bar that also serves beer and wine. They serve their own products as well as other brands such as Sipsmith (page 71), Tanqueray and Monkey 47.

As we went to press, Tom and Rory were in the process of bringing production in house at The Spirit Works. They had also just bought some mini pot stills for their new gin school, which they hoped to open in winter 2019.

Pin Gin and Bottomley Distillers

Louth, Lincolnshire
Distillery, shop and gin school

ESSENTIAL INFORMATION

Key botanicals (Pin Gin): juniper, liquorice root, cinnamon, black peppercorn, orange peel, cucumber, rose petal, lavender

Output: 15,000 bottles a year

Location: 6 Bolingbroke Court, Bolingbroke Road, Louth, LN11 0ZW

Telephone: 01507 600410

Email: info@bottomleydistillers.co.uk

Website: www.bottomleydistillers.co.uk

Facebook: www.facebook.com/ PinGinClassic

Instagram: @pin_gin_

Twitter: @BottomleyDistil

Opening hours:
Monday-Saturday 0800-1700

Other reasons to go: Hubbard's Hills, Louth Museum, St James' Church

Husband and wife team Alan Bottomley and Amy Conyard founded Bottomley Distillery in March 2017. In the 1990s Alan had learned distilling from his father, who made whisky. After a career in engineering, Alan decided to revisit these skills, turning the garage in their town house in Louth into a distillery and experimenting for a year with a 35-litre alembic still called Dotty.

Starting with 19 different recipes, Alan whittled them down to two, with the help of local chef Steven Bennett. He then played around with the botanicals, re-distilling five versions of each until he was happy with the flavour. He produces around 15,000 bottles a year in two stills: a 100-litre copper pot still called Rose and a 500-litre copper pot still, Stansfield, named after Alan's father.

The botanicals of Bottomley's signature product, Pin Gin London Dry, (left) are steeped for 24 hours before distilling. Amy came up with the name, combining Alan's two projects: growing Christmas trees ('Pin' comes from pine needles) and producing gin. They recommend serving Pin Gin with a quality tonic, strawberries, lime and plenty of ice.

They also produce Pin Gin Premium Pink, an infusion of strawberries and the London Dry Gin, and a limited edition Sloe Gin.

The gins can be bought from Bottomley's on site shop, which is open Monday to Saturday from 10 am to 3 pm.

In October 2018, Bottomley moved into a larger premises in Louth, where they offer a gin school once a week by appointment only.

Two Birds Gin and Union Distillers

Market Harborough, Leicestershire
Distillery and gin school

ESSENTIAL INFORMATION

Key botanicals (Two Birds London Dry Gin): juniper, coriander, citrus, plus one secret ingredient

Output: 95,000 bottles a year

Location: E7 Welland Business Park, Valley Way, Market Harborough, LE16 7PS

Telephone: 01858 463758

Email: sales@twobirdsspirits.co.uk

Website: www.twobirdsspirits.co.uk

Facebook: www.facebook.com/twobirdsspirits

Instagram: @twobirdsspirits

Twitter: @twobirdsspirits

Opening hours:
Monday-Friday 0900-1700

Other reasons to go: Harborough Museum, St Mary in Arden Church, Kelmarsh Hall

David T. Smith writes: Union Distillers is in the Leicestershire town of Market Harborough which was also home to a 17thC grammar school and was the staging place for royalist troops before the decisive Battle of Naseby during the English Civil War.

The modern-day distillery was founded by partners Mark Gamble and Lyn Taylor. Mark's first career was working in a business that designed and fabricated equipment for the food service industry, experience which he found useful when creating his first still, Gerard, which continues to be used every day.

Union Distillers released their first product in 2013, a classic London Dry Gin called Two Birds Gin (bottom left). This was followed in 2014 by Two Birds Speciality Cocktail Gin (opposite, top right), a more intensely botanical spirit. Although bottled at 40%, it has a powerful flavour which is ideal for mixing with fruit juice or, if you like powerful flavour, enjoying neat.

Perhaps the pinnacle of the distillery's work is their Sipping Gin (opposite, top middle), which was a labour of love for distiller Mark and is aged in barrels with pecan wood staves. The result is also particularly complex, ideal for sipping neat.

The distillery runs a Gin Workshop (opposite, top left and bottom left) at weekends: in a three-hour session, you are taught the basics of gin production and flavour profiles, before having a go at making

a gin to your own recipe using the distillery's miniature copper pot stills.

In addition to their in-house brand, Two Birds, Union Distillers have worked with a range of other companies, assisting in both production and product development. They have also created bespoke bottlings for a number of retailers, restaurants, and bars.

Burleighs Gin and 45 West Distillery

Nanpantan, Leicestershire
Distillery, bar, shop and gin school

ESSENTIAL INFORMATION

Key botanicals (Burleighs Gin): juniper, coriander seed, cardamom, orange peel, burdock root, silver birch

Output: 110,000 bottles a year

Location: The Collection Yard, Bawdon Lodge Farm, Charley Road, Nanpantan, LE12 9YE

Telephone: 01530 245402

Email: enquiries@45w.co.uk

Website: www.burleighsgin.com

Facebook: www.facebook.com/burleighsgin

Instagram: @burleighsgin

Twitter: @burleighsgin

Opening hours:
Sunday-Thursday 1030-2330
Friday-Saturday 1030-0130

Other reasons to go: Great Central Railway, Beacon Hill Country Park, Charnwood Museum, Manor Farm Park and Woodlands

Ella Carr writes: Burleighs Gin was launched in June 2014 by Graham Veitch. Graham had a background in scrapping and selling breweries and distilleries but the craft gin revolution shifted his interest to distilling. He joined forces with Jamie Baxter in October 2013 to build a distillery in Leicester but when the city site fell through, the distillery was moved to its current location at Bawdon Lodge Farm.

The surrounding countryside is the inspiration for their signature gin (bottom left) – in particular Burleigh Wood. They knew they wanted to produce a traditional London Dry, with classic botanicals such as orris and angelica root, juniper and cardamom, but they struggled to make it stand out from the crowd. Walking through the wood one day Jamie came across burdock, dandelion, silver birch and elderberries, all of which made their way in to the final recipe – and inspired the Burleighs name. The sturdy black bottle with white lettering and a Union Jack reflects its crisp, classic taste and British identity – it's distilled, bottled and sealed at the Leicestershire site. The distillery's quaint location belies a savvy operation by two seasoned businessmen.

If Burleighs is classic, Burleighs London Dry Gin Pink Edition (opposite, bottom right) is unique, inspired by Jamie's visit to Tokyo during cherry blossom season. Bringing back as much preserved cherry blossom (*sakura*) as he could lay his hands on, he distilled this with the other 11 Burleighs botanicals – as well as rose petals, hibiscus and chamomile. The first batch of 600 bottles sold out within four days.

Burleighs recently moved their Gin School (opposite top and bottom left) to Leicester's old town. Sessions last three hours, and include a cocktail masterclass, complimentary Burleighs G&Ts, a chance to blend botanicals and devise a recipe, before distilling, bottling and taking it

home (£145 for the Shared Experience; £115 for the Single). Down the road from the Gin School is their flagship store, 45 West Bottle Shop and Bar. The bar is stylish and contemporary, with sultry lighting and carefully crafted Burleighs cocktails, served by knowledgeable bar staff. Alongside Burleighs, the adjoining Bottle Shop serves a well-presented collection of spirits, wines and craft beers.

Redsmith Gin and Distillery

Nottingham, Nottinghamshire
Distillery

ESSENTIAL INFORMATION

Key botanicals (Redsmith London Dry Gin): juniper, coriander, orange, plus six secret ingredients

Output: 10,000 bottles a year

Location: Unit 33 Avenue C, Nottingham, NG1 1DW

Telephone: 01158 712545

Email: office@redsmithdistillery.com

Website: www.redsmithdistillery.com/

Facebook: www.facebook.com/RedSmith-Distillery

Instagram: @redsmithgin

Twitter: @RedSmithDistill

Opening hours: visits by appointment only

Other reasons to go: Nottingham Castle, Wollaton Hall, City of Caves

*D*avid T. Smith writes: Redsmith Distillery is in the bustling Creative Quarter of Hockley in the City of Nottingham. This area is also known as The Soho of Nottingham and is home to various fashion and record shops, as well as trendy bars and restaurants.

The distillery was founded in 2015 by Wayne Asher and started life in the small village of Ruddington, before moving to Nottingham in early 2017. Wayne had previously studied engineering, worked in the aerospace industry, and set up a plumbing and heating business. The name Redsmith is a nod to Wayne's metalworking past and comes from the name for someone who works with copper, in contrast to a blacksmith, who works with iron or steel.

This experience also gave him the skills to build his own first still, Jenny (above). Jenny was custom-built and designed over a period of 12 months and includes a ten-plate rectifying column, as well as a carterhead to allow the vapour distillation (page 254) of botanicals. Wayne also created a smaller still, named Tiny Tess, to assist with product research and development.

The distillery's flagship gin, Redsmith London Dry (left), was launched in 2016 and has won a Double Gold at the San Francisco World Spirits Competition. A year later, Wayne resurrected a forgotten style of gin: Apple Gin, which was popular in the first half of the 20thC, and disappeared

sometime in the 1960s. Redsmith Dry Apple Gin (right) is made using Bramley apples that originate from Southwell in Nottinghamshire. These are peeled and cored before being infused in the gin.

He also produces Barberry Gin (top), made with barberry root, bark and berries, which give it a pink hue.

The distillery works closely with a local pub to offer gin tastings and educational sessions, as well as tours of the distillery (by appointment only).

Oxford Dry Gin and The Oxford Artisan Distillery

Oxford, Oxfordshire

Distillery

ESSENTIAL INFORMATION

Key botanicals (Oxford Dry Gin): juniper, coriander, liquorice root, cubeb, lemon peel, orange peel, bitter orange peel, nutmeg, meadowsweet

Output: 21,000 bottles a year

Location: Old Depot, South Park, Cheney Lane, Oxford, OX3 7QJ

Telephone: 01865 767918

Email: info@spiritoftoad.com

Website: www.spiritoftoad.com

Facebook: www.facebook.com/thespiritoftoad

Instagram: @spiritoftoad

Twitter: @thespiritoftoad

Opening hours:

Monday-Friday 1100-1500

Saturday 1100-1700

Sunday 1400-1630

Other reasons to go: Oxford Castle, Radcliffe Camera, Oxford University Museum of Natural History

What do *The Wind in the Willows*, craft gin and Oxford have in common? Answer TOAD: The Oxford Artisan Distillery (bottom left), founded by Tom Nicholson, Cory Mason and Tagore Ramoutar. Kenneth Graham, who wrote *The Wind in the Willows*, went to school in Oxford where TOAD can be found, next to Oxford Brookes University.

TOAD opened as Oxford's first craft distillery in 2017.

They don't cut corners: TOAD is one of a handful of pioneers making gin from grain to bottle (see also page 56). Most craft distillers buy in ready-made neutral grain spirit and then complete the gin process by adding their own botanicals. In addition, TOAD is the only distillery we know of to use ancient populations of grain, grown locally by archaeo-botanist John Letts. These old grains are hardier than modern strains and can be grown without pesticides.

The two stills, Nautilus and Nemo, are also one-offs, designed by Cory, TOAD's Master Distiller, and Paul Pridham, a steam boiler specialist on the South Devon Railway, whose past projects include repairing *The Flying Scotsman*. In most ways, TOAD's gin is handmade and unique.

Cory also has an impressive pedigree. Born in California, he worked on the New York bar scene mixing cocktails for ten years, including a managerial job at Employees Only, voted the best cocktail bar in the world. On the side he grew a cult following for his bootlegged absinthe.

Before finally joining TOAD's team he completed an MSc in Brewing and Distilling at Heriot-Watt University.

TOAD's Oxford Dry Gin (above) has a classic botanical taste, showing off the integrity of its purist and traditional distilling values. The Oxford Botanic Garden Physic Gin (below right) follows in the footsteps of other garden gins, such as Edinburgh (page 228) and Kew, and is one of the few to harvest its botanicals (above right) from its own garden.

We think their most exciting gin is the Ashmolean Dry Gin (opposite, top right), inspired by Oxford's famous museum, one of the oldest in the world. Inspired by the museum's collections of ancient artefacts, its botanicals include Persian, Middle Eastern, Greek and Roman ingredients – such as jara lemon, saffron, cardamom, rose and, most exotically, myrrh.

You can choose from three tours a day (£20), or one a week with one of the founders (£50).

Costwolds Gin and Distillery

Shipston-on-Stour, Warwickshire
Distillery, shop, café, tasting room and gin school

ESSENTIAL INFORMATION

Key botanicals (Cotswolds Dry Gin):
juniper, coriander seed, cardamom seed,
black pepper, lime zest, pink grapefruit
zest, bay leaf, Cotswolds lavender
Output: 172,000 bottles a year
Location: Phillip's Field, Whichford Road,
Stourton, Shipston-on-Stour, CV36 5HG
Telephone: 01608 238533
Email: info@cotswoldsdistillery.com
Website: www.cotswoldsdistillery.com
Facebook: www.facebook.com/
cotswoldsdistillery
Instagram: @cotswolds_distillery
Twitter: @Cotswoldistill

Opening hours:
Distillery Shop
Monday-Saturday 0900-1700
Sunday 1030-1700

Other reasons to go: Whichford Pottery,
Hidcote Manor Garden

David T. Smith writes: The Cotswolds Distillery (bottom left) sits in one of England's most charming locations for a distillery, surrounded by rolling hills and picturesque villages. It's a 25-minute drive from Banbury and the M40, while 20 minutes to the south are Blenheim Palace and The Feathers Hotel in Woodstock, the inaugural record holder for the world's largest commercial gin collection – see page 156.

The distillery was founded by Dan Szor – originally from New York, he worked in London for a year in finance before starting the distillery in July 2014.

The first Cotswolds Gin (opposite, bottom right) was released in October 2014. Produced on a Holstein still, it is made using a classic mix of botanicals (opposite, top left) combined with pink grapefruit and lime zest, black pepper, and locally grown lavender (opposite, top right).

Since then, Cotswolds has released a wide range, starting with 1616 Barrel Aged Gin in 2016, released to commemorate the 400th anniversary of the death of William Shakespeare. This gin was created in the style of a 17thC genever and was cask aged. The following year, they released Baharat Gin, a spice-forward gin featuring botanicals such as cardamom, cumin, clove, cinnamon, black pepper, chilli, and Jaffa orange.

Next came Hedgerow Gin, made by infusing gin with local fruits and berries before being gently sweetened. Cotswolds Ginger Gin was released in the autumn of 2018 and is the resurrection of an old gin style that was once made by gin heavyweights such as Booths. It is an aged version of their classic gin, infused with candied ginger and sweet oranges.

The distillery is open for tours seven

days a week, with typically three tours per day. A tour includes a look at both the gin and whisky stills, as well as the rack (barrel) house and bottling hall, before a trip to the tasting room. In early 2019, Cotswolds opened a new visitors' centre, providing additional space to accommodate more visitors to the distillery, as well as new facilities such as a café. They also introduced gin blending masterclasses, allowing visitors to make their own recipe.

Cotswolds has shops in three different locations: one at the distillery (see opposite for opening times), one in Bourton-on-the-Water, and another in Broadway. They are open Monday to Saturday 9.30 am to 5.30 pm and Sunday 10.30 am to 5 pm.

Cotswolds also makes single malt whiskies and speciality spirits.

Stratford Gin and Shakespeare Distillery

Stratford-upon-Avon, Warwickshire
Distillery and gin school

ESSENTIAL INFORMATION

Key botanicals (Stratford Gin): juniper, coriander seed, lemon peel, orange peel, rosemary, lovage seed, lemon balm, rose

Output: not disclosed

Location: Unit A, Drayton Manor Drive, Stratford-upon-Avon, CV37 9RQ

Telephone: 01789 336335

Email: info@shakespearedistillery.com

Website: www.shakespearedistillery.com

Facebook: www.facebook.com/ shakespearedistillery

Instagram: @shakespearedistillery

Twitter: @shakedistillery

Opening hours:

Wednesday-Saturday 1000-1700

Sunday 1000-1600

Advanced booking advised for tours and Gin School

Other reasons to go: Shakespeare's birthplace, Anne Hathaway's cottage, Church of the Holy Trinity, Stratford Butterfly Farm

A distillery in Stratford-upon-Avon calls, of course, for Shakespeare in its name and Simon Picken also pays homage to The Bard by using botanicals in Stratford Gin (bottom left) that were well known in Tudor England. For example, lovage, known at the time as love ache, was used in love potions and as a deodorant. Lemon balm was used for dressing wounds. Tudor England was an interesting time in gin history: at first, distilling was confined to the monasteries and the product was used mainly for medicinal purposes. After the Dissolution of the Monasteries, distilling became a nationwide industry and all social classes started to drink spirits.

As we went to press, the distillery had recently moved from the 4,000-acre Alscot Estate in Preston-on-Stour to the Drayton Manor Farm Estate on the outskirts of Stratford-upon-Avon. They use the one-shot method (page 68) – all ingredients are added to the still at the same time. The environmentally friendly still, Portia (named after *The Merchant of Venice*'s heroine), has a 250-litre capacity and combines heavy insulation to preserve energy with a computer-controlled cooling condenser that lets in just enough water to cool down the vapour (opposite, top left). As in many stills, copper is placed in the vapour path so every drop of alcohol comes into contact with it before leaving the still, creating a clean, smooth spirit. At the new

distillery, Portia has been joined by her 500-litre big sister, Ophelia (named after the protagonist's love interest in *Hamlet*).

Distillery tours are run throughout the week (see website for dates and times) and at weekends Shakespeare also offers a Gin School (right and bottom right) where you make your own recipe in a 2.5-litre copper still, before bottling and labelling it.

The Shakespeare Distillery website sells the gins plus several gift sets, including Stratford Gin and Tonic, Mulberry Gin and Tonic and Rhubarb Gin and Ginger Ale sets for £10 each. The Mulberry Gin and Prosecco set is £12.50 and a Three Gins gift set £20.

For the perfect G&T, add 50 ml of Stratford Gin to 100 ml of tonic water. Serve over ice with a fresh slice of lemon and a sprig of rosemary. Shakespeare also produces Mulberry Gin, combining mulberries with Stratford Gin and leaving them to steep for several months. This is great in a cocktail, or to sip on its own. The newest edition is flavoured with rhubarb – juice is pressed from the fruit and blended with the gin. Try adding this to lime and ginger ale for a fresh, fruity summer thirst quencher.

Shropshire Gin Company

Telford, Shropshire
Distillery

ESSENTIAL INFORMATION

Key botanicals (Tiger Gin): juniper, coriander seed, liquorice root, cassia bark, cinnamon bark, lemon peel, orange peel, nutmeg, plus two secret ingredients

Output: not disclosed

Location: Telford, Shropshire

Telephone: 01952 250360

Email: sales@tigergin.co.uk

Website: www.tigergin.co.uk

Facebook: www.facebook.com/tigergin.uk

Instagram: @thetigergin

Twitter: @TheTigerGin

Opening hours: not open to the public

JJ Lawrence launched Shropshire Gin Co. alongside its first product, Tiger Gin (bottom left), in early 2016 after a rocky start – the producers of Tiger Beer challenged his trademark, but JJ came out victorious after a long court case.

JJ had always loved gin and, when he decided to make his own, turned to Alcohols LTD to help him create the recipe – he wanted to train himself, but thought it would take too long.

JJ wanted his gin to be sweet and smooth enough to sip on its own and, to achieve this, Tiger Gin has a higher than usual amount of liquorice root. The gin is made at Langley Distillery near Birmingham using seasonal botanicals from around the world which are steeped in neutral grain spirit overnight. The product is then distilled for nine hours to produce an 80% strength gin before it's cut with water to 40%. Try it in a G&T with an orange slice, or in a Martini.

Shropshire Gin Co. also produces Ruby Gin, a pink gin made with British rhubarb, best served over ice with rose lemonade, or ginger ale.

The gins can be bought from Majestic Wine shops around the country, as well as the Master of Malt website (www.masterofmalt.com).

Nelson's Distillery and School

Uttoxeter, Staffordshire
Distillery and gin school

ESSENTIAL INFORMATION

Key botanicals (Nelson's Rhubarb and Custard Gin): juniper, liquorice, green cardamom, cinnamon, vanilla, caraway seed, lemongrass, natural rhubarb extract

Output: 20,000 bottles a year

Location: 5A Grindley Business Village, Uttoxeter, Stafford, ST18 0LR

Telephone: 07399 455436

Email: enquiries@nelsonsdistillery.co.uk

Website: www.nelsonsdistillery.co.uk

Facebook: www.facebook.com/nelsonsgin.co.uk

Instagram: @nelsonsdistillery

Twitter: @Nelsonsgin

Opening hours:
Monday-Saturday 0900-1500

Other reasons to go: Alton Towers theme park, Uttoxeter racecourse, Sudbury Hall

"In a world of proliferating craft gins", former chef Neil Harrison (next page, bottom left, left-hand side) claims to stand out because he has the "vision and the palate to be exceptional."

His No.7 gin (bottom left, middle bottle and next page, bottom right) is intended to be clean, fresh, but complex and this could be partly because he uses ingredients usually associated with cooking, such as lemongrass, vanilla and cinnamon, alongside more standard gin botanicals. Neil's best seller is a rhubarb and custard flavoured gin (bottom left, left-hand bottle) which might well be the only one in the country. He also produces Timur Gin (bottom left, right-hand bottle), named after its key ingredient, the Timur pepper, found in the mountains of Nepal – it's not spicy but leaves a tingly feeling in the mouth along with a citrus flavour similar to grapefruit.

In the heart of the Midlands, the distillery is more than 100 miles from the sea – so why is it named after the great admiral? Answer, Neil's grandfather was called Nelson James Harrison. By now you may suspect Neil and his partner Greg Kimber (next page, bottom left, right-hand side) have strong marketing instincts, and you would be right. Even the water used to dilute their spirit is described with melodramatic relish: "We start with water. And a reed bed." The reeds, explains Neil, filter unwanted elements out of the water which is then tested in a filtering system. "And then. Our work can begin." The gin's flavour is "like notes in concerto" – and so on. The reed pond is on the distillery site and complements its eco-friendly production methods.

The other thing they do here with

gusto is the gin school (above and right). Sessions start at 10 am with coffee and an introductory talk and tour, taking in the main still which of course is named Victory after Nelson's flagship at the Battle of Trafalgar. At 11.30 you get down to distilling your own gin, whose recipe they keep on record so it can be replicated for re-order after you leave – a nice touch which few other distilleries we've come across are offering. At 12.15 there is a lunch break and a talk on gin history. At 2, distilling complete, you bottle and label your spirit for a 3 pm finish.

Grain Store Gin Emporium and Kitchen

Wolverhampton, West Midlands
Bar

ESSENTIAL INFORMATION
Location: 2-3 King Street, Wolverhampton, WV1 1SX
Telephone: 01902 219535
Email: kelly@thegrainstorewolverhampton.co.uk
Website: www.thegrainstorewolverhampton.co.uk
Facebook: www.facebook.com/ Grainstorewolverhampton
Instagram: @thegrainstorewolves
Twitter: @TGS_Wolves

Opening hours:
Monday-Tuesday 1130-2200
Wednesday 1130-0400
Thursday 1130-0000
Friday-Saturday 1130-0230
Sunday 1200-2100

Other reasons to go: Wolverhampton Art Gallery, National Trust Wightwick Manor and Gardens, Royal Air Force Museum

Opened in May 2017, Grain Store Emporium (bottom left) stocks over 40 gins, plus their own in-house infusions. Their Gin Guide has two menus – the first is The Ginventory, which is split into sections: Classic & Dry; Smooth; Citrus; Floral; Herbal; Fruity; and Unique to help find a gin suited to your palate. Each gin has a description and details of its perfect serve. The second menu, The Signature Serve, is like a gin cocktail menu, with offerings such as Gin Sangria and Gin Fizz Royale (a juniper take on the classic Pornstar Martini). They also offer a Gin Tree, where you can order 12 Signature Serve gins at a time – why not?

As we went to press, Grain Store had eight different in-house infusions made with JJ Whitley Gin. These include Cherry Bakewell using Luxardo cherries, roasted almonds and cherry syrup, Apple and Blackberry Crumble, made with blood orange extract and zest, and Piña Colada, infused with coconut cream and fresh pineapple.

They also offer 'G & Tea' where, for £15 per person, you get a teapot filled with one of their Signature Serve gins, plus everything you'd expect from a classic afternoon tea.

Grain Store is a location in itself – during the day, it's a casual lunch spot that becomes a lively bar as the evening draws in. On the weekends it transforms into a Shoreditch-style nightclub complete with resident DJs, and there's a terrace for sipping G&Ts in the warmer months (above).

The Feathers Hotel Gin Bar

Woodstock, Oxfordshire
Bar

ESSENTIAL INFORMATION
Location: Market Street, Woodstock, OX20 1SX
Telephone: 01993 812291
Email: reception@feathers.co.uk
Website: www.feathers.co.uk/pages/
    kitchen/gin-bar.html
Facebook: www.facebook.com/
    TheFeathersWoodstock
Instagram: @featherswoodstock
Twitter: @FeathersHotel

Opening hours:
Monday-Saturday 1100-2300
Sunday 1200-2230

Other reasons to go: Blenheim Palace, The
Oxfordshire Museum, St Martin's Church,
Soldiers of Oxfordshire Museum

Gin 'n history. Visit this pretty market town eight miles NW of Oxford not just for one of the country's best gin bars but for a serious slice of historic interest.

On the edge of town is Blenheim Palace (the only non-royal palace in England, leaving out bishops' palaces). Its owners, the Dukes of Marlborough, are the family that produced Winston Churchill; and before the first Duke of Marlborough was given the Palace in the early 1700s for winning the Battle of Blenheim, the town had long been associated with the English monarchy. Woodstock Palace, which stood on the site of Blenheim Palace before being cleared away for the new building was a favoured residence of several medieval kings and queens.

Today, the town thrives on tourism, many of whom choose to stay in The Feathers (featured in Duncan Petersen's *Charming Small Hotel Guide to Britain* – opposite, top left). It's a charming place to stay, stylishly decorated in a vividly colourful 'boutique' style with a notable collection of stuffed birds – hence feathers.

The gin bar (left), its most intimate space packed with nearly 450 gins, was for a while certified by *The Guinness Book of Records* as having the largest choice in the UK (these days The Gin Pantry at nearby Clanfield, page 131, has a similar number). Around 45 per cent of the gins are British, including locals from Oxford's Artisan Distillery (Spirit of Toad, page 146). The rest are from around the world.

As we went to press Octavian (opposite, bottom left), the impeccable barman, was still in place. He told us that he comes from a wine-making family in Romania so with a

background in wines, spirits and hospitality he has the expertise – and the friendly manner – needed to guide punters through the mind-bending choices. If you can't make up your mind, maybe go for his own favourite, Citadel by Old Tom Gin (right), great with a slice of orange.

Or you could settle for The Feathers signature G&T, which they call The Ultimate G&T, made with Cotswolds Dry Gin (page 148), 1724 tonic and a slice of fresh grapefruit.

The Ely Gin Company

Ely, Cambridgeshire
Distillery and shop

ESSENTIAL INFORMATION

Key botanicals (Ely Special London Dry Gin): juniper, coriander seed, liquorice root, cinnamon, cassia bark, lemon peel, orange peel, nutmeg

Output: not disclosed

Location: 2/3 Buttermarket, Ely, CB7 4NZ

Telephone: 01353 968871

Email: info@elygin.co.uk

Website: www.elygin.co.uk

Facebook: www.facebook.com/elyginco

Instagram: @elyginco

Twitter: @ElyGinCo

Opening hours:
Monday-Saturday 1000-1700

Other reasons to go: Ely Cathedral, Oliver Cromwell's house, The Stained Glass Museum, Ely Museum

Husband and wife team James and Nancy Clark started The Ely Gin Company in 2011. James (bottom left), a software engineer of 20 years, was looking for a change and wanted to run his own company. In his spare time, he made hedgerow wines and sloe gins, successfully infusing the gins with different fruits. After a year of experimenting, Ely Special London Dry Gin was launched on the 26th March 2012 at the Saturday market in Ely.

James specializes in flavoured gins, using the vapour infusion method (page 254) to distil botanicals – many of which are from the Ely market – with the London Dry. He produces a standard selection of ten gins, including Breakfast Marmalade, Afternoon Tea and Chocolate Orange. He also produces four to six special edition gins each year under the 'Whimsies' brand, which are sold in 250-ml bottles. As we went to press, the latest release was St Clement's Gin, made with oranges, lemons and clementines.

Besides being a genuine small batch gin maker, Ely is also a serious and well-established operation that makes gin under contract for several large drinks companies.

The gins can be bought online or from their shop in Ely, which also stocks more than 52 tonics. Nancy specializes in tonics and makes bespoke G&Ts to suit every palate.

Tasting evenings (above) are hosted by James once a month, where you learn about the history of gin and how Ely Gin is made. You taste at least five different gins and receive a goodie bag to take away – see the website for booking details.

Archangel Gin and Distilleries

Fakenham, Norfolk
Distillery

ESSENTIAL INFORMATION

Key botanicals (Archangel Gin): juniper, cardamom, cinnamon, grains of paradise, orange peel, cloves, ginger, verbena, sea buckthorn, plus three secret ingredients

Output: 12,000 bottles a year

Location: The Distillery, Dunton Hall, Fakenham, NR21 7PG

Telephone: 01328 744436

Email: distiller@archangel-distilleries.co.uk

Website: www.archangel-distilleries.co.uk

Facebook: www.facebook.com/ ArchangelDistilleries

Instagram: @archangeldistilleries

Twitter: Archangel_Gin

Opening hours: visits by appointment only

Other reasons to go: Norfolk Coast, Pensthorpe Natural Park, Langham Glass merchant, Thursford

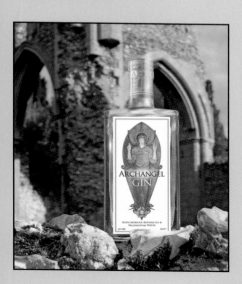

Archangel's co-founders, Peter Allingham and Jude De Souza, met in 1994 at ITV in London where Peter's IT company did consultancy work and Jude worked as a statistician. A mutual friend Craig Penn, who runs The Wrecking Coast Distillery (page 323), inspired them with the success of his venture and suggested they work together. Their first move was to travel to Holland to learn about distilling. Then they converted some disused stables on Peter's family farm into a distillery.

Archangel lies on the last section of the old pilgrimage route to Walsingham Abbey from Castle Acre Priory. Peter and Jude are Roman Catholics, conscious of the monastic tradition of making beers and spirits, so the religious brand name came naturally. There are angels on the labels, and a 19thC Dutch crucifix hangs on the wall of the bottling room. Religion is part of the distillery's life: lauds and vespers – monastic prayers held in the morning and evening – are said most days.

Peter and Jude use a genever-style recipe to reflect the Dutch influence in Norfolk during the 16th to 19thC. They use local verbena and juniper picked from bushes planted by Peter 15 years ago. In 2016, they planted another 200 juniper bushes (next page, middle), plus 50 sea buckthorn and, in 2019, 2, 500 blackthorn bushes were planted for sloes. The grain spirit and botanicals are distilled using the one-shot method (page 68), after which pure Walsingham water is used to cut the spirit down to 45%.

The first batch of Archangel Gin (left) was made in February 2017. Their ambition was to sell 4,000 bottles in the first year, but the demand was 6,000 in the

Above: the Norfolk countryside. Archangel Gin is made from grain to bottle in Norfolk.

first ten months. To enjoy Archangel at its best, mix 50 ml of the gin with a couple of orange slices, 150 ml of Fever-Tree tonic and plenty of ice. Archangel also works well as a cocktail base: add 50 ml of the gin to 25 ml of Campari, 75 ml of fresh orange and lemon juice, 2 tbsp of Peruvian marmalade (Seville will do) and a dash of Angostura orange bitters to make a Paddington Bear (above, right).

They also produce a limited edition Rhubarb Gin Liqueur (bottom right), made with Norfolk rhubarb steeped in their own vodka for at least four weeks. The product is then blended with Arhchangel Gin before being filtered twice. This is best served chilled and neat, or with ginger ale, or Prosecco to make a Rhubarb Royale. Their special winter release, Sloe and Mulberry Liqueur, is made with local fruit and is great as a sipping gin or when added to Prosecco.

The gins can be bought from the online shop and can also be found in various shops, bars and restaurants around Norfolk.

They also offer bookable tours – see the website for details.

Cambridge Gin and Distillery

Grantchester, Cambridgeshire
Distillery, shop and tailor-made gins

ESSENTIAL INFORMATION

Key botanicals (Cambridge Dry Gin):
   juniper, lemon verbena, basil, rosemary,
   blackcurrant leaf, rose petal

Output: not disclosed

**Location: 20-22 High Street, Grantchester,
   CB3 9NF**

Telephone: 01223 751146

Email: info@cambridgedistillery.co.uk

Website: www.cambridgedistillery.co.uk

**Facebook: www.facebook.com/
   CambridgeDistillery**

Instagram: @cambridgegin

Twitter: @CambridgeGin

Opening hours:
The Showroom
Monday-Saturday 1000-1800
Tuesday 1100-1800
Sunday 1000-1600

**Other reasons to go: River Cam,
Trumpington Meadows, Shepreth Wildlife
Park, Wandlebury Country Park**

This is a polished operation that claims to be 'the world's first gin tailors'. By this, founders William and Lucy Lowe mean that the distillery enables you (for £400) to create your own 'bespoke' blend. You get a two-hour consultation with William, Master Distiller, and blind tastings to define your palate. This forms the basis for your gin. After making the first bottle (or bottles), the recipe is then filed so that you can order more. A similar deal is offered by Nelson's Distillery and School on page 153.

The distillery uses fresh botanicals from the countryside outside Cambridge – where possible – to make their signature product, Cambridge Dry Gin (bottom left). Each botanical is distilled individually by the partial vacuum method (page 53), in less than two-litre batches, to preserve the freshest possible flavour.

They also produce a Seasonal Gin, costing £90 a bottle, which is only made twice a year. The Spring/Summer 2018 edition featured magnolia blossom, lemon balm and local honey and the Autumn/ Winter 2018 included juniper, anise hyssop flower and leaf, yarrow, meadowsweet and lemon balm. Other gins include Japanese Gin (next page, bottom right, right-hand bottle), combining juniper with traditional Japanese botanicals such as yuzu peel, shiso leaf, sansho pepper and sesame seed.

William Lowe has 20 years' experience in the drinks industry, and managing director Lucy has a marketing and events background. Despite the distillery's international reputation, every bottle is still produced by hand, so it can claim to be a small batch distiller. Curator's Gin (next page, bottom right, left-hand bottle), their collaboration with Cambridge University

Botanic Garden, was only available as we went to press as an experimental batch of just 600 bottles. The botanicals were picked from the university's Botanic Garden and include lavender, green ginger rosemary, Newton's apple, and lemon balm. A visit to Cambridge itself (which has produced more Nobel prizewinners than France, especially for scientific achievements) combined with a visit to the nearby village of Grantchester, makes an interesting day out. The distillery is in Grantchester, but wasn't offering tours as we went to press. However, you can visit their Gin Laboratory (top) at 10 Green Street, Cambridge – see page 322.

Roundwood Gin and Distillery

Huntingdon, Cambridgeshire
Distillery and tasting room

ESSENTIAL INFORMATION

Key botanicals (Roundwood Gin): juniper, coriander seed, orange peel, bitter orange peel, elderberry, elderflower

Output: not disclosed

Location: Unit 1, Wennington Lodge Farm, Huntingdon, PE28 2LP

Telephone: 01487 829149

Email: info@roundwooddistillery.co.uk

Website: www.roundwooddistillery.co.uk

Facebook: www.facebook.com/ roundwoodgin

Instagram: @roundwoodgin

Twitter: @roundwoodgin

Opening hours:
Gin Discovery sessions
Friday and Saturdays evenings
(booking required)

Other reasons to go: Houghton Mill National Trust, Cromwell Museum, Hinchingbrooke Country Park

Emily Robertson (next page, bottom right) had been a software developer for several years and was looking for a drastic life change to get her away from commuting and desk work. She shared a love of gin with her partner and co-founder, Rupert (next page, bottom left), and they wanted to make a product that represented rural Cambridgeshire. The result? Roundwood Gin (above right and bottom left), launched in May 2018.

The couple moved to Huntingdon in 2014 for Rupert's job as a manager on the De Ramsey Estate, where they now live, outside of Abbots Ripton, on one side of Wennington Wood, a 180-acre woodland area which they say formed the inspiration for their brand. The woodland has no footpaths, so you have to walk round it, hence Roundwood. They rented a crumbly brick building on the other side of the wood to house the distillery.

While the product was launched in 2018, the process of turning the building into a distillery and perfecting the recipe took 18 months. Emily collated every botanical she'd come across, distilling each individually to find the flavours she enjoyed most. She wanted to create a London Dry that incorporated botanicals inspired by the Wennington woodland and she found that elderberries lifted the dryness of the juniper, providing a sweetness to the gin, while elderflower gave a subtle floral finish.

Emily uses a combination of the maceration and vapour infusion (page 254) →

methods to ensure the subtle flavours of each botanical (right) are extracted during distillation. The unique copper still has a rectifying column with adjustable bubble plates to increase the reflux rate and maximize the copper contact. This removes unwanted flavours, creating a clean, smooth spirit. The result is a fruity twist on a classic London Dry that's smooth enough to sip neat, but Emily also recommends serving Roundwood with plenty of ice, a quality Indian tonic water, orange peel and a sprig of thyme.

In October 2018, Roundwood started offering bookable Gin Discovery sessions (top left), available on Friday and Saturday evenings – see the website. You learn about how Roundwood Gin is produced and have a tutored tasting. Also watch out for their gin wagon (right) at shows and festivals around the country.

The Newmarket Gin and Bedford Lodge Hotel and Spa bar

Newmarket, Suffolk
Bar

ESSENTIAL INFORMATION
Key botanicals (The Newmarket Gin):
    juniper, coriander, orange, wild chive,
    Devil's Dyke orchid petal, alfalfa,
    wild horseradish, bay leaf, almond,
    assorted wildflowers
Output: approximately 756 bottles a year
Location: Bedford Lodge Hotel & Spa, Bury
    Road, Newmarket, CB8 7BX
Telephone: 01638 663175
Email: info@thenewmarketgin.co.uk
Website: www.thenewmarketgin.co.uk
Facebook: www.facebook.com/
    thenewmarketgin
Twitter: @TheNewmarketGin

Opening hours:
Hotel bar
Monday-Sunday 0000-0000

Other reasons to go: Palace House
museum, Bill Tutte Memorial museum,
Newmarket's famous racecourses

Originally produced for Bedford Lodge Hotel & Spa, The Newmarket Gin (bottom left) was launched at the Gin Guild's Ginposium in June 2016 on the 350th anniversary of horse racing at Newmarket.

It's made using the one-shot method (page 68) in a copper pot still. The botanicals are steeped English grain spirit, distilled from East Anglia sugar beet to make vodka, which is then re-distilled to make a base for the gin. One of the more unusual botanicals, alfalfa, is used not just for its mild nutty flavour but for its connection to horse racing – it's fed to Newmarket's pedigree racehorses.

In honour of the 350th anniversary (see above) the bottle has a hand-made leather collar with a ribbon tag in the Newmarket stripe, made by locals, Gibson Saddlers, to resemble riding tackle. At the top of the label are three horses racing in the 'Classics', and the bottom is in the style of a vintage betting slip.

At £70 a bottle, it's one of the pricier gins in the guide. Buy it from Bedford Lodge Hotel & Spa (top), Corney and Barrow wine shop in Newmarket, or at Majestic wines in Newmarket, Bury St Edmunds and Cambridge.

Bullards Gin and The Anchor Distillery

Norwich, Norfolk
Distillery, bar and gin school

ESSENTIAL INFORMATION

Key botanicals (Bullards London Dry Gin):
juniper, coriander, liquorice, cardamom,
cassia bark, black pepper, orange peel,
lemon peel, tonka bean

Output: 20,000 bottles a year

Location: 24 Cattle Market Street,
Norwich, NR1 3DY

Telephone: 01603 928585

Email: hello@bullardsspirits.co.uk

Website: www.bullardsspirits.co.uk

Facebook: www.facebook.com/bullardsgin

Instagram: @bullardsgin

Twitter: @BullardsGin

Opening hours:
Monday-Sunday 0900-2300

Other reasons to go: Norwich Castle
Museum and Art Gallery, Norwich Cathedral

The Bullards brand was originally established in 1837, producing beer and spirits for more than a hundred years, until production ceased in the late 1960s. Some 50 years later, Russell Evans, who had worked with Bullards in his youth, wondered what had become of it. He discovered that no one owned the brand, so he bought it, invested in a 120-litre still and opened The Ten Bells pub in 2015, resurrecting Bullards with a focus on gin. He brought in Craig Allison for his knowledge of the industry – he had a background of running bars around the world – and launched Norwich's first Gin Palace in 2013. Keen to stand out from the crowd, Craig liked the idea of incorporating the vanilla and marzipan flavours of the tonka bean into the recipe.

The rest was left in the capable hands of head distiller, Peter Smith, who had just completed an internship at The Cotswolds Distillery (page 148) when he joined the Bullards team. Peter used his knowledge to build a London Dry recipe, experimenting with the botanicals until he found a combination that worked with tonka beans.

All of the botanicals are added to the base spirit 12 hours before distillation to extract as much flavour as possible. The product is then distilled for 12 hours in a unique 600-litre copper still to produce 60 litres of undiluted gin, which is then cut with water to 42.5% to create Bullards London Dry Gin (left).

Bullards also produces Strawberry and Black Pepper Gin (opposite, middle), made with fresh strawberries infused for 72 hours before distillation to give the gin its pink colour. Black pepper is added for warmth. Bullards recommends adding this

to Prosecco for a refreshing cocktail. Their third product is Old Tom Gin (bottom right), created by Bullards distiller Rory Smith, whose mixology background enabled him to create a gin that could be used in cocktails or sipped neat. He added his own twist, introducing honey, mango and Demerera sugar to produce a caramel hue. Other botanicals include pink pepper, black pepper, cassia bark, grapefruit peel and vanilla. This is best served neat over ice, or with a quality tonic water.

The gins can be bought from their distillery and online shop, each costing £40 for a 70-cl bottle.

In August 2019, Bullards moved to The Anchor Distillery on Cattle Market Street in Norwich (top). As well as frequent tours, they hold tasting masterclasses where you get a brief history of gin and the Bullards brand. You then learn to make a perfect serve with their three signature gins. They also hold a Gin School, where you make your own recipe – visit their website for prices and booking information. There's a gin bar where you can sample their latest experiments – as we went to press they were working on a samphire and seaweed concoction to join a Cold Brew Coffee Gin and a Distilled Negroni Gin.

Norfolk Gin

Norwich, Norfolk
Distillery

ESSENTIAL INFORMATION

Key botanicals (Norfolk Gin): juniper,
   coriander, green cardamom, citrus peel,
   plus three secret ingredients
Output: 10,000-12,000 bottles a year
Location: N/A
Telephone: 01603 559047
Email: jonathan@norfolkgin.co.uk
Website: www.norfolkgin.co.uk
Facebook: www.facebook.com/NorfolkGin
Instagram: @norfolk_gin
Twitter: @norfokgin

Opening hours: not open to the public

Norfolk Gin was started in 2014 by husband and wife Jonathan and Alison Redding (bottom left) in the kitchen of their home in Norwich. After leaving the army as a major in 2001, Jonathan worked in government and for local charities, watching the gin craze as it gathered momentum. Alison, also working in local government, shared Jonathan's passion for craft gin and together they set about researching gins, botanicals and investing £400 in ingredients to get the project underway.

They got advice from the craft gin community, and were heartened by its warmth, encouragement and enthusiasm. Soon they realised that while stills are beautiful, they are expensive too. Having sampled some excellent 'bathtub' gins they decided to try that approach. The botanicals are prepared by hand (never chopped or mashed) and slowly steeped in a neutral (bought-in) grain spirit imparting a subtle straw-like colour, resulting in an aromatic premium gin. Jonathan knows of two or three other UK gin makers using this supremely simple method, which nonethless takes time (several days) and care to introduce the botanicals in the right sequence.

They experimented with hundreds of flavour combinations, and with immersing the botanicals for different lengths of time. Friends and family came to many a tasting session, until everyone agreed on the final recipe (number 55 out of 56) and the signature taste was established.

They launched in 2015, with their first retail outlet at Harper Wells, the Norwich wine merchant. The first batch of 15 bottles sold out in three days, so a waiting list was started.

Demand soon outgrew the couple's kitchen, so they set up a gin studio in their

back garden. Gin is still made there, with two other buildings – Matilda the English Shepherd Hut and Jennifer the bottling shack (above) – also allowing production to expand.

They see Norfolk Gin (right, being bottled) as appealing to today's gin drinkers while also respecting the past, with a traditional herbaceous flavour, like genever, alongside a gentle sweetness typical of Old Tom. Juniper and herb aromas are balanced with a touch of spice, sweetness and citrus: smooth, easy drinking.

They keep the full recipe secret but say that of the seven botanicals two are grown by Jonathan in the garden. Croatian juniper, green cardamom and fresh lime are key, complemented by the secret combination of herbs.

The distinctive handcrafted Wade Ceramics bottle is considered by many too pretty to bin: people like to re-use their empties, or turn them into lamp bases. Empties can be topped up at Reno Wine in Wymondham and the Jarrold department store in Norwich city centre, where a handcrafted iron refilling machine has been installed.

Alison and Jonathan still measure, pour, fill, seal and label every bottle before manning their Morgan three wheeler, electric powered BMW i3 or Renault Twizy to deliver bottles in person (right).

Suffolk Gin and Distillery

Sudbury, Suffolk
Distillery

ESSENTIAL INFORMATION

Key botanicals (Suffolk Dry Gin): juniper, coriander, cassia bark, liquorice, cinnamon, citrus, plus four secret ingredients

Output: 1,200 bottles a year

Location: 38 Long Pastures, Glemsford, Sudbury, CO10 7SS

Telephone: 01787 280958; 07387 561871

Email: sales@suffolkdistillery.co.uk

Website: www.suffollkdistillery.co.uk

Facebook: www.facebook.com/ thesuffolkgin

Instagram: @thesuffolkgin

Twitter: @thesuffolkgin

Opening hours: not open to the public

Gary Wilkinson worked for large corporate distillers for most of his career. He had qualified as an applied chemist and in various roles was involved in cutting-edge distillation and botanical extraction techniques.

Like many a would-be craft gin maker wanting to quit the rat race, he saw the craft gin craze an opportunity and went for it – perhaps encouraged by his wife who had a good job and supported them both through the first months of debt and no pay. Like many another gin maker, he didn't regret his decision because although well paid (plus company car) he had no job satisfaction.

Now he does, but the catch is having to do everything in the business from paying bills to marketing, warehousing packing and dealing with HMRC.

He says his main gin, Suffolk Dry (bottom left, left-hand bottle), is a homage to his home county, which he loves, and its climate. He describes the gin as 'an honest, traditional juniper-led dry gin, upfront on the juniper but then developing a dry citrus character' – with mellow spicy elements. The finish is fresh and fruity 'ending in a crescendo of sweet liquorice and warm spice, with a long lingering floral, citrus heady mix of ripened, intense berries.'

He also produces a Navy Strength (57% – left, right-hand bottle): 'think blustery seaside walks and crisp winter evenings followed by a nightcap by the fire,' enthuses his website.

He also makes mandarin and cranberry (left, middle bottle); strawberry & cucumber and rhubarb gins, the last using local rhubarb 'grown on the banks of the Stour.'

As we went to press his ambition was to grow the business to enable him to offer tours and tutorials.

Cuckoo Gin and Brindle Distillery

Brindle, Lancashire
Distillery and gin school

ESSENTIAL INFORMATION

Key botanicals (Brindle Cuckoo Gin):
juniper, coriander, liquorice, cardamom,
cinnamon, cassia bark, ground almond,
lemon, orange, grapefruit, chamomile,
porridge oat

Output: 50,000 bottles a year

Location: Holmes Farm, Sandy Lane,
Chorley, PR6 8LZ

Telephone: 01772 323313

Email: info@brindledistillery.co.uk

Website: www.brindledistillery.co.uk

Facebook: www.facebook.com/cuckoogin

Instagram: @cuckoogin

Twitter: @CuckooGin

Opening hours:
Monday-Friday 0900-1700

Other reasons to go: Leyland Market, The
British Commercial Vehicle Museum, South
Ribble Museum and Exhibition Centre,
Hoghton Tower, Worden Park, Astley Hall

People born and bred in Brindle call themselves Brindle Cuckoos. Local lore maintains that in medieval times the townsfolk had the improbable idea of building a wall around a field where they heard a cuckoo calling. They wanted to capture it because they thought it would give them spring all year round, but they didn't build the wall high enough and the cuckoo escaped. A dotty story, for sure, but it's behind the name of the distillery's core product.

Started in March 2016, the family-run distillery is based on Gerard (bottom left) and Cath Singleton's Holmes Farm. The farm needed an extra, sustainable source of income and when Gerard visited the Cotswolds Distillery (page 148), he realized that they could grow their own barley and wheat on the farm to make alcohol and use the natural spring water from the land to brew, distil and cut the alcohol to strength.

Two months later, they took the plunge, turning a cowshed into a distillery. It took 13 months, during which son-in-law Mark also studied alcohol production and gin distilling. Big gin fans, the Singletons used their favourite brands as a reference and started experimenting with botanicals. Cuckoo Gin (left) was launched at a gin event in Skipton in June 2017.

The Singletons are very sustainability conscious. All the raw materials come from the farm or are brought in from local farmers, and the botanicals are ethically sourced. They even heat their still (next page, bottom right) by biomass boiler, and any by-products are fed to the cows and chickens, or are composted. The straw is used in bedding or for transporting the glass bottles. The still is called Maggie, after a great aunt.

→

For the perfect G&T, the Singletons suggest garnishing Cuckoo with orange peel and a slice of fresh ginger. The flavour is juniper led, followed by a mixture of citrus, cinnamon and liquorice, with an aftertaste of coriander. They also make a spicy version, with clove, ginger and cinnamon and there's Cuckoo Sunshine Gin, made with honey from the farm, which gives it a smooth texture. Infused with raspberries, it makes a great summer tipple.

For £95 Brindle offers a three- to four-hour workshop experience (top) where you hear the distillery's story and learn how they make gin. There is a distillery tour, you can drink up to four gin cocktails, and pick your own botanicals to create a gin recipe to distil in a mini pot still. You then package your 70-cl bottle and have it signed off by the Master Distiller. For £24, Brindle also offers a simple once-monthly gin tour.

Batch Gin and Batch Brew Ltd

Burnley, Lancashire
Distillery

ESSENTIAL INFORMATION

Key botanicals (Batch Signature Gin):
juniper, coriander, cardamom, cinnamon, dried orange peel, nutmeg, allspice, cloves, lemongrass, frankincense, myrrh

Output: 9,000+ bottles a year

Location: Unit 10 Habergham Mill, Coal Clough Lane, Burnley, BB11 5BS

Telephone: 01282 701473

Email: info@batchbrew.co.uk

Website: www.batchbrew.co.uk;
www.innovations.batchbrew.co.uk

Facebook: www.facebook.com/BatchBrew

Instagram: @batch_brew

Twitter: @BatchBrew

Opening hours:
Monday-Friday 0930-1600

Other reasons to go: Towneley Art Gallery and Museum, Gawthorpe Hall National Trust, Singing Ringing Tree sculpture, Thompson Park

Phil Whitewell started his career in the drinks industry making craft beers for bars and restaurants around Hampshire. With the market getting saturated, he started looking for a new venture. A trip to Madrid in 2012 exposed him to Spain's rich gin culture while craft gin was just taking off in the UK, so he turned his hand to distilling. In November 2012, he got a distiller's licence and started building the recipe for what was Lancashire's first gin.

The basic recipe was taken from the internet and he taught himself to distil – having no previous experience – combining infusion with vapour infusion (page 254). He thought this was the norm, but later discovered he'd made a happy mistake, as this hybrid procedure is one of the things that makes Batch Gin unique.

Production began in his nephew Ollie's basement in Burnley, with 40 bottles produced at a time. Ollie was a cobbler looking for a change in direction and quickly learned the craft from his uncle, later taking over as head distiller. They didn't want to make yet another London Dry and, as it was Christmas, Phil wanted to incoporate frankincense and myrrh, enjoying the seasonal link and the spicy, earthy flavours the ingredients brought to the gin. He then spent a year experimenting to get the balance of flavours right.

Batch Signature Gin (left) was launched at a gin festival in 2015. Ollie's local was one of the first to stock it, and the word spread. Orders started coming in from abroad and they soon outgrew the basement, moving into a renovated mill with space in which to welcome visitors.

They have four small (25-litre) stills: Tom, Dick, Harry and The Other One (next

page, bottom right). Each run produces around 160 70-cl bottles of well-balanced gin, good enough to sip neat. Try it with a quality tonic water plus lime peel and a crushed frozen raspberry to emphasize the orange flavour.

With new premises came new flavours. First was Whinberry Gin (right), whinberry being the local term for bilberry. The bilberries are steeped in Batch Signature Gin and aged in a former Cognac barrel. They also produce Batch Industrial Strength Gin (top left), their take on a Navy gin which pays homage to the industrial history of Burnley. This is less spicy and more juniper led than Batch Signature Gin and is best served with a quality tonic, sage and dried apricots.

The gins can be bought from their online shop or, for £35 a month, you can subscribe to Batch Innovations, where you receive an experimental spirit each month, for example, Absinthe Gin (above, right-hand bottle).

Liverpool Gin Distillery

Liverpool, Merseyside
Distillery, bar and gin school

ESSENTIAL INFORMATION

Key botanicals (Liverpool Gin): juniper, coriander seed, liquorice root, cardamom, cassia bark, lemon peel, orange peel
Output: not disclosed
Location: 52-54 Castle Street, Liverpool, L2 7LQ
Telephone: 01514 815555
Email: info@liverpoolgindistillery.com
Website: www.liverpoolgindistillery.com
Facebook: www.facebook.com/ LPLGinDistillery
Instagram: @liverpoolgindistillery
Twitter: @LPLGinDistiller

Opening hours:
Sunday-Thursday 1200-0000
Friday-Saturday 1200-0100

Other reasons to go: Royal Albert Dock, Museum of Liverpool, International Slavery Museum, Liverpool Waterfront

Launched in 2013, Liverpool Gin was initially produced in Huyton, across the road from one of Liverpool's oldest distilleries, the former Bank Hall Distillery. In November 2018, they moved to a larger premises on bustling Castle Street, where it's now produced in a 600-litre copper still called Margaret, visible from the gin bar on the ground floor.

The botanicals, inspired by spices brought to the UK via old trading routes running through Liverpool's port, are steeped in a base spirit overnight by head distiller John O'Dowd. The result is then distilled for an hour, using the vapour infusion method (page 254). John uses only the heart of the run which they cut with water to 43%. Try serving Liverpool Gin with a quality tonic and a wedge of watermelon.

John also produces Liverpool Gin Lemongrass and Ginger, using juniper, lime, lemongrass, ginger, allspice and kaffir lime leaves. Liverpool Gin Valencian Orange was made to celebrate his son's wedding day, with a nod to his new daughter-in-law's home town of Valencia, while the most recent release (as we went to press) was Liverpool Gin Rose Petal.

The distillery (left) offers three visitor experiences: the Distillery Tour; the Distillery Tour and Gin Tasting, including a sampling of the whole Liverpool Gin range; and the Distillery Tour, Tasting and Gin Lab Experience. The last costs £70, for which you get a G&T on arrival, learn the process of distilling, get a brief history of gin, and Liverpool Gin, and explore botanicals before making your own recipe.

Whitley Neill Gin

Liverpool, Merseyside
Distillery

ESSENTIAL INFORMATION

Key botanicals (Whitley Neill Original Gin): juniper, coriander seed, cassia bark, lemon peel, orange peel, Cape gooseberry, baobab powder

Output: 1,000,000 bottles a year

Location: The Sovereign Distillery, Wilson Road, Huyton Business Park, Liverpool, L36 6AD

Telephone: 01514 808800

Email: customer.services@halewood-int.com

Website: www.whitleyneill.com

Facebook: www.facebook.com/WhitleyNeill

Instagram: @whitleyneillgin

Twitter: @WhitleyNeill

Opening hours: not open to the public

Whitley Neill Gin (from The Sovereign Distillery) was officially released in 2010 but its history goes as far back as the 18thC. Founder Johnny Neill, also the founder of Mary-Le-Bone Gin (page 88), is an eighth-generation distiller whose family has been distilling since 1762. He first encountered gin at his grandmother's house when he found a collection of bottles under the stairs. He liked what he found, his grandmother taught him how to make the spirit, and he discovered its extraordinary ability to combine with different flavours.

When he decided to make his own gin, he wanted to acknowledge both his family's distilling history and his wife's South African roots, so he uses a mix of classic English botanicals and South African ones such as Cape gooseberry and baobab to make Whitley Neill Original Gin (left).

All botanicals except the Cape gooseberry (it's too delicate) are steeped in neutral grain spirit overnight, before being distilled in Constance, their 100-year-old copper pot still. The gin is then cut with pure water to 43%. Johnny recommends serving the gin with Lamb & Watt Hibiscus tonic water, two lemon wedges and a handful of raspberries.

Whitley Neill had a range of 11 other flavoured gins as we went to press. Among them are Blackberry, Parma Violet (above), and Pink Grapefruit, a pink gin released in time for Valentine's Day in 2019. Quince Gin was made to honour Johnny's grandad, Freddie, an army officer who spent time in Palestine and Pakistan where he developed a taste for the fruit. The gins can be bought from the online shop.

Forest Gin, Distillery and Bar

Macclesfield Forest, Cheshire
Distillery and bar

ESSENTIAL INFORMATION

Key botanicals (Forest Gin): juniper, coriander seed, liquorice root, vanilla, blackberry, raspberry, wild bilberry, wildflower, spruce, pine, Peak District moss

Output: 75 bottles per batch

Location: Chambers Farm, Bottom of the Oven, Macclesfield Forest, SK11 0AR

Telephone: 01260 253245

Email: distillery@forestgin.com

Website: www.forestgin.com

Facebook: www.facebook.com/forestgin

Instagram: @forest_gin

Twitter: @ForestGin

Opening hours:
Bar
Tuesday-Friday 1300-1700
Distillery Tours (booking required)

Other reasons to go: Shining Tor, Shutlingsloe, Peak District National Park

Ella Carr writes: It was the bottle (bottom left) that first grabbed my attention. Hand crafted from Staffordshire porcelain, with an intricate floral design radiating from a weasel motif, it's one of the finest gin vessels I've seen. Whimsical and earthy, it reflects how Forest Gin is made.

Karl and Lindsay started as complete amateurs, producing a number of less-than-palatable versions until their young daughter Hattie brought home some freshly picked berries. Karl substituted these for his dry ingredients, and from then on the gin flourished with foraging at its core.

They originally only planned to sell to the local pub and farmer's market, but things kicked off when they became the first gin brand to win two Double-Gold Medals at the San Francisco World Spirit Awards. They now distil full time with three helpers, and their gin is stocked by high-end retailers and restaurants such as Harvey Nichols and Heston Blumenthal. They also export to New Zealand, China and Japan.

The well above-average price tag of £50 (or more) is doing little to hold back sales, perhaps helped by the reusable ceramic vessel made by Wade Ceramics, with artwork by Suzy Taylor.

I'd recommend first sipping the gin neat, to fully appreciate its aroma of the forest. The initial taste is of juniper and citrus, sliding into the sweetness from the berries, with herbal hints of flower and pine, and a satisfying earthy finish from the moss. As a G&T it's best served with a sprig of rosemary and sliver of grapefruit. It also makes an excellent Negroni. The family hold intimate weekend tours, including two drinks, plus neat samples and a gin talk for £20 per person.

Atlas Bar

Manchester, Greater Manchester
Bar

ESSENTIAL INFORMATION
Location: 376 Deansgate, Manchester,
    M3 4LY
Telephone: 0161 8342124
Email: enquiries@atlasbarmanchester.com
Website: www.atlasbarmanchester.com
Facebook: www.facebook.com/AtlasBar
Instagram: @theatlasbar
Twitter: @TheAtlasBar

Opening hours:
Monday-Wednesday 0800-2300
Thursday 0800-0000
Friday 0800-0100
Saturday 0900-0100
Sunday 0900-2300

Other reasons to go: Old Trafford stadium,
Science and History Museum, National
Football Museum, Manchester Cathedral

Elaine and Mark Wrigley (both opposite, middle, far right) run their bar (bottom left) in the railway arches on Deansgate, the longest road in the city, specializing in gins from all over the world. They had a collection of more than 480 gins (opposite, top left) as we went to press, growing with a new addition every week. One of Elaine's favourites is Colonsay Gin from Wild Thyme Spirits (page 276). Her best-selling gin of 2018 was 5th Gin Fire and she reckons her most unique gin is Manchester Zymurgorium Vigil Gin (above) – a limited edition of just 300 bottles was created to raise funds for the arena bombing victims. Atlas was also the first in the UK to sell Vaione Gin, imported from New Zealand.

The bar offers gin and cocktail masterclasses, which take you through the history of gin from genever, Old Tom and Plymouth Navy Strength to London Dry. They also have a mobile gin bar (opposite, far right) which can be sent to your home or any other location. There's a Gin Supper Club every month, where they serve a welcome G&T, followed by a three-course dinner with three 'perfect serves' (ie with the ideal mixer and garnish) to complement each dish. The suppers are hosted by different distillers and brand ambassadors, who present the gins' histories, how they're made and their botanical content.

Future plans include their newly upgraded all-weather terrace (opposite, bottom left), a gin masterclass booth, and a

178

new online bottle shop (www.ginbible.co.uk) where you can learn about all the gins on offer, including their history, botanicals and recommendations for perfect serves. As we went to press, they were working on an Atlas 100 Club, where customers can subscribe and get a discount at the bar, access to special events and be among the first to try their new gin releases.

Jack and Gin

Ormskirk, Lancashire
Bar

ESSENTIAL INFORMATION
Location: Unit 9/10 Burscough Wharf,
    Liverpool North Road, Burscough,
    Ormskirk, L40 5RZ
Telephone: 01704 895564
Email: rob@jackandgin.co.uk
Website: www.jackandgin.co.uk
Facebook: www.facebook.com/
    jackandginbar
Instagram: @jackandginburscough

Opening hours:
Wednesday-Thursday 1200-2330
Friday 1200-0200
Saturday 1000-0200
Sunday 1130-2200

Other reasons to go: Martin Mere lake,
Mere Sands Wood, Burscough Bridge

Jack and Gin opened in 2016 on the cobbled streets of Liverpool's Burscough Wharf. The name refers to the bar's range of Jack Daniels whisky and gins, while the subtitle 'by the canal' (below left) refers to the location on the bank of the Leeds and Liverpool canal, completed in the late 18thC. The exterior (bottom left) resembles the stable that stood here more than 150 years ago and while the interior has been completely renovated, there is still a feeling of times past, perhaps especially in the small antique chandeliers. The bare wooden bar and wooden ceiling beams echo, perhaps, the interior of a canal boat.

The bar functions as a café during the day, selling cakes and pastries but easily transforms into a night-time haunt serving tapas. If you're looking for gin, don't be put off by the neon sign reading 'Jack lives here' – Jack Daniels is not the main focus – the range of 40 different gins has a strong presence too.

As we went to press, Jack and Gin were holding an annual Gin Festival and Soul Train event in June, where gin producers from across the country come together to give a masterclass on how their gins are distilled, plus small tastings, suggestions for perfect serves and discounted prices. Tickets can be bought on the Jack and Gin website for £15 and include a G&T on arrival. Tastings are advertised on Jack and Gin's Facebook page.

Willie Hogarth Old Tom Gin and Hogarths bar

Preston, Lancashire
Bar

ESSENTIAL INFORMATION
Key botanicals (Willie Hogarth Old Tom Gin): juniper, coriander, liquorice, cardamom, citrus
Output: 140 bottles a year
Location: 140 Church Street, Preston, PR1 3BU
Telephone: 01772 253010
Email: info@ambertaverns.co.uk
Website: www.ambertaverns.co.uk/pub/hogarths-preston
Facebook: www.facebook.com/HogarthsPreston
Instagram: @hogarthspreston
Twitter: @HogarthsPreston

Opening hours:
Sunday-Wednesday 1100-2300
Thursday 1100-0000
Friday-Saturday 1100-0100

Other reasons to go: 45 West Distillers Bar

Hogarths (bottom left) is an interesting choice of name for a gin bar. It's a reference, of course, to the English artist William Hogarth and his famous prints *Beer Street and Gin Lane* (1751). They depict gin as the catalyst of social decline, and beer as one of prosperity; Hogarth supported the prohibition of the liquor.

Opened in December 2014, this Preston bar was the second of 14 Hogarths bars and has recently been refurbished. The so-called Gin Palace stocks over 140 different brands of gin, including their own small batch varieties – Hogarths London Dry and Hogarths Old Tom, developed with the help of Union Distillers (page 140). The London Dry has a subtle hint of vanilla and is best served with plenty of ice, Fever-Tree tonic water and a cucumber slice or a quarter slice of citrus fruit. Their signature gin, Old Tom, is slightly sweeter, with a notable taste of liquorice and is best served with ice, Fever-Tree tonic, and an orange twist. They also produce rhubarb, strawberry, vanilla and sloe gins, and two gin liqueurs, flavoured with passion fruit or, of all things, bubblegum.

Hogarths offers a 'gin tray' tasting experience, where you can pair five of the big name gins with a choice of tonics and garnishes. There is also a summer edition, incorporating fruity flavours associated with the warmer months, including garnishes such as strawberries, raspberries, and pink grapefruit, as well as an elderflower tonic. They also showcase new products in their 'Gin of the Week' and 'Cocktail of the Month.'

The Lakes Gin and Distillery

Setmurthy, Cumbria
Distillery

ESSENTIAL INFORMATION

Key botanicals (The Lakes Gin): juniper, coriander seed, liquorice, cassia bark, lemon, orange and bitter orange peels

Output: not disclosed

Location: Setmurthy, near Bassenthwaite Lake, CA13 9SJ

Telephone: 017678 788850

Email: info@lakesdistillery.com

Website: www.lakesdistillery.com

Facebook: www.facebook.com/ thelakesdistillery

Instagram: @lakesdistillery

Twitter: @LakesDistillery

Opening hours:
Shop and distillery tours
Monday-Sunday 1000-1800
Bistro
Monday-Sunday 1000-2300

Other reasons to go: Wordsworth House and Garden, Castlegate House Gallery, Cockermouth Castle, Percy House Gallery

Whisky is the main focus here but The Lakes Distillery's range of two gins and four gin liqueurs makes them worth an entry. The distillery (bottom left) was founded in 2014 by Paul Currie, whose aim was to create spirits that reflect the surrounding Cumbrian countryside, while maintaining a low carbon footprint by using biomass boilers and recycling by-products as animal feed for local farmers.

The botanicals for the main gin, The Lakes Gin (above right), are steeped in British wheat spirit for up to 18 hours before distillation takes place in a 1,200-litre copper pot still, Chemmy. The spirit is then cut with water from The River Derwent to 43.7% to make a smooth, classic London Dry. Try it neat over ice.

The latest release, The Lakes Explorer Gin, is made with Earl Grey tea and cracked pepper to create a herbal flavour with a spicy finish. They also produce a range of gin liqueurs: Rhubarb and Rosehip Gin Liqueur infuses extracts of these botanicals with The Lakes Gin to create a fruity and floral, pink-hued gin which works well with Prosecco. The Elderflower edition is best served with tonic, lemon, lime and cucumber slices. The Lakes also makes Damson and Sloe gin liqueurs – all can be bought from the online shop.

The Lakes Distillery holds tours where you learn about the production of their whisky, gin and vodka before taking part in a guided tasting of the three spirits. Tours last around an hour for groups of up to 15 people and cost £12.50 – best to book ahead.

Trippets Lounge Bar

Sheffield, South Yorkshire
Bar

ESSENTIAL INFORMATION
Location: 89 Trippets Lane, Sheffield,
    S1 4EL
Telephone: 01142 762930
Email: ginandjazz@outlook.com
Website: www.trippetsloungebar.co.uk
Facebook: www.facebook.com/TrippetsBar
Instagram: @trippetsloungebar
Twitter: @TrippetsBar

Opening hours:
Wednesday-Thursday 1200-2230
Friday-Saturday 1200-0000
Sunday 1200-1600

Other reasons to go: Sheffield Cathedral,
City Hall and Peace Gardens

A stone's throw from Sheffield Cathedral and the City Hall, this independent jazz bar has become something of a landmark since it opened in 2015. Trippets Lounge Bar (bottom left) stocks 89 gins ranging from mainstream brands such as Bombay Sapphire (page 115) to craft gins such as Cotswolds Dry Gin (page 148).

The beauty of this place is that you don't have to be a gin connoisseur to drink here, nor should you feel overwhelmed by the vast choice of gins – Debbie, the owner, and her bar staff know their stuff and have been known to offer tasting samples and spontaneous gin masterclasses to help you find what zaps your buds.

The food is also a hit here – Carl, the chef, provides a tapas-type menu, but with reasonably priced starter-sized portions. On Friday and Saturday nights there's a live jazz band, with staff happy to bring drinks to your table.

As we went to press, Trippets was holding an Autumn Gin Festival at which for £25 a ticket you can meet the distillers of ten different brands and sample and buy their gins. Exchange a portion of your ticket at the bar (top) for a gin of your choice, served and garnished expertly by the knowledgeable bar staff.

Why 89 gins? Because they're based at 89 Trippet Lane.

Spital, Wirral
Distillery and shop

ESSENTIAL INFORMATION

Key botanicals (Bakewell Gin): juniper, coriander, cardamom, almond, raspberry, cherry, hibiscus

Output: 120,000 bottles a year

Location: Claremont Building, Old Clatterbridge Road, Spital, CH63 4JB

Telephone: 01513 349784

Email: info@wirraldistillery.com

Website: www.wirraldistillery.com

Facebook: www.facebook.com/WirralDistillery

Instagram: @wirraldistillery

Twitter: @WirralDistiller

Opening hours:
Monday-Sunday 1030-1630

Other reasons to go: Wirral Peninsula, Lady Lever Art Gallery, Hilbre Islands, Mersey Ferries

Wirral Distillery is in the grounds of Poulton Hall in an 18thC brewhouse on the NE side of the main house. The Poulton Lancelyn family settled here in the 12thC and legend has it that the grounds are haunted by the ghost of a nun (The White Nun) who was murdered in the 1700s when travelling from Liverpool to Chester Cathedral. The Poulton Lancelyn surname became Lancelyn Green in the 16thC, and the same family produced the writer Robert Lancelyn Green.

Wirral distils more than 50 unique gins using copper stills and the vapour extraction method (page 254). The botanicals hang in muslin bags above the boiling liquid, producing a fresh, sulphate-free flavour. Sulphates can be released when botanicals are simply boiled.

The distillery claims to be the home of the original Bakewell Gin (bottom left – White Peak produces a Bakewell Pud Gin – see page 123), which they recommend serving with a quality tonic water and a cherry.

Among the distillery's signature gins is Wirral Gin, made with bog-myrtle which literally defines the place in which it's distilled. Wirral means 'myrtle corner' referring to bog-myrtle which can be found in the area. Wirral also makes Violetta Parma Violet Gin (opposite, top left), a purple, pearlescent, shimmering spirit – the first of its kind. Released in 2016, it uses natural flavours and colours. They recommend adding it to Prosecco. Along similar lines is Strawberry Candy Floss Gin (opposite, middle), a pink gin best served with lemonade and sliced strawberries.

Wirral's most popular edition is, however, Pink Dog Gin (opposite, top right), which has a hint of rose and a soft

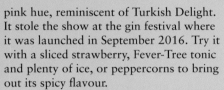

pink hue, reminiscent of Turkish Delight. It stole the show at the gin festival where it was launched in September 2016. Try it with a sliced strawberry, Fever-Tree tonic and plenty of ice, or peppercorns to bring out its spicy flavour.

You can subscribe to their Friday Night Gin Club, where for £3 a week you get a new 40-ml bottle of either craft gin or gin liqueur direct through your door. You will also receive a £5 voucher to spend on a full bottle of gin from the website.

You can buy Wirral Gin directly from the distillery in Claremont Courtyard, and the distillery's shop in Brimstage Craft Centre, also in Wirral.

Shed 1 Gin and Distillery

Ulverston, Cumbria
Distillery

ESSENTIAL INFORMATION

Key botanicals (Cuckold's Revenge):
   juniper, green cardamom, star anise,
   lemon zest, orange zest, nutmeg
Output: not disclosed
Location: 70 Sunderland Terrace, Ulverston,
   LA12 7JY
Telephone: 07397 180486
Email: shed1distillery@gmail.com
Website: www.shed1distillery.com
Facebook: www.facebook.com/shed1gin
Instagram: @shed_1_gin
Twitter: @Shed1Gin

Opening hours: not open to the public

Occupying a small (7 x 7 foot) shed in Ulverston since 2016, Shed 1 was Cumbria's smallest gin distillery as we went to press. Co-founders Andy and Zoe met in Korea, while he was touring as an actor and she was teaching. Cuckold's Revenge Gin (bottom left, right-hand bottle), layered with citrus and spice, is named after a character Andy especially enjoyed playing – the cuckolded Master Ford in *Merry Wives*. It's produced in 50-cl bottles in batches of 36 bottles per run. For the perfect G&T, Andy recommends adding a non-flavoured tonic (herbal infusions tend to clash with the botanicals) and a couple of ice cubes.

Giggle in the Ginnel Gin (bottom left, left-hand bottle) is an elderberry and fresh orange zest concoction created for a party they had in the ginnel (alleyway) by the distillery. They also produce Fancy Frolic Gin (bottom left, middle bottle), made with strawberry, lime and ginger. Zoe recommends serving the gins neat with a couple of ice cubes.

Their Festive Tipple Gin combines the classic flavours of Christmas: cinnamon, nutmeg, and cloves. It's available from late October to mid-January and they also have a gin for Valentine's Day, Shed Loads of Love. This limited edition is available from January to February and includes rose petals, lavender, strawberries and chilli.

In September 2018 they launched Chilli Fest Gin for the local chilli festival. It was so well received that they continue to produce it at intervals. Later in 2018 they released a limited edition of Festive Bramble Gin Elixir, a blend of their Festive Tipple Gin with locally foraged blackberries and apples.

Andy and Zoe bought new premises in December 2018 and were hoping to move in by the end of 2019.

Alnwick Gin and Northumberland Spirits

Alnwick, Northumberland
Distillery

ESSENTIAL INFORMATION

Key botanicals (Alnwick Gin): juniper, rosehip, lavender, fennel, plus seven secret ingredients

Output: 10,000+ bottles a year

Location: Blacksmiths Hall, Rock, Alnwick, NE66 3SB

Telephone: 01665 579100

Email: office@northumberlandspirit.co.uk

Website: www.alnwickgin.co.uk

Facebook: www.facebook.com/RealAlnwickGin

Instagram: @alnwickgin

Twitter: @NorthlandSpirit

Opening hours:
Monday-Friday 0900-1700

Other reasons to go: Alnwick Castle, The Alnwick Garden, Bailiffgate Museum

Neil Osborne discovered his love for gin after his wife introduced him to the classic G&T, which thereafter became his favourite summer nights tipple. It reminded him of his grandfather, who once allowed him into his garden shed where he made beer, cider and gin – illegally. Forty-five years later, Neil was coming to the end of a job contract and looking for his next venture, when he had a light-bulb moment – to reproduce his grandad's gin, which had been so popular with locals all those years ago.

He founded The Northumberland Spirit Company in June 2016, and spent many months of trial and error to get as close to his grandfather's recipe as possible. After being sampled and approved by friends and locals, Alnwick Gin (below left) was finally launched in October 2016. The reaction was so positive, that he had to set up a website and online shop within days to meet demand. He sold his first batch – 200 bottles – in three days. Within the first couple of weeks, he realized he would need a bigger premises than the garden shed so bought two garages where he continued production. In July 2017, The Northumberland Spirit Co. moved to their current premises at Blacksmiths Hall.

As well as Alnwick Gin, they also produce three gin-based fruit liqueurs (next page, bottom right): Rhubarb and Strawberry, Lime and Ginger, and Raspberry and Vanilla, plus a sloe gin

(previous page, top right). In January 2019, they released Firestorm Gin (top right) made with ten botanicals including juniper, lemon, lime, apple, lavender and horseradish. The name is a combination of the distillery's history as a blacksmiths hall and the subtle heat that comes from the horseradish. They also produce bespoke, limited edition gins for several businesses and organizations.

The bottle is possibly the most exciting we've seen so far, made of stone with a label made of pewter (above middle) – a nod to Alnwick Castle and its history as the home of the Earls and Dukes of Northumberland.

Masons Gin and Distillery

Bedale, North Yorkshire
Distillery

ESSENTIAL INFORMATION
Key botanicals (Masons Yorkshire Gin):
   juniper, coriander, cardamom, citrus peels,
   fennel seed, bay leaf, Szechwan pepper
Output: not disclosed
Location: N/A
Telephone: 01677 426467
Email: info@masonsyorkshiregin.com
Website: www.masonsyorkshiregin.com
Facebook: www.facebook.com/
   MasonsYorkshireGin
Instagram: @masonsyorkshiregin
Twitter: @MasonsGin

Opening hours: not open to the public

Ella Carr writes: It was only a matter of time before Yorkshire, a county with a robust sense of itself, brought forth a representative Yorkshire gin. In 2013, Karl and Cathy Mason (next page, bottom right) – gin enthusiasts with no prior knowledge of the industry – single-handedly revived the Yorkshire distilling tradition when they set out to make an artisan, craft-made gin that stood out from the crowd.

Their Original Masons Gin (next page, top left, middle bottle) was launched on World Gin Day that same year, from their small distillery in picturesque Bedale. Fast forward to 2019 and Masons has grown into one of the UK's leading premium craft gin distillers.

Despite Masons' growth, the essence of its gin remains the same as when it started: all the gins are distilled in copper stills in small batches, using a traditional, London Dry, slow distillation method and just the right balance of botanicals (above) to create a distinctive gin. Every batch is taste tested, both neat and with tonic, to ensure they meet high standards.

Their core gins are Original, Lavender (next page, top left, right-hand bottle), Tea (next page, top left, left-hand bottle), and Peppered Pear (next page, top right), while 'Special Edition' gins have included Slow Distilled Sloe, and Steve's Apple. Most use Yorkshire products, including, of course, Yorkshire Tea.

To enjoy Masons gin, pair with premium

tonic, plenty of ice and a complementary garnish: try orange peel with the Original (previous page, bottom left), lemon peel with the Tea edition and lime peel with Lavender. Alternatively, try the Lavender with ginger ale, or Tea with bitter lemonade.

Unfortunately, on the 2nd April 2019, the Masons Distillery was destroyed in a fire. The next day, the team gathered around Karl and Cathy's dining room table, unfazed, to work out how to keep the brand going. As we went to press, Karl and Cathy were still distilling.

Purple Ram Gin and Yorkshire Dales Distillery

Colburn, North Yorkshire
Distillery

ESSENTIAL INFORMATION

Key botanicals (Purple Ram Gin): juniper, pink grapefruit peel, local honey, plus four secret ingredients

Output: not disclosed

Location: Unit 7C, Easton Way, Colburn, Catterick Garrison, DL9 4GA

Telephone: 01748 518070

Email: helloram@yorkshiredalesdistillery.com

Website: www.yorkshiredalesdistillery.com

Facebook: www.facebook.com/ yorkshiredalesdistillery

Instagram: @yorkshiredalesdistillery

Twitter: @homeoftheram

Opening hours:
Monday-Friday 0900-1700

Other reasons to go: Bolton Abbey Estate, Bolton Castle, Dales Countryside Museum, Black Sheep Brewery

Tony Brotherton and his wife Sarah founded the family-run Yorkshire Dales Distillery in April 2016, with the aim of producing a range of smooth spirits using hand picked, locally sourced ingredients. In November of that year, they moved the distillery into a former wine warehouse. One of their main objectives was to provide jobs for the long-term unemployed, ex-offenders, the young, and veterans. Tony had previously served in the Royal Artillery for 18 years but, as we went to press, he was studying for his Master's in Brewing and Distilling at Heriot-Watt University to revitalize his long-term passion for distilling – he was once caught brewing beer at school.

Yorkshire Dales' first product, Purple Ram London Dry Gin (bottom left), was released in February 2017. Initially, distillation took place on a 30-litre still, producing 50 bottles per run. A year on, demand saw Tony invest in another still ten times the size of the original, which produces 80 cases of gin per batch. The gin has floral, citrus and honey flavours, best served with basil and a wedge of grapefruit over ice.

Their second offering was Desert Ram 'Army Strength' Gin (next page, bottom right, middle bottle). Bottled at 50%, this is a nod to Tony's time in the army. Made with bitter orange, rose and cardamom, this works well with grapefruit rind and ice. Their third gin is another dry gin: Wild Ram 'Yorkshire Berry' Gin (next page, bottom right, second bottle from left), made with locally sourced gooseberries, redcurrants, blackcurrants and heather. Try it with a quality tonic, ice and a fresh blackberry. All of Yorkshire Dales' spirits are quadruple distilled and vapour infused

→

(page 254) before they are cut with natural mineral water from the Dales.

In addition to their core 'Ram' range, Yorkshire Dales also produces a niche collection of gins – their YD range (top). These include Honeyed Rhubarb Gin, Bramble Berry Gin, and Strawberry and Thai Basil Gin. All products can be bought direct from their distillery or the online shop.

Durham Gin and Distillery

Durham
Distillery

Durham Distillery was founded by Jon Chadwick (next page, middle), who was inspired by a trip to the USA's East Coast where he found there was a growing taste for gin that mirrored the craft beer movement in the UK. Using the redundancy money from his previous job in the NHS (in a team that spread awareness of the dangers of alcohol abuse) Jon decided to make his own gin. He and his then Master Distiller spent about a year developing a recipe and Durham Gin (below left) was launched with the opening of the distillery in 2014.

Head distiller Jess Tomlinson (next page, top left) uses a combination of pot distillation and vapour infusion (page 254). She crushes the juniper (above) by hand and adds it to Lily, their 400-litre copper pot still, along with the more robust botanicals, such as angelica and pink peppercorn. The botanicals are left to infuse in Durham spring water and pure grain spirit overnight before the coriander and orris root are added, and the mixture heated. The vapour produced is used to distil the more delicate botanicals such as elderflower, celery seed, cardamom and citrus peels, which sit in a basket at the top of the still. Distillation takes five to six hours, after which the head and tail of the run are removed (the tails are recycled in the production of their vodka – next page, bottom right, right-hand bottle) and the gin is cut with water to 40%

to produce 300 bottles of London Dry style gin. Try it in a Negroni.

Jess also produces Strawberry and Pink Pepper Liqueur, made by soaking the peppercorns in Durham Gin for 24 hours before blending the spirit with fresh strawberry juice. This works well in a Strawberry Collins cocktail: add 50 ml of the gin to 25 ml of lemon juice, 10 ml of grenadine syrup and top with soda water, with lemon slices and cocktail cherries to garnish.

Each year, Jess produces a different Cask Aged Gin (right, left-hand bottle). As we went to press, this was Durham Gin rested for nearly 18 months in a combination of American Bourbon and Spanish Oloroso Sherry casks to produce a fruity, honeyed flavour with hints of vanilla and citrus zest. She produces just over a thousand bottles each year, and it's best served neat with ice. She also makes a Damson, Blackberry and Ginger Liqueur, a winter warmer made with Durham Gin. All the gins can be bought from the online shop.

As we went to press, Durham Distillery had recently secured new premises in the heart of Durham city centre. They will open a visitors' centre and offer a range of tours and events from spring 2020.

Tin of Sardines

Durham
Bar

ESSENTIAL INFORMATION
Location: 18 Elvet Bridge, Durham,
    DH1 3AA
Telephone: 01913 741666
Email: info@tinofsardines.co.uk
Website: www.tinofsardines.co.uk
Facebook: www.facebook.com/
    tinofsardinesdurham
Instagram: @tinofsardinesdurham
Twitter: @tinofsardines

Opening hours:
Sunday-Tuesday 1200-2300
Wednesday-Saturday 1200-2330

Other reasons to go: Durham History Tour,
The National Museum of the Royal Navy,
Bolton Castle

Opened by Ben Davis in May 2017, Tin of Sardines (bottom left) covers an area of just 68 square feet, making it one of the smallest bars in the world – hence the name. Despite its size, the bar boasts an impressive collection of gins – around 200 different brands – including Carounn Gin (page 282), Drumshanbo Gunpowder Irish Gin (page 306 – top right) and Isle of Harris Gin (page 270), plus 50 mixers.

The bar offers a Gin Tasting Experience led by ginologist and barman Connah Jarvis-Reed, where for £30 you get a brief history of gin, 4 G&Ts suited to your palate, and nibbles. The premises is also available to hire for an hour for up to 15 people, with sessions including a gin tutorial.

Tin of Sardines serves a G&T of the Week at a discounted price of £4.95. They have an online shop (www.etsy.com/TinofSardines) where you can buy homemade gin products, as well as garnishes.

They also have a bar at 3 High Street, Poole, Dorset (01202 677435).

Steampunk Gin and Steampunk Spirits

Gateshead, Tyne and Wear
Distillery and gin school

ESSENTIAL INFORMATION

Key botanicals (Steampunk Extremely Rare Dry Gin): juniper, cardamom, three types of citrus peel, plus three secret ingredients

Output: 120,000 bottles a year

Location: 3 Earksway Trade Park, Earlsway, Team Valley Trading Estate, Gateshead, NE11 0QG

Telephone: 01914 870698

Email: customer@steampunkspirits.co.uk

Website: www.steampunkspirits.co.uk

Facebook: www.facebook.com/SteampunkGin

Instagram: @steampunkspirits

Twitter: @SteampunkGin

Opening hours: only open for tasting events – see website for information

Other reasons to go: Gateshead Millennium Bridge, Saltwell Park, Newcastle Castle

Husband and wife team Charlie (opposite, middle) and Julie Gibbs founded Steampunk Spirits in 2014 with the aim of making spirits accessible to everyone and turning gin sceptics into gin lovers. Using a recipe from 1892, Charlie started producing Steampunk Extremely Rare Dry Gin (bottom left) in his kitchen, but in 2016 they moved into a larger premises on the Team Valley in Gateshead.

The gin is made using the one-shot method (page 68) on a stainless steel pot still. Charlie recommends serving the gin with smashed basil leaves, a quality tonic and a few ice cubes.

Steampunk also produces two spirits made with their Extremely Rare Dry Gin at 20% bottle strength: Prudence, a rose petal flavoured gin, works well with Prosecco; and Florence, which has a parma violet flavour. Try this in an Aviation cocktail: mix equal measures (15 ml) of Florence, maraschino liqueur, and lemon juice with 40 ml of Steampunk Extremely Rare Dry Gin.

In 2018, they released the 'Explorer' range (opposite, top left) in partnership with B&M Retail. These include Bone Dry, Rhubarb and Blood Orange gins which were made to appeal to a wider audience in both taste and price, sold at around £15 a bottle. These are bottled at a strength of 37.5% and are sold exclusively from licensed B&M stores.

Steampunk hosts private gin tastings for up to eight people where you get a tour of the distillery, and a talk on gin production and its history before sampling five different gins, ending with a farewell Steampunk G&T served in a Copa de Balón glass, which you take home. The experience lasts around two hours and costs £25 per person.

Email sales@steampunkspirits.co.uk to book.
They also offer a Gin School for those who want to make gin on a commercial scale. This is a one-day course where you learn about setting up a business, dealing with HMRC, and the distilling process. Classes cost £250 – visit the website to register.

Whittaker's Gin and The Harrogate Distillery

Harrogate, North Yorkshire
Distillery

ESSENTIAL INFORMATION
Key botanicals (Whittaker's Gin): juniper, coriander, lemon citrus, thyme, hawthorn berry, bilberry, bog-myrtle
Output: 25,000 bottles a year
Location: Harewell House Farm, Dacre Banks, Harrogate, HG3 4HQ
Telephone: 01423 781842
Email: enquiries@whittakersgin.com
Website: www.whittakersgin.com
Facebook: www.facebook.com/ whittakersgin
Instagram: @whittakersgin
Twitter: @WhittakersGin

Opening hours:
Monday-Friday 1000-1700
Saturday 1000-1600

Other reasons to go: Turkish Baths, Royal Pump Room, RHS Garden Harlow Carr

*D*avid T. Smith writes: Harrogate Distillery (opposite, top left), makers of Whittaker's Gin, is part of a growing powerhouse of excellent gin producers in Yorkshire. Currently located on the family farm near Harrogate, the distillery was founded by husband and wife team Jane and Toby Whittaker in 2015. Toby had previously worked in property and finance; Jane had run her own house-building company.

The stills are housed in an old pig shed, originally built in the 1950s, and has plenty of homespun charm, with chinks of sunlight coming through the walls, illuminating Toby's self-built stills (opposite, middle). Despite its rustic nature, the quality of the gin speaks for itself and their original gin (bottom left) was awarded a Double Gold by the American Distilling Institute in their 2018 Judging of Craft Spirits.

Whittaker's first gin was launched in 2015 and features a mix of classic botanicals as well as jammy hawthorn and bilberries and earthy bog-myrtle. They then released their Navy Strength Gin, followed in 2016 by Pink Peculiar Gin (opposite, bottom right): this bolder, more contemporary gin is made using botanicals such as pink peppercorns and pink hibiscus flower.

Whittaker's also make Clearly Sloe Gin, which is a dry take on the traditional sloe gin liqueur. In their version, the sloe berries are distilled rather than infused; additionally, no sugar is added and it is colourless. In 2017, Whittaker's partnered with That Boutique-y Gin Company to produce a Double Sloe Gin, which is the result of a mix of distilled and infused sloe berries. The following year, they launched their spiced Winter Solstice Gin (opposite, bottom left), which is made using botanicals

such as cinnamon, star anise and cloves.

In addition to the range listed above, Harrogate Distillery have also made bespoke gins for other customers, such as Fortnum & Mason, and are currently expanding into whisky production.

As we went to press, the distillery was expanding into a purpose-built structure that will house gin and whisky production, as well as a visitors' centre. This will teach visitors about the process of both gin and whisky production, and offer the opportunity to sample the Whittaker's spirits range, including some of Toby's latest creations.

Hepple Gin and Moorland Spirit Co.

Morpeth, Northumberland
Distillery

ESSENTIAL INFORMATION

Key botanicals (Hepple Gin): purple juniper, green juniper, coriander seed, liquorice, lemon, fennel seed, blackcurrant, blackcurrant leaf, douglas fir, lovage

Output: not disclosed

Location: The Old Coach House, Hepple Whitefield, Morpeth, NE65 7LN

Telephone: N/A

Email: hello@moorlandspirit.com

Website: www.moorlandspirit.co

Facebook: www.facebook.com/hepplegin

Instagram: hepple_spirits

Twitter: @Hepple_Spirits

Opening hours: not open to the public

Other reasons to go: Whitehouse Farm Centre, Morpeth Chantry Bagpipe Museum, Plessey Woods Country Park, Kirkley Hall Zoological Gardens

David T. Smith writes: The Moorland Spirit Company is based on the Hepple Estate (bottom left) in the wilds of Northumbria, 15 miles from the Scottish border, on Northumberland moorland (opposite, top left), a windswept but beautiful landscape of heather, peat bogs and ancient woodland. For gin lovers, perhaps its main feature is the juniper bushes that thrive in the harsh terrain.

Hepple Gin (right) was created by a collaboration of several people: Walter Riddell, whose family have been long-time residents and owners of the Hepple Estate; Valentine Warner, cook, food writer and broadcaster; Nick Strangeway, award-winning bartender and flavour expert; and Cairbry Hill, an expert on and researcher into the distillation process and techniques. Their distinct backgrounds and skill-sets enabled them to make a unique contribution to the development of the gin.

The team (left and opposite, middle) wanted to create a 'high fidelity' gin with great complexity. Their access to local juniper provided an obvious focus, but in fact the gin is made using juniper from three sources: Macedonia, Italy, and green juniper from the Hepple Estate, each adding a different character to the gin, resulting in a multi-depth juniper flavour.

Master Distiller Chris Garden (opposite, bottom left) uses three different production methods: pot distillation, vacuum distillation (page 53), and supercritical extraction, which uses super-chilled carbon dioxide to extract flavour from the juniper.

As well as making a high-quality gin, the distillery is also focussed on ecology and the environment, and is only too aware of the plight of juniper in the UK, where it is one of the country's three native conifers. In recent decades, the amount of juniper growing in the country has dwindled due to infection by the juniper blight fungus and by the clearing of bushes to liberate grazing land for sheep. In collaboration with Northumberland National Park, the Moorland Spirit Company aims to plant at least 200 seedlings a year to help revive the local juniper population.

The Continental Gin Palace

Newcastle upon Tyne, Tyne and Wear
Bar

ESSENTIAL INFORMATION
Location: 29 Collingwood Street, Newcastle
   upon Tyne, NE1 1JE
Telephone: 01912 211333
Email: info@thecontinental.co.uk
Website: www.thecontinental.co.uk
Facebook: www.facebook.com/www.
   thecontinental.co.uk
Instagram: @thecontinentalnewcastle
Twitter: @Continental_NCL

Opening hours:
Monday-Wednesday 1600-2330
Thursday-Saturday 1200-0000
Sunday 1200-2230

Other reasons to go: The Cathedral Church
of St Nicholas, Tyne Bridge, Newcastle Castle

Co-founders and husband and wife Toni Almiron and Claire Elwell opened El Torero, the first of two Spanish restaurants, in Newcastle in 2001. In October 2013, Toni (from Granada) wanted to bring his Spanish thirst for gin to Newcastle, so the duo opened Dacantus Gin Lab (see opposite). Expanding on its success, they opened The Continental on the 25th November 2016, stocking more than 500 gins, including Whitley Neill (page 176), Apothecary Rose (page 236) and Drumshanbo Gunpowder Irish Gin (page 306), plus an amazing 30 tonics.

The Continental's building was used as an insurance company office in the early 20thC and you'll see some of the original features: marble- and wood-panelled walls in the main bar and the original safe and secure room in the basement, which can be seen on the way to the loos. A new and central feature is the alabaster colour-changing bar (left), a mesmerising focal point.

The Continental offers private gin tastings for a minimum group of four. For £20.95 per person, you try three different gins: Hayman's London Dry, Durham (page 193) and Brockman's followed by a G&T of your choice. For an extra £3 you can upgrade to the 5 Gin Tasting where you can also taste Hayman's Old Tom Gin and Bulldog Gin.

Dacantus Bar and Restaurant

Newcastle upon Tyne, Tyne and Wear
Bar

ESSENTIAL INFORMATION
Location: 30-32 Grey Street, Newcastle
   upon Tyne, NE1 6AE
Telephone: 01912 618111
Email: serve@dacantus.com
Website: www.dacantus.com
Facebook: www.facebook.com/Dacantus
Instagram: @dacantus_newcastleuk
Twitter: @Dacantus

Opening hours:
Sunday-Thursday 1200-2330
Friday-Saturday 1200-0100

Other reasons to go: Newcastle Cathedral,
Theatre Royal, Newcastle Castle

Toni Almiron and wife Claire Elwell opened Dacantus (right) in October 2013 with the aim of bringing to Newcastle informal dining reminiscent of a typical Spanish bar in Granada (Toni's home city). It's located on Grey Street, known to locals as the Platinum Strip, named as one of the most beautiful streets in the UK because of its sandstone-fronted buildings.

The bar (below left) stocks around 400 gins and 30 tonics which could be overwhelming but for the Speciality G&T Menu which tells you which gin pairs best with which tonic and garnish. The gin is served in large 'fishbowl' style glasses, as in Spain, with oversized ice cubes. Shaun, the manager, says the larger ice cubes melt more slowly so the gin doesn't dilute. You also receive a complimentary tapas dish with your drink, as is customary in Granada.

Dacantus hosts gin tastings in their 'Gin Lab' similar to those held at its sister bar, The Continental (see opposite).

Dacantus? A play on acanthus – a type of Mediterranean leaf which features in the bar's interior decoration, including the ceiling which is shaped to resemble an acanthus leaf.

Newcastle Gin and Bealim House

Newcastle upon Tyne, Tyne and Wear
Distillery and bar

ESSENTIAL INFORMATION

Key botanicals (Newcastle Gin): juniper, coriander, orange peel, sumac, ginger, rose petal, hibiscus, plus three secret ingredients

Output: not disclosed

Location: 17-25 Gallowgate, Newcastle upon Tyne, NE1 4SG

Telephone: 01912 212266

Email: bealimhouse@vaulkhardgroup.co.uk

Website: www.bealimhouse.co.uk

Facebook: www.facebook.com/BealimHouse

Instagram: @bealimhouseofficial

Twitter: @bealimhouse

Opening hours:
Monday-Thursday 1130-2300
Friday 1130-0000
Saturday 1100-0000
Sunday 1200-2230

Other reasons to go: Beamish – the Living Museum of the North, Gateshead Millennium Bridge, Angel of the North, Hadrian's Wall Path

Bealim House claims to be the first authentic gin distillery, bar and eatery in Newcastle for more than 200 years. Its interior pays homage to the building's former life as a print works, with wooden flooring, antique leather furnishings, vintage tiles and varnished brick walls. Now, it's home to the Newcastle Gin Company and the city's only working in-house gin still (450 litres – opposite, top left), which can be seen on the ground floor from the bar (bottom left) behind bullet proof glass.

The main spirit, Newcastle Gin (above and opposite, bottom right), is distilled on the premises and gets some of its character from African botanicals. In common with several other distilleries in this guide (see pages 123 and 254), the more delicate botanicals, such as rose petal, are distilled in a vapour basket which distillers claim avoids loss of flavour. Each batch is created over two days, starting with the maceration of the 'hard' botanicals and alcohol for 48 hours. The 'soft' botanicals are then added before they are distilled for five hours. Finally, Newcastle City water is added to dilute the product from a strength of 85% to 43%. The result is a gin with a subtle taste of rose and hibiscus, which make it easy to sip on its own.

Bealim House also recommends serving Newcastle Gin with elderflower tonic and a dash of elderflower cordial and, in the warmer months, they serve their own summer cocktail, mixing the gin with fresh

strawberries, a drop of strawberry syrup and Fentiman's herbal tonic water. The gin also works well in a mojito, adding a punchy, floral dimension to the classic cocktail. They also produce other gin flavours including apple and cinnamon, rhubarb and ginger, and damson.

The distillery offers two gin tasting packages: the Newcastle Distillery Experience costs £18 and includes a welcome cocktail, a G&T and a brief introduction to distilling and how Newcastle Gin is made. The experience lasts approximately 45 minutes. Priced at £33, the Gin Tasting Experience includes the same as the first package but you also taste your way through the history of gin, finishing with a guided tasting of Newcastle Gin. This experience lasts 90 minutes and includes a selection of nibbles.

Newcastle Gin is available to drink in many bars around its home city but as we went to press was only available to buy for £38 by the bottle from Bealim House, the Newcastle Gin website and at certain festivals from the Newcastle Gin van.

Poetic License Gin and Distillery

Roker, Tyne and Wear
Distillery and bar

ESSENTIAL INFORMATION

Key botanicals (Northern Dry Gin): juniper, cardamom, pepper, Persian lime

Output: not disclosed

Location: Roker Hotel, 21-24 Roker Terrace, Roker, SR6 9NB

Telephone: 01915 103564

Email: chinchin@poeticlicensedistillery.co.uk

Website: www.poeticlicensedistillery.co.uk

Facebook: www.facebook.com/PoeticLicenseDistillery

Instagram: @poeticlicensedistillery

Twitter: @PoeticLicenseUK

Opening hours:
Distillery
Monday-Friday 0800-1600
Roker Hotel bar
Monday-Sunday 0000-0000

Other reasons to go: National Glass Centre, Sunderland Museum and Winter Gardens, Hylton Castle, Ryhope Engines Museum, Seaburn Beach

David T. Smith writes: Poetic License Distillery and Bar is located in the Roker Hotel, one of the longest-established hotels in Sunderland, overlooking a beach (opposite, bottom right). Their still, Gracie (bottom left), is a focal point in the bar. In addition to Poetic License, the hotel is also home to the 'Let There Be Crumbs' tea and cakery room, Poetic License Restaurant and Italian restaurant Antico.

The distillery was opened in 2015 by Mark Hird, owner of The Roker Hotel. He already owned a brewery, S43 in Coxhoe, Durham, and created Poetic License for "the wild spirits – those who do not conform to the norm."

The first gins were released in the summer of 2015. Northern Dry Gin (opposite, top, middle bottle) uses 13 botanicals and is relatively spice-forward because it contains cardamom and a variety of peppercorns. The Old Tom Gin (opposite, top, second bottle from left) is botanically sweetened and barrel rested. More recent additions include the Spiced Fireside Gin (opposite, top, right-hand bottle), and Strawberry and Cream Gin (opposite, top, left-hand bottle).

Several times a year the distillery releases limited edition gins under 'The Rarities' range: examples include Pink Grapefruit and Tonka Bean, and Raspberry and Buddha's Hand, released for World Gin

Day 2019. For those with a sweet tooth, the distillery also produces a selection of gin-based liqueurs.

The distillery bar is open throughout the week and visitors may often get the chance to see the senior distiller Lewis Hendry (opposite, top right) in action and maybe have a chat. More formal tours take place at the weekend and include the story of the distillery and its 'wild spirit' philosophy, plus a welcome drink, a tasting (which includes some of the latest limited editions), and a farewell drink. Poetic License also offers Gin Masterclasses in the bar, every Saturday from 12 pm. Booking is essential – email events@rokerhotel.co.uk.

Cooper King Gin and Distillery

Sutton-on-the-Forest, North Yorkshire
Distillery and bar

ESSENTIAL INFORMATION

Key botanicals (Cooper King Dry Gin): juniper, coriander seed, green cardamom, lemongrass, lavender, honey

Output: 5,000 bottles a year

Location: The Old Stable, Stillington Road, Sutton-on-the-Forest, YO61 1EH

Telephone: 01347 808232

Email: info@cooperkingdistillery.co.uk

Website: www.cooperkingdistillery.co.uk

Facebook: www.facebook.com/cooperkingdistillery

Instagram: @cooperkingdistillery

Twitter: @CKdistillery

Opening hours:
Saturday 1000-1800

Other reasons to go: Castle Howard, York Bird of Prey Centre, the Yorkshire coast, York city centre

*D*avid T. Smith writes: Yorkshire is becoming a hub for distillers. Cooper King, a recent addition, is about 10 miles north of York, sitting between the Howardian Hills and the Yorkshire Dales National Park. York has a number of gin bars and the record-breaking Evil Eye Gin Shop, which stocks more than 1,100 different gins.

Cooper King was founded by Dr. Abbie Neilson (opposite, top left), a biomedical scientist, and Chris Jaume (opposite, top right), a chartered architect. The pair were inspired by distillers they had visited on a trip to Australia and Tasmania, where they studied with Bill Lark, a prolific distiller.

The distillery takes its name from Chris' great-great-grandfather, a lieutenant colonel in the Royal Marine Artillery whose family tree is rooted in Yorkshire.

The distillery was built by Chris and Abbie with help from friends, family, and founder supporters. It's proud of its environmental credentials and sustainable spirits, running exclusively on green energy and recycling water and waste. It is also part of the '1% for the Planet' initiative, which means that one per cent of sales are used to plant trees in the Yorkshire Dales. In the initiative's first year, over 4,600 square metres of new woodland was planted, offsetting 230 tonnes of CO2 and improving the area's landscape and biodiversity.

Cooper King is currently open to the public on Saturdays, guided tours taking place in the afternoon. Visitors can learn

about making gin and whisky, bring back an empty bottle for a gin refill, and have a G&T or cocktail at the snug bar (bottom left). You can also stay overnight in the distillery's bed and breakfast.

The distillery's original Dry Gin (opposite bottom left), launched 2018, is made using the vacuum distillation method (page 53 – above right) with a combination of wheat and malt spirits and botanicals that include locally sourced lavender, and honey from the distillery's own beehives. It has also produced a number of special editions in collaboration with high-end designers and Michelin-starred restaurants.

Crow Man's Gin and The Kelso Gin Company

Ancrum, Scottish Borders
Distillery and shop

ESSENTIAL INFORMATION

Key botanicals (Crow Man's Gin): juniper, cardamom, plus five secret ingredients

Output: 70 bottles a day

Location: Harestanes, Ancrum, Jedburgh, TD8 6UQ

Telephone: 01573 226883

Email: thekelsogincompany@gmail.com

Website: www.kelsoginco.com

Facebook: www.facebook.com/thekelsogincompany

Instagram: @kelsogincompany

Twitter: @kelsogin

Opening hours:
Distillery and shop
Friday-Sunday 1000-1700

Other reasons to go: Dryburgh Abbey, Monteviot Gardens, Fatlips Castle

Kelso Gin Co. was established in 2017 and claims to be the first distillery in the Scottish Borders since 1837. Their debut product, Crow Man's Gin (bottom left), was named after head distiller Andrew Crow and their advertising and labelling is based on the folk tale of The Crow Man – a 17thC travelling plague doctor in the Borders who offered special herbal mixes said to help those who had been infected with the Black Death.

Crown Man's Gin is made with locally foraged botanicals blended with an organic pure grain base spirit in a copper still. Andrew uses only the heart of the distillation, disposing of the tails which some distilleries recycle (see Salcombe Gin on page 47).

Andrew also produces Kelso Elephant Gin, named after the local legend that an elephant is buried under Kelso Square. He mixes oriental spices with local ingredients to create a zingy taste that works well with ginger ale. The third product in their core range is Crow Man's Lovage Gin, a herby spirit made with lovage sourced from the Teviot Valley, plus olives and orange zest. Try this in a Dry Martini.

The gins can be bought from the online shop, as well as the Master of Malt website and various bars around the Borders. The distillery offers mobile gin tastings where, for £250, 'The Crow Man' comes to a venue of your choice (within a 25-mile radius of Kelso) with various products to sample – see website for booking information. They also have a Founders Club. For £500 you receive a bottle of the first batch made each year, for the next ten years. Members are also invited to exclusive first-batch tastings and special events throughout the year.

Oro Gin and
The Distillery at Dalton

Dalton, Dumfries and Galloway
Distillery and tasting rooms

ESSENTIAL INFORMATION

Key botanicals (Oro Gin): juniper,
   coriander, Malaber cardamom,
   cinnamon, cassia bark, ground
   almond, lemon peel, orange peel, pink
   peppercorn, lemongrass, fennel, and one
   secret ingredient

Output: not disclosed

Location: The Distillery, Dalton, near Lockerbie,
   DG11 1DU

Telephone: 01387 840381

Email: info@theorogin.com

Website: www.orogin.co.uk

Facebook: www.facebook.com/theorogin

Instagram: @oro_gin

Twitter: @oro_gin

Opening hours:
Wednesday 1300-2000
Thursday 1300-2200
Friday-Saturday 1300-0000
Sunday 1300-2000

Other reasons to go: Annandale Whisky
Distillery, Dryfesdale Cemetery

Oro Gin was launched in December 2017 by the Clynick family, whose aim was to create a gin using scientific knowledge of different flavour compounds and how they interact with each other. *Oro* is Spanish for gold and the bottle labels feature gold concentric circles to represent the atomic structure of the element.

The botanicals are macerated for 24 hours before being distilled for 15-17 hours with a neutral grain spirit using the one-shot method (page 68). Before they are cut with water, most London Dry recipes are 70% after distilling. Oro Gin (bottom left, left-hand bottle), however, is cut at a higher strength to ensure an even cleaner, purer spirit. It's then diluted to 43% with pure water.

The Clynicks also produce Oro Gin V (bottom left, right-hand bottle), using lavender as a smoothing agent. Try mixing this with an elderflower tonic and a slice of lemon.

The distillery's Tasting Rooms include a bar with a growing collection of gins and a tapas menu. There's also a courtyard and a conservatory for the warmer months.

The Lab releases limited edition seasonal products such as aged and fruit gins. With most fruit gins, the fruit flavours are added after distillation. However, the Clynicks make theirs in a London Dry style, which means that only water can be added after distillation. Many flavours won't distil, particularly red fruits and berries, so they use chemistry to extract those botanicals into alcohol, stabilizing the flavour compounds in order to distil them with the botanicals.

They can also design bespoke products for special occasions or businesses. Tours are available by appointment from Monday to Friday 10 am to 4 pm – see website for booking information.

ChiQuiOui Gin and Rutherfords Micropub

Kelso, Scottish Borders
Bar

ESSENTIAL INFORMATION

Key botanicals (ChiQuiOui Gin): juniper, plus 11 secret ingredients

Output: not disclosed

Location: 38 The Square, Kelso, TD5 7HL

Telephone: 07803 208460

Email: rutherfordltd@googlemail.com

Website: www.rutherfordsmicropub.co.uk

Facebook: www.facebook.com/ Rutherfordsmicropub.co.uk

Instagram: @rutherfordsmicropub

Twitter: @R_fordsMicropub

Opening hours:

Monday-Thursday 1200-2200

Friday-Saturday 1200-2300

Sunday 1200-2200

Other reasons to go: Floors Castle and Gardens, Kelso Abbey, Roxburgh Castle, Springwood Park

Rutherfords was opened by Debbie and Simon Rutherford in summer 2015 and is Scotland's only micropub. They stock over 20 gins, including their own creations.

They started producing their own gin in October 2017, under the name DeliQuescent, which means 'becoming liquid', apt for a team of spirits producers specializing in unusual gins. Their signature taste, ChiQuiOui Gin (bottom left), pronounced Cheeky Wee and served on draught via a microscope tap, is juniper led with a kick of citrus, best served with a quality tonic and a wedge of pink grapefruit or orange.

As we went to press, their most recent release was Haggis Gin, launched on Burns Night 2019. The gin's tagline is 'there's nothing offal in our gin', comically reassuring the drinker that only spices reminiscent of the Scottish delicacy are used, with not a hint of meat. Haggis Gin works best neat but Debbie and Simon also recommend serving it in true Scottish style – with a splash of Irn Bru.

They also produce seasonal gins: in winter 2018, they released Christmas Pudding, GINgerbread and GINgle Bells gins; in spring, a limited edition Hot Cross Bun Gin, using sultanas, citrus and spice.

The gins can be bought from Rutherfords micropub or their online shop. Debbie and Simon also sell at Kelso's farmer's market on the third Saturday of most months from 10 am to 1.30 pm – check their website for dates.

Rutherfords offers an Afternoon G&T where three gins of your choice are served alongside cucumber sandwiches, manchego and parma ham, and handmade sweets – call or email to book.

Brodie's Gin and Coffee Lounge

Moffat, Dumfries and Galloway
Bar

ESSENTIAL INFORMATION
Location: 1-2 Altrive Place, Holm Street,
    Moffat, DG10 9EB
Telephone: 01683 222870
Email: whatscooking@brodiesofmoffat.co.uk
Website: www.brodiesofmoffat.co.uk
Facebook: www.facebook.com/
    BrodiesofMoffat
Instagram: @brodiesofmoffat
Twitter: @BrodiesofMoffat

Opening hours:
Monday-Tuesday 1000-1600
Wednesday-Thursday 1000-2200
Friday-Saturday 1000-late
Sunday 1030-2100

Other reasons to go: Moffat Museum,
Moffat Community Nature Reserve, Station
Park, Frenchland Tower, The Devil's Beef Tub

Lincolnshire-born Russell Pearce opened Brodies, named after Sculptor William Brodie, in April 2011 with his wife, Danyella. As an award-winning chef, he'd cooked for the Queen and former US President Bill Clinton during his 12-year career at Rudding Park Hotel in Harrogate. It made sense to open his own restaurant.

Brodies opened as a restaurant and wine bar, with the idea of offering a dining experience for every budget – people could come for a three-course meal or just a casual drink. In summer 2016 they expanded into the neighbouring building to open up the Gin Lounge (left and top), initially stocking 27 – mainly Scottish – gins. Now, they offer more than 50 brands including Pickering's (page 234), Caorunn (page 282) and Rock Rose (page 265), plus around 15 tonics.

The lounge offers informal tastings where you try three different tonics, ranging from one with a strong quinine taste to a sweeter one, with the aim of discovering how they affect the taste of the gin. You then try four different gins, learning about botanicals, different types of gin and the history of the spirit.

Hills & Harbour Gin and Crafty Distillery

Newton Stewart, Dumfries and Galloway
Distillery, café and shop

ESSENTIAL INFORMATION

Key botanicals (Hills & Harbour Gin):
  juniper, coriander seed, liquorice root,
  orange peel, green sichuan pepper seed,
  bay leaf, mango, noble fir tree needle,
  bladderwrack seaweed

Output: 30,000 bottles a year

**Location: Wigtown Road, Newton Stewart,
  DG8 6AS**

Telephone: 01671 404040

Email: info@craftydistillery.com

Website: www.craftydistillery.com

**Facebook: www.facebook.com/
  craftydistillery**

Instagram: @craftydistillery

Twitter: @craftydistills

Opening hours:
January-March
Tuesday-Saturday 1000-1730
April-December
Monday-Saturday 1000-1800

**Other reasons to go: Dark Skies Park, 7
Stanes Mountain Biking, Wigtown Book
Festival, Newton Stewart Museum**

Newton Stewart, home town of Crafty's founder Graham Taylor, is in Dumfries and Galloway, the area sometimes loosely described as South-West Scotland, an unspoiled, out-of-the way corner of the British Isles. The town is known as the 'Gateway to the Galloway Hills' and with over 200 miles of coastline in the region, there's a good reason Crafty's gin is called Hills & Harbour (opposite, middle).

The wittily named Crafty Distillery (bottom left) is artfully dovetailed into the local tourist scene, providing what could be one of the pleasantest distillery experiences in southern Scotland. This is mainly down to the Tree Bar and Café (opposite, bottom right), a relaxing, airy stopping place for lunch or tea with big views over the Galloway Hills (opposite, top right). It serves light dishes, tea and coffee, and cakes, or there's the picnic option: you're given a chopping board on which to arrange a choice of cheeses, salads, smoked foods, bread and preserves. If the weather is right, take it outside for a picnic.

The Tree Bar (opposite, top middle) is a draw in its own right, but combine it with a distillery tour (opposite, top left) plus a visit to the shop and you have a worthwhile expedition. Tours run Tuesday to Saturday at 12 pm and 3 pm from January to March, and Monday to Saturday at 11 am, 1 pm and 3 pm from April to December.

The distillery also organizes the Gin Escape experience: join a guided tour of the hills and coastlines to forage for botanicals, then head back to the distillery at the end of the day for a tour and two cocktails prepared by your guide from the ingredients you foraged.

And the gin? Also a deliberately

commercial concept: most craft gins strive for uniqueness, but Hills & Harbour was developed for the widest possible appeal. Graham and his friend Craig Rankin, distillery manager, say they tested 90 different recipes over 14 months to get the final formula, which they then made in three different styles – one modern, one light and one sweet. Next they tested these on the general public and made final adjustments. The result, 'a vibrant, balanced and easy drinking gin' is a deliberate move away from 'fussy niche gin' in order to turn new punters on to craft spirits. It's a 'grain-to-spirit gin' – no bought-in spirit is used.

The bottle says to drink Hills & Harbour however you like, but for a perfect serve put 25 ml in a tumbler with plenty of ice. Add 100 ml of Franklin & Sons tonic (or another mellow tonic such as Bon Accord or Fever-Tree Mediterranean). Finish with a slice of fresh mango, which complements the mango used in distillation, but is also low in sugar and citrus. This allows the gin's flavour to take centre stage.

The Central Bar

Peebles, Scottish Borders

Bar

Roddy MacKay (bottom left) runs this bar in Peebles, the Scottish Borders market town 23 miles S of Edinburgh. It's where Eddleston Water joins the Tweed and was once a key contributor to the woollen industry, but is now mainly a commuter dormitory town. Tourists come to see its old buildings such as St Andrew's Church, founded 1195, and the Old Parish Church of Peebles (above) on the High Street. Just a hundred metres away, on the adjacent street Northgate, is The Central Bar.

As we went to press, Roddy was stocking around 48 gins from craft spirits such as Pickering's (page 234) to big names such as Brockmans. One of his favourites is Bombay Sapphire (page 115) served in a tall glass with tonic and plenty of ice. Central Bar's best-seller is Boë Violet Gin, which Roddy recommends mixing with soda, ice and a selection of fresh fruit. He also stocks Hendrick's limited edition Summer Solstice Gin and locally distilled Kelso Elephant Gin (page 210). He says his most unique gin is Garden Shed Gin, made in Glasgow by two former Scotland rugby players who decided to make gin in the shed at the bottom of their garden.

The bar top (left) is surfaced with 1,600 old pennies, some dating back to 1862, a talking point for customers.

Gilt Gin and Strathleven Distillers

Dumbarton, West Dunbartonshire
Distillery

ESSENTIAL INFORMATION

Key botanicals (Gilt Gin): juniper, coriander, liquorice, cardamom, cassia bark, lemon, orange
Output: not disclosed
Location: Vale of Leven Industrial Estate, Dumbarton, G82 3PD
Telephone: 01389 298755
Email: enquires@strathlevendistillers.com
Website: www.strathlevendistillers.com
Facebook: www.facebook.com/ StrathlevenDistillers
Instagram: @strathlevendistillers6908
Twitter:@GiltGin

Opening hours: not open to the public

Launched in 2012 by Ricky Christie, Strathleven's Gilt Gin (bottom left) is a proudly Scottish creation – the first thing you'll notice on the striking green bottle is the heraldic lion of Scotland etched on to the glass and, naturally, the spirit is distilled in Scotland, near Loch Lomond.

Strathleven describes the spirit as a 'single malt gin', referring to its pure barley base, the same that would be used to make a Scotch whisky. The barley is combined with water from the River Spey, and the result distilled five times. As with many of the stills in this guide, Strathleven's has been designed specifically to meet the requirements of the product – it has its own chill filtration system which reduces the temperature of the spirit to -12°C, after which it's passed through their 'secret' charcoal filters. The distillers claim this method makes the purest spirit. The result is a London Dry-style gin that is not too floral, and great for sipping on its own.

Some say Gilt Gin is best served as a Martini, Negroni or even an Old Fashioned (on account of its whisky character) rather than a G&T. This is because of the potency of its grass and coriander flavours, which have a bitter tang. Strathleven recommends mixing 25 ml of the gin with equal parts of Green Chartreuse, Maraschino liqueur, lime juice and plenty of ice to create The Last Word cocktail.

You can buy Gilt Gin from the Strathleven website for £35 as well as their famous Valt Vodka.

Alston Bar & Beef

Glasgow
Bar

ESSENTIAL INFORMATION

Location: Unit 19, Caledonia Centre,
   Central Station, Glasgow, G1 3SQ
Telephone: 01412 217627
Email: info@alstonglasgow.co.uk
Website: www.alstonglasgow.co.uk
Facebook: www.facebook.com/
   alstonglasgow
Instagram: @alstonglasgow
Twitter: @alstonglasgow

Opening hours:
Monday-Saturday 1200-0000
Sunday 1200-2200

Other reasons to go: Glasgow Central
Station, The Lighthouse

Ella Carr writes: A discrete door by the Alston Street entrance to Glasgow Central Station takes you down into Alston Bar & Grill (bottom left): a long arched brick cellar, painted white and suffused with blue neon light. First impressions are of a seedy dive, not helped by the station location. It feels odd for a steakhouse, or a gin bar, and in any case the two are an unusual pairing. But, the unsettling atmosphere aside, it has a good reputation for serving sustainable melt-in-the-mouth steaks, and with a collection of about 150 gins (above), there's no denying they're serious about the juniper flavoured spirit.

They also serve impressive cocktails, keeping the menu short, sweet and classic: come here for a Martini or a Gimlet without trendy millennial frills. Even the creative cocktails are restrained, which is always sensible in my opinion: particularly interesting were the Gin & Gingerbread and the Tonka Bean Old Fashioned.

Their Gin Masterclass includes a historical run-through, a gin cocktail on arrival and a tasting of six gins, one of which will be the original Dutch genever. I liked the historical element, and at £30 you get plenty for your money (pay an extra £20 to get a three-course meal). Rather than come here just for the Alston Bar, get to the station early before catching your train and treat yourself to a *bon voyage* cocktail – there's a departure screen in the bar. Choose the Grand Margarita if you're keen to try genever without doing the Masterclass.

beGIN

Glasgow
Bar

ESSENTIAL INFORMATION
Location: 383 Byres Road, Glasgow,
    G12 8AU
Telephone: 01413 416516
Email: beginbar@outlook.com
Website: www.beginglasgow.com
Facebook: www.facebook.com/
    beginglasgow
Instagram: @beginglasgow
Twitter: @beGINGlasgow

Opening hours:
Monday-Thursday 1600-0000
Friday 1600-0100
Saturday 1200-0100
Sunday 1200-0000

Other reasons to go: Glasgow Necropolis,
Kelvingrove Art Gallery and Museum, Pollok
Country Park

Ella Carr writes: You have to applaud beGIN's (bottom left) commitment to gin. As we went to press this was the newest gin bar to open in Glasgow, and it hosts a roster of events to entice diehard gin heads as well as newbies. The bar holds around 100 gins, with a special emphasis on Scottish and local gins (flowers are displayed in Garden Shed Gin bottles (right), a gin made by two local rugby players in – you guessed – their garden shed). You can tailor your own G&T with a selection of garnishes and tonics, or opt for their perfect serve. If you're struggling which to choose, go for the Gin Flight: different gins themed The Bold, The Beautiful, The Best and Scottish. Membership of their Gin Club is free, giving you access to exclusive events such as Meet the Makers each month (soon to include a Gin Masterclass).

Black walls and ceilings with pink inserts (apparently referencing the pink gin craze) make this a proper late night joint – speakeasy style. The staff, who personally gutted and re-did the place when it was bought in 2016, have added a touch of industrial chic, with copper pipe glass racks (next page, top left), purple lights and the odd copper still (next page, top right). At night, especially on weekends when DJs are brought in, the bar is rammed – the place to sample Glasgow's famous nightlife.

On my mid-week afternoon visit, the bar was significantly more sedate. I settled back with a Makar Scottish G&T (when in Rome – page 225) – not my favourite,

though I enjoyed the chilli garnish (below right). Perhaps more exciting ones to try here include Hills & Harbour (page 214), a grain-to-bottle variety recommended by the barman; Bakewell Gin (page 184), a spicy gin with hints of ground almond and cherry jam; and Four Pillars Bloody Shiraz, a deep purple, richly jammy gin hailing from Australia, made from Yara Valley Grapes.

Crossbill Gin and Distillery

Glasgow
Distillery, shop, gin school and visitors' centre

ESSENTIAL INFORMATION

Key botanicals (Crossbill Gin): juniper, rosehip

Output: not disclosed

Location: Unit 1 BAaD, 54 Calton Entry, Glasgow, G40 2SB

Telephone: 0141 237 4664

Email: enquiries@crossbillgin.com

Website: www.crossbillgin.com

Facebook: www.facebook.com/CrossbillGin

Instagram: @crossbill_highland_distilling

Twitter: @CrossbillGin

Opening hours:
Monday-Friday 0900-1700

Other reasons to go: Kelvingrove Art Gallery and Museum, Glasgow Cathedral, Riverside Museum, Gallery of Modern Art

David T. Smith writes: Crossbill Gin's story began in 2012 in a converted shed on an estate near Aviemore, Scotland, a characterful location which was awarded Shed of the Year by Channel 4 in 2015.

In 2017, the distillery moved to a new home near Barras Market (above) in the Trongate area of Glasgow, quickly transforming itself from a remote, rural distillery to a bustling urban one. The new home enables people to get to know the gin via the visitors' centre and shop. This runs The Gin School course (next page, top left and bottom right) three times a week, offering participants an interactive session covering the distillery's background, spirit production, and how to impart flavour to spirits. You get a tutored tasting of Crossbill products, before making your own gin using the custom pot still. Unusually for a gin school, the stills have vapour baskets, so participants can also explore vapour botanical distillation (page 254).

Crossbill Gin (left, left-hand bottle) is made using only two botanicals and 100 per cent of them are sourced from Scotland. Common juniper comes from the Cairngorms and, whilst this is the same variety that many other distilleries source from Tuscany and the Mediterranean, the differences in climate affect the character of the juniper. The Scottish berries are more aromatic

and slightly lighter. The second botanical is rosehip (above right): a plant that commonly grows near juniper and also works well in gin, adding its own resinous character.

Crossbill 200 (previous page, second bottle from left) is a special annual release: a true vintage gin made exclusively from juniper berries harvested from a single 200-year-old juniper bush and the rosehips that grow around it.

In 2017, Crossbill teamed up with That Boutique-y Gin Company to produce 3D Juniper Gin, made using both green and purple juniper berries, juniper wood, and needles.

The Finnieston

Glasgow
Bar

ESSENTIAL INFORMATION

Location: 1125 Argyle Street, Glasgow, G3 8ND

Telephone: 01412 222884

Email: hello@thefinniestonbar.com

Website: www.thefinniestonbar.com

Facebook: www.facebook.com/ thefinniestonbar

Instagram: @thefinniestonofficial

Twitter: @The_Finnieston

Opening hours:

Monday-Thursday 1100-0000

Friday 1100-0100

Saturday 1000-0100

Sunday 1000-0000

Other reasons to go: Kelvingrove Art Gallery and Museum, Escape Rooms Scotland, Cameronians War Memorial

Ella Carr writes: The Finnieston gin bar and seafood restaurant (bottom left) opened in 2007, but the building itself is steeped in history. Dating from the 1800s it started out as a drover's tavern, then changed hands between a cabinet makers, a hotel and a dairy farmer. With beautiful low coffered ceilings and rich wood panelling, it bursts with historic atmosphere as well as a jovial vibe – making this my favourite Glasgow gin bar.

Alongside sustainable seafood, The Finnieston's speciality is classic cocktails such as the Martini. However, the bar also prides itself on having been run by some of the most innovative bartenders in Scotland, all of whom have contributed their own twists to the menu. There are usually around 70 gins behind the bar, with new names added every few months. I chose the Fallen Star gin and tonic, made with Bombay Sapphire (page 115), a twist of orange peel and some star anise. Despite its low-key presentation in a long tumbler it was one of the most delicious G&Ts I've ever drunk.

With its scuffed leather settees and vintage wooden furniture, The Finnieston is a great mix of historic and ramshackle – like Glasgow itself. The bar is on Argyle Street, which was once quite rough and run-down, but is now a rising star since the SSE Hydro Stadium opened in 2011. Known simply as The Strip, Argyle Street is also home to bars such as Lebowski's, Ben Nevis and Kelvingrove Cafe, and attracts a gang of experimental bartenders who are good at exchanging ideas. A top spot for a bar crawl.

Gin71

Glasgow
Bar

ESSENTIAL INFORMATION
Location: 71 Renfield Street, Glasgow, G2 1LP
Telephone: 0141 353 2959
Email: contact@gin71.com
Website: www.gin71.com
Facebook: www.facebook.com/gin71bar
Instagram: @gin71bar
Twitter: @Gin71Bar

Opening hours:
Sunday-Thursday 1700-2300
Friday-Saturday 1700-0000

Other reasons to go: The Glasgow School of
Art, George Square, Glasgow Cathedral

Ella Carr writes: Gin71's three Glasgow branches are named after its original flagship on 71 Renfield Street (bottom left), which was Glasgow's first-ever dedicated gin bar. This branch is the prettiest of the three, located in a high-ceilinged listed building featuring enormous marble arches lined with Indian tiles: an elegant tea room by day, and a candle-lit gin bar by night. The other two branches resemble it little in decoration, but they all stock 71 gins at any one time, bringing in new gins on rotation as they're discovered by the knowledgable staff.

Their all-day gin bar is, rather eccentrically, located in the House of Fraser shopping mall on Buchanan street. With burnished gold-look walls, mismatched tassel lamps and jungle-theme decoration, it makes for an odd but cosy stop off. Isle of Harris' beautiful gin bottles (page 270) are used on each table as water bottles – an inspired touch. They also have a branch in Merchant City, around Ingram Street, where you'll also find The Gin Spa – you can treat yourself to a selection of massages and facials inspired by gin botanicals. Gin71 provides tasting dinners as part of The Gin Spa's package.

All three bars hold gin tastings, providing six perfect-serve gins and an introduction to gin's history. They also offer a comprehensive cocktail list, divided into Classics, Favourites, Modern and Martinis. I'd recommend the 'Martinez' made with Arbikie Kirsty's Gin (page 248), Cocchi di Tonno, Maraschino Liqueur and Bitters. This is a little-known ancestor of the Martini, perfect for novice gin drinkers. Arbikie Gin, Scotland's first 'grain-to-bottle' gin made using Scottish botanicals, is a clear favourite throughout the menu.

Makar Gin and
The Glasgow Distillery Company

Glasgow

Distillery and tasting room

ESSENTIAL INFORMATION
Key botanicals (Makar Original Dry Gin):
   juniper, liquorice, cassia bark, black
   pepper, lemon, rosemary
Output: not disclosed
Location: 8 Deanside Road, Glasgow,
   G52 4XY
Telephone: 0141 404 7191
Email: info@glasgowdistillery.com
Website: www.glasgowdistillery.com
Facebook: www.facebook.com/
   glasgowdistillery
Instagram: @glasgowdistillery
Twitter: @GlasgowDC

Opening hours:
Monday-Sunday 0900-1800

Other reasons to go: Kelvingrove Park,
Kelvingrove Art Gallery and Museum,
Glasgow Cathedral

Ella Carr writes: After a century-long hiatus, Glasgow Distillery are on a mission to bring gin distilling back to the city – taking their name from the original Glasgow Distillery Company founded in 1770, back when Glasgow was a thrumming centre for trade, and Scotland was home to 150 licenced distilleries. The Great Depression in 1933 managed to decimate Glasgow's remaining distilleries, and while whisky made a comeback after the Second World War, gin distilling floundered in the wings.

Until 2011, that is, when founders Liam, Mike and Ian envisaged its renaissance: a new whisky and gin distillery in one (next page, top right). They teamed with Professor Michael Moss (an archivist at the University of Glasgow) to unearth the story of the original Glasgow Distillery Company, before opening in 2013.

Located in a run-down Glasgow suburb, their large industrial site isn't much to look at. They do a monthly tour in collaboration with a local brewery, and have a general five-year plan to construct a welcome centre/shop and bar, but this wouldn't be my first choice for a distillery experience. They are, by their own admission, much more focussed on the spirit itself, which they take mighty seriously – they are, for example, the only distillery in Britain with a full-time cooper on hand.

I went upstairs to sample their Makar range of gins (next page, bottom right), taking its name from the Scots word for craftsman, or 'maker'. First up is their juniper-led Makar Original Dry Gin (left, right-hand bottle), with hints of warm pepper spice and rosemary, followed by their more unusual cask-aged gins. Both →

of these are produced identically to the Original; one of them is then aged in a mulberry wood cask (previous page, bottom left, middle bottle), the other in an oak cask (previous page, bottom left, second bottle from right) to produce full-bodied gins that can be sipped straight, but are also rather good with ginger ale.

Makar Old Tom (previous page, bottom left, second bottle from left) is made by replacing the cassia and rosemary in the Original with honey, almond and orange for a sweeter gin. My surprise favourite was the Makar Cherry Gin (previous page, bottom left, left-hand bottle), made by soaking ripe cherries and pink peppercorns, before pressing them. The result is a relatively viscous spirit with hints of dried cherry and warming spice, surprisingly good paired with cheese.

Dine Restaurant and
The Travelling Gin Professor

Edinburgh

Bar

ESSENTIAL INFORMATION

Location: First Floor, 10 Cambridge Street, Edinburgh, EH1 2ED

Telephone: 01312 181818

Email: restaurant@dine.scot

Website: www.dineedinburgh.co.uk

Facebook: www.facebook.com/ DineEdinburgh

Instagram: @dineedinburgh

Twitter: @DineEdinburgh

Opening hours:
Monday-Thursday 1200-2300
Friday-Saturday 1200-0100
Sunday 1200-2100

Other reasons to go: Edinburgh Castle, Palace of Holyroodhouse, Arthur's Seat, Calton Hill, Usher Hall

*E*lla Carr writes: Don't be put off by the multiplex exterior: tucked behind Usher Hall, Dine shares a rather shabby building with Traverse Theatre. But once you've made it up the washed-out stairwell, you'll find a romantic, classical restaurant with a *faux* apple tree sprouting from its centre. Dine brasserie has already won awards for its menu featuring premium Scottish produce, but it was only in August 2017 that owner Paul turned his attention to adding a gin bar (bottom left).

For this, he brought in serious gin chops, for example Alessandro Borelli – aka The Travelling Gin Professor – who became a gin fanatic when he made his first pink gin in Italy. He bartended at the Sheraton Hotel in Milan before being transferred to its Edinburgh address. Here, he transformed their bar One Square (page 233) into one of Edinburgh's top gin bars, while also travelling the country as the Gin Prof on a mission to heighten awareness of craft gin.

Since my visit, Alessandro has left Dine, but his legacy remains – he designed the bar's Martini menu which offers sweet, sour, salty and bitter flavour categories, as well as a Martini Experience – your chance to become an expert in the supremely alcoholic cocktail. Over the course of two hours it includes a history of the Martini plus five different cocktails to taste, with bespoke garnishes. At the end, pupils get behind the bar to prepare their own signature Martini.

This gin bar is still in its infancy, and the interiors reflect that: leopard-print carpets and tired leather settees make it look a bit *faux* fancy. It still feels like an afterthought to the restaurant, but with an upcoming revamp and the launching of events such as Ginuary, owner Paul is hoping to develop it into something special in its own right.

Edinburgh Gin

Edinburgh
Distillery and bar

ESSENTIAL INFORMATION

Key botanicals (Edinburgh Gin): juniper, coriander, bitter orange, mulberry, lavender, pine, milk thistle

Output: not disclosed

Location: 1a Rutland Place, Edinburgh, EH1 2AD

Telephone: 0131 656 2810

Email: info@edinburghgin.com

Website: www.edinburghgin.com

Facebook: www.facebook.com/edinburghgin

Instagram: @edinburghgin

Twitter: @Edinburgh_Gin

Opening hours:
Monday-Sunday 0900-1645

Other reasons to go: Heads and Tales gin bar, Dean Village, The Edinburgh Dungeon, Edinburgh's lively bar scene

*E*lla Carr writes: Descend the stone steps on the corner of Edinburgh's Rutland Place and you'll find yourself in what is, by day, the Edinburgh Gin Distillery (and by night, Heads and Tales bar – page 230): an arched dungeon cellar leading into a steampunk lair, replete with sultry lighting, black panelling and velvet furnishings (opposite, top middle). It's an atmospheric setting in which to sit back and enjoy the Gin Connoisseur Experience. You hear the history of gin in Edinburgh from one of their lively tour guides, then a brief history of Edinburgh Gin itself (bottom left), founded by husband-wife team Alex and Jane Nicol in 2005, who quit their jobs to launch Spencerfield Spirits. They started out with whiskies, but the end-game was always going to be gin. Edinburgh Gin was launched in 2010 before the couple retired and sold the company to Ian Mcleod Distillers in 2016.

Visitors get a tour of the distillery in which two small stills named Flora and Caledonia (opposite, top left and bottom right) are tucked into a narrow, sauna-hot corridor at the back of the bar. These stills do the brunt of the work for EG's small batch gins, while their Classic Gin and core range is made in their second distillery, The Biscuit Factory, down the road in Leith.

The most exciting part of the experience is of course the tasting session, for which the group are taken into one of the cave-like alcoves laden with glistening bottles. It includes a perfect serve G&T made with their London Dry followed by several straight samples. These can vary but when I visited they included Edinburgh Gin Seaside, a satisfyingly sea-salty tipple made with Bladderwrack; and 1670, an

aromatic garden gin made in partnership with Edinburgh's Botanical Gardens, with a kick of Tasmanian Mountain Pepper, best served with a sprig of thyme. My favourite, however, was their navy-strength Cannonball. Made with twice the amount of juniper to create a thicker, whisky-like texture, it warms the mouth with hints of pepper – a real pleasure to sip neat. Finally, the group are invited to try two of EG's range of fruit gin liqueurs, which come in flavours such as Rhubarb & Ginger and Pomegranate & Rose. These didn't taste much like gin and are best added to sparkling wine.

The Gin Connoisseur experience is good value at £25: you'll leave feeling not a little giddy, with a free bottle of gin liqueur.

Heads and Tales

Edinburgh
Distillery and bar

ESSENTIAL INFORMATION

Key botanicals (Edinburgh Classic Gin): lime peel, orange peel, cobnut, lemongrass, mulberry, lavender, pine bud

Output: not disclosed

Location: 1A Rutland Place, Edinburgh, EH1 2AD

Telephone: 01316 562811

Email: info@headsandtalesbar.com

Website: www.headsandtalesbar.com

Facebook: www.facebook.com/ HeadsandTalesBar

Instagram: @headsandtalesbar

Twitter: @HaTGinBar

Opening hours:

Sunday-Thursday 1700-0100

Friday-Saturday 1700-0300

Other reasons to go: Auld Toun walking tours, Church of St John the Evangelist, Royal Scots Regimental Museum

Ella Carr writes: Edinburgh Gin's microdistillery (page 228) by day becomes Heads and Tales bar by night (or rather, from 5 pm onwards). Tucked away in the basement of the Rutland Hotel, styled as a sort of steampunk speakeasy, this is in many ways the perfect Edinburgh bolt hole. With blacked out mirrors and lush velvet and leather armchairs, there are plenty of cosy candle-lit corners to settle into, and the bar has the added charm of sharing space with the distillery – Flora and Caledonia, Edinburgh Gin's two stills, glow behind two neon-illuminated screens (bottom left).

Alternatively you can reserve a booth – one of the cave-like alcoves in the corridor – where Edinburgh Gin hold their gin tastings. With their hint of Edinburgh Gothic, these are ideal for bigger parties wanting to get in the mood for a night out.

Heads and Tales do their own Gin Masterclasses. They include a history of the spirit, with a sampling of four gins with tonics, while also learning how to make a perfect serve. There's a fairly comprehensive menu of gins to guzzle through, though it feels a little rude not to go for the gin in residence (I recommend Edinburgh Gin's navy strength Cannonball). There's also talk of a Heads and Tales Edinburgh Gin collaboration.

But above all, this is a late night joint and it's the cocktails you should seek out. I recommend Losing Days, a combination of Hayman's Old Tom, peach, orgeat, dandelion and burdock bitters, citrus and tonic; or, for something truly off centre, Imperial Haar, made with Jinzu Gin, Umeshu Japanese liqueur, plum and vanilla, cherry bitters, lemon and ginger tea, and a citric acid solution.

The Jolly Botanist

Edinburgh
Bar

ESSENTIAL INFORMATION
Location: 256-260 Morrison Street,
    Edinburgh, EH3 8DT
Telephone: 01312 285596
Email: info@thejollybotanist.co.uk
Website: www.thejollybotanist.co.uk
Facebook: www.facebook.com/
    The-Jolly-Botanist
Instagram: @thejollybotanist
Twitter: @jolly_botanist

Opening hours:
Sunday-Thursday 1000-0000
Friday-Saturday 1000-0100

Other reasons to go: St Mary's Cathedral,
Edinburgh Castle, Gladstone Memorial,
Edinburgh International Conference Centre

Ella Carr writes: Sandwiched between Haymarket Station and Edinburgh's International Conference Centre, The Jolly Botanist (bottom left) opened four years ago as an after-work watering hole for the area's professionals, and first port for arrivals at the station. As such, the bar doesn't offer the most attractive Edinburgh street views, but its artful ramshackle interior is appealing: walls hung with mismatched mirrors and old prints alternate between exposed brick and washed-out Tuscan-yellow plaster. The ground level revolves around a handsome wooden bar, with plenty of comfy leather settees to sink into with a G&T. The slightly raised level at the back – their gin palace of sorts, with floor-length windows and a Georgian cornice – is especially cosy.

When PG Taverns bought the bar they scoured the globe to assemble an exotic collection of gins, which currently stands at 87. I tried some of the bar's favourites, including Drumshanbo Gunpowder Irish Gin (which uses Gunpowder Tea as a key botanical, distilled in medieval copper pot stills – page 306), as well as Monkey 47, which famously uses 47 botanicals. Unsurprisingly the Scottish gins also do well with customers, in particular Edinburgh Gin (page 228) and its edgier alternative Electric Spirit. The menu is impressively comprehensive and informative, including the brand, region, style, tonic and garnish of each gin. To increase the choice, the bartenders also mix a cocktail of the week. I'd recommend the 'Gin Thyme', a heady concoction of Gin Mare, St Germain, basil, black pepper, olive brine, toasted thyme and egg white.

Juniper

Edinburgh

Bar

ESSENTIAL INFORMATION
Location: 20 Princes Street, Edinburgh,
   EH2 2AN
Telephone: 01316 527370
Email: kirsty@twentyprincesstreet.co.uk
Website: www.juniperedinburgh.co.uk
Facebook: www.facebook.com/
   JuniperEdinburgh
Instagram: @juniperedinburgh
Twitter: @JuniperEdin

Opening hours:
Sunday-Thursday 1200-2330
Friday-Saturday 1200-0030

Other reasons to go: Scott Monument,
Royal Yacht Britannia, The Edinburgh
Dungeon, The Scotsman Hotel

Ella Carr writes: While other Edinburgh gin bars have gone down the speakeasy route, Juniper defines itself as a sophisticated cocktail bar, with blacked out mirror walls, foliage installations and a flashy silver-and-black panelled bar (bottom left). By comparison, their sleek shiny surfaces lack character, but there's a decent view on to Princes Street, the Scotsman Hotel and the Scott Monument – a snippet of Edinburgh's main sites, as well as its main thoroughfares. It's on the building's first floor.

Their gin count is a respectable 54, many sourced from local distilleries. Bartender Thomas (top right), who originally worked at Heads and Tales (page 230) – one of Edinburgh's premier gin bars – recommends I go for G-Vine, a French gin made from grapes and vine blossoms. But, really, it's the cocktails you should try. My favourite was Kwai Thai – with Ancho Reyes, chilli liqueur, Aluna coconut, Kwai Fei lychee liqueur, lime, sugar and lemongrass. If you're feeling theatrical, opt for 'Strawberries & Steam', a strawberry-infused Brokers gin cocktail that comes with dry ice for effect.

The bar is bang opposite Waverley station, meaning you could kill time before your train with a *bon voyage* gin cocktail – but really it's a night-time joint, ideal for pre-drinks before hitting the tiles.

One Square

Edinburgh
Bar and gin school

ESSENTIAL INFORMATION

Key botanicals (One Square Gin): juniper, coriander, liquorice, cardamom, cinnamon, star anise, lemon, lime, grapefruit, cloves, fennel, Scottish heather, bog-myrtle

Output: 728 bottles a year

Location: Sheraton Grand Hotel and Spa, 1 Festival Square, Edinburgh, EH3 9SR

Telephone: 01312 216422

Email: info@onesquareedinburgh.co.uk

Website: www.onesquareedinburgh.co.uk

Facebook: www.facebook.com/ OneSquareEdinburgh

Instagram: @onesquareedinburgh

Twitter: @OneSq

Opening hours:
Monday-Friday 0630-0100
Saturday-Sunday 0700-0100

Other reasons to go: Usher Hall

Ella Carr writes: This is the bar of the formidable Sheraton Grand Hotel and Spa in Edinburgh's Festival Square. It's slightly tainted by the stuffy grandeur typical of a grand hotel bar: tinkling muzak, shiny surfaces and well above-average prices. While you might prefer the off-centre character of Edinburgh's other gin bars, One Square (bottom left) nevertheless has a solid reputation when it comes to gin. This is partly because it was one of the first original gin bars in the city, with a respectable collection of 90 gins – but mostly because of its Gin Experience, the 'Ginnasium', in tandem with One Square's launch of its own-brand gin. At £35 per person (surprisingly fair value), the Experience includes a tasting of four gins paired with tonics, a demonstration of the gin-making process by the resident gin expert, and the opportunity to make your own miniature One Square Gin to take home.

The bar's own gin was launched in 2015 in partnership Summerhall Distillery (page 234). It also makes a 'globetrotting' gin incorporating 15 botanicals from around the world (a nod to Edinburgh's port of Leith, with its long history of global trade) plus the defiant Scottish twist of heather and bog-myrtle. The gin is made using the one-shot method (page 68) to produce a clean, citrusy London Dry. The aroma is fresh and zesty with hints of star anise, the taste on the tongue is gently juniper with a pleasant sweetness and the finish is warm and dry. Best served with grapefruit peel and a sprig of thyme. I also liked the classic gold-flecked bottle, sealed with gold wax.

Pickering's Gin and Summerhall Distillery

Edinburgh
Distillery and bar

ESSENTIAL INFORMATION
Key botanicals (Pickering's Gin): juniper, coriander, cardamom, lemon, lime, star anise, clove, fennel
Output: 438,000 bottles a year
Location: Summerhall, Edinburgh, EH9 1PL
Telephone: 0131 290 2901
Email: enquiries@pickeringsgin.com; tours@pickeringsgin.com
Website: www.pickeringsgin.com
Facebook: www.facebook.com/Pickeringsgin
Instagram: @pickeringsgin
Twitter: @pickeringsgin

Opening hours:
Distillery shop
Monday-Friday 0900-1700
Saturday-Sunday 1100-1800

Other reasons to go: Summerhall, The Queen's Hall, National Museum of Scotland

Ella Carr writes: Pickering's robust and spicy gin comes with an equally robust backstory – ever more important if a craft gin wants to stand out from the crowd. For starters, the distillery building (bottom left) was home to The Royal Dick Veterinary College of Edinburgh University between 1917 and 2011, and still bears the signs of 95 years of wear and tear – cat cages remain to this day stacked behind the stills, and until recently there were dog kennels in the bottling room. In 2012 Matthew Gammel and Marcus Pickering were brought in by the new owner – and founder of the abutting Royal Dick pub (opposite, top left) – to advise on transforming the rickety old building. Despite only ever distilling gins as a hobby, the pair spotted an opportunity.

The plan got legs when, in 2012, Marcus' father died and his old Indian friend got in touch, offering condolences and bequeathing them his old family recipe for gin, handed down over generations. They received it in the post on a scrap of brown paper dated 1947, which now hangs framed in the distillery. The list of ingredients didn't come with any indication of quantity needed, so there was a laborious process of recipe development before they hit upon their 'red top' Pickering's Gin: a spicy yet smooth gin, with a hint of sweetness. In fact, the recipe listed nine pretty standard gin botanicals, such as coriander, fennel, cinnamon and star anise, but it's not a bad story, and the spice-oriented gin certainly deserves its 'Bombay style' tagline.

When Matt and Marcus launched Pickering's in 2014 they unwittingly made history, establishing the first exclusive gin distillery in Edinburgh for more than 150 years. They quit their day jobs and went

into distilling full time, turning Summerhall Distillery into a serious operation, producing 1,200 bottles a day. However, Pickering's is still bottled, corked and labelled on the premises, and the nicely shaped bottles made from quality glass – Matt was previously in the glass and crystal industry.

Because of the building and the gin's colourful history, Summerhall Distillery offers a compelling gin tour to visitors. It begins with a G&T in the eclectically decorated Royal Dick pub after which a spirited tour guide reels off the Pickering's story and makes introductions to their two stills, Gertrude (above right) and Emily. Then you get a generous tasting of some of Pickering's favourites, including Pickering's Gin (called 'red top' for its wax seal), as well as Pickering's Original 1947 Gin, which follows the Bombay recipe even more precisely, and boosts the cardamon for an extra spicy kick. Next you'll try Pickering's Navy Strength (above right) which comes with a little fluffy hat for the bottle, and a serious kick from its 57% strength. Afterwards, browse their extensive special editions, including Pickering's Gin with Scottish Botanicals and Pickering's sloe. During the festive season they also do Pickering's Gin Baubles (right) – one of their most popular items.

Secret Garden Gin and The Old Curiosity Distillery

Edinburgh
Distillery and café

ESSENTIAL INFORMATION

Key botanicals (Secret Garden Apothecary Rose Gin): juniper, coriander, winter savory, Apothecary rose

Output: 12,000 bottles a year

Location: 32A Old Pentland Road, Edinburgh, EH10 7EA

Telephone: 01312 856833

Email: info@theoldcuriosity.co.uk

Website: www.theoldcuriosity.co.uk

Facebook: www.facebook.com/oldcuriositydistillery

Instagram: @oldcuriosity

Twitter: @OldCuriosity_

Opening hours:
Monday-Friday 0900-1700
Saturday-Sunday bookings only

Other reasons to go: Edinburgh Castle, Royal Mile, Arthur's Seat, National Museum of Scotland

*E*lla Carr writes: As often happens, Hamish Martin's (opposite, top right) road to distilling gin was indirect and almost entirely accidental. He and his wife Liberty opened Secret Herb Garden in 2014 – a specialist herb nursery at the foot of the Pentland hills, just outside Edinburgh – which combined his passion for herbalism with her dream of opening a café and shop full of vintage furniture, wine and beer. It was only after the council threatened to revoke their wedding licence that they turned to gin as a way to fund their garden. Success quickly followed after the alcohol buyer for M&S tried one of their herbal gins at a wedding, and invited them to make the brand's British Rose Colour Changing Gin. The Old Curiosity Distillery's own range of colour-changing gins now includes Apothecary Rose (bottom left), Lavender and Echinacea (opposite, bottom right), and Chamomile and Cornflower.

Gins may have started as a sideline, but Hamish's success as a distiller is not surprising. Before getting an MSc in herbology and opening his herb garden, he founded the acclaimed wine merchant Inverarity Vaults (sold on as Inverarity Morton). His gins stand out from the crowd because of their colour-changing properties, achieved with herbs which Hamish and Liberty grow, dry and harvest themselves.

The gin project is still relatively new, but Hamish has ambitious plans. At the back of the garden, rows of juniper plants are beginning to rear their heads for harvesting, while the 700 different types of herbs and flowers in the garden promise huge scope for flavour experimentation. As we went to press, tours and tasting classes were under way – see their website.

And, of course, it's not just about the gin. The 7.5 acres of herb garden (above), bordered by native hedgerows and a gentle stream, are a joy to visit in their own right. The Glasshouse – a wonderful canopied greenhouse furnished with antique furniture – is a great spot to eat seasonal food. Next to the herb drying room Hamish holds classes in herb-growing, bee-keeping, candle-making and foraging. To complete the bucolic scene, there's a baby animals pen, and pigs and geese wandering around freely. Children will be easily distracted while you enjoy the lovely herbal gin.

South Loch Gin and 56 North bar

Edinburgh
Distillery and bar

ESSENTIAL INFORMATION

Key botanicals (Juniper, Citrus and Lime Flower Gin): juniper, lemon peel, orange, grapefruit, pink peppercorn, lime flower, sichuan pepper

Output: not disclosed

Location: 2 West Crosscauseway, Edinburgh, EH8 9JP

Telephone: 01316 628860

Email: info@fiftysixnorth.co.uk

Website: www.fiftysixnorth.co.uk

Facebook: www.facebookcom/56edinburgh

Instagram: @56northedinburgh

Twitter: @fiftysixnorth

Opening hours:
Monday-Sunday 1100-0100

Other reasons to go: Five Sisters Zoo, Linlithgow Palace, Bo'ness and Kinneil Railway, National Museum of Scotland

Ella Carr writes: Despite its dated interior decoration (opposite, bottom right) and unassuming location (near Edinburgh University's main buildings) this is definitely the place for gin fanatics – and has gained a steady reputation as such since opening its doors ten years ago, back when gin was relatively unfashionable. Owner James has amassed a whopping range of 400 gins – which can claim to be the largest collection in Scotland.

The menu is a veritable gin bible. As well as the usual Spicy, Herbal and Floral chapters, there are sections devoted to Oriental Spice & Teas; Scottish Botanicals; Colour Changing Gins and Grain to Bottle gins. Among the exotic and the experimental are, of course, a comprehensive range of Scottish gins. If you can't make up your mind, there's a spinning wheel (bottom left) to make the decision for you.

In the last couple of years the bar has produced its own 56 North Gins, made in the two stills on display in the bar (opposite, top left and right). The range is currently only served in the bar, but will give birth to a new brand – as we went to press, South Loch (named after the loch in Edinburgh which was drained in the 1770s to make way for The Meadows park) was due to be launched in June 2019. The gin, James stresses, won't become more important than the bar, it will just give him some creative freedom. Master Distiller, Lindsay Blair, brought over from Daffy's, will mastermind production.

They give their signature product, a 42% Juniper, Citrus and Lime Flower Gin, a local connection by saying it's inspired by the limes that grow in The Meadows park. In fact, they flavour it with bought-in lime

flowers and citrus fruits. The second gin will be Black Raspberry Old Tom, a sweeter gin infused with black and pink Scottish raspberries which give it a pink hue.

During my visit, I opted for a G&T with 56 North Woodland & Ocean gin, chosen because of its especially Scottish profile: botanicals include dandelion burdock, nettle, meadowsweet, pine resin, heather, elderflower and orange blossom. It is wonderfully piny herbaceous, perfectly lifted with a sprig of rosemary.

Come here for ginducation, either by attending a masterclass or a gin tasting. Or simply work your way through the reasonably priced menu.

NB Gin and Distillery

North Berwick, East Lothian
Distillery

ESSENTIAL INFORMATION

Key botanicals (NB London Dry Gin):
   juniper, coriander seed, cardamom, grains
   of paradise, cassia bark, lemon peel
Output: 16,000 bottles a year
Location: Halflandbarns, North Berwick,
   EH39 5PW
Telephone: 01620 894744
Email: sales@nbgin.com
Website: www.nbdistillery.com
Facebook: www.facebook.com/NBDistillery
Instagram: @nb_distillery
Twitter: @NB_Distillery

Opening hours:
Distillery
Monday-Friday 1000-1600
The Connoisseur Tour (booking required)
Friday 1700-1900
Saturday 1400-1600
Taster Tour
Wednesday-Thursday at 1130, 1330 and 1530
Friday at 1130

**Other reasons to go: Scottish Seabird
Centre, Tantallon Castle, Seacliff Beach**

NB Gin was launched in 2013 by husband and wife team Steve and Viv Muir, both lawyers. They secured a distiller's licence in 2011 and started experimenting in their kitchen, infusing botanicals and water in a pressure cooker to see which flavour combinations worked best. They enlisted the help of Charles Maxwell of Thames Distillers to help with the recipe, and once finalized, bought a proper still, which was later replaced by another, custom built in London. At first they distilled in batches of 100 litres, but they now produce around 16,000 bottles a year.

NB Gin (bottom left, middle bottle) is made from 100% British neutral grain spirit, using the one-shot distillation method (page 68). The result is a 42% London Dry-style gin that works well with Fever-Tree tonic and a slice of lime. They also produce a Navy Strength Gin (bottom left, left-hand bottle) at 57%.

In April 2018, Steve and Viv moved the distillery to a small premises in North Berwick (where the brand gets its name). Here, they offer experiences such as The Connoisseur Tour where you learn about their production process and the history of the brand. You also taste their gins, vodka and rum, then snack on canapés with a drink of your choice. This tour must be booked in advance and is held on Fridays from 5 pm and Saturdays from 2 pm. It lasts around two hours and costs £36 – see the website for booking information. For half the price, you can join the drop-in Taster Tour, held on Thursdays at 11.30 pm, 1.30 pm and 3.30 pm. This experience lasts an hour and includes a distillery tour and a brief talk on their London Dry distillation process.

Persie Gin and Distillery

Bridge of Cally, Perthshire
Distillery and bar

ESSENTIAL INFORMATION
Key botanicals (Persie Zesty Citrus Gin):
 juniper, lime, orange zest
Output: not disclosed
Location: Glenshee Road (A93), Bridge of
 Cally, PH10 7LQ
Telephone: 01250 886798
Email: snifter@persiedistillery.com
Website: www.persiedistillery.com
Facebook: www.facebook.com/persiegin
Instagram: @persiegin
Twitter: @PersieGin

Opening hours:
Saturday-Thursday 1200-1800

Other reasons to go: Glasclune Castle, River
Ardle, Loch of Clunie

David T. Smith writes: Persie Distillery (bottom left and next page, bottom left) is in the Scottish Highlands, housed in an old coaching inn 25 miles N of Perth. This distillery is a warm and cosy space with a small bar and can cater for groups of up to 20 people. From the tasting room (next page, bottom right), visitors have a great view of the distillery's gleaming Mueller still, as well as the original brickwork of the building behind. In the tasting room, they can find out more about the gin-making process, including learning about different botanicals and how flavours and aromas interact with one another. Visitors then get the chance to taste the standard Persie gin range (next page, top left), as well as a selection of spirits exclusive to the distillery's tasting room.

Persie Distillery was founded by Simon Fairclough, who had previously worked in media and marketing, including some work with Scottish distilleries in the 1980s. Whilst deciding upon an approach to his own gin, he observed that distillers tended to fall into two groups: those who developed a spirit based simply upon flavour, and those who tried to capture the essence of the distillery's locality. Simon, however, chose a third way: he decided to investigate what combinations of flavours appeal most to gin drinkers. The tastings and gin-themed events that he set up for this purpose quickly became Gin Club Scotland, which has now run hundreds of events and helped people sample thousands of shots of gin.

Simon's research helped him to identify three popular areas of aroma and flavour, which formed the basis of the distillery's inaugural launch of gins: Zesty Citrus Gin (the best seller – next page, top left, third

bottle from left), Herby & Aromatic Gin (above, third bottle from right), and Sweet & Nutty Old Tom (above, second bottle from right), first launched in 2016.

In 2018, the distillery released a new limited edition range of gins in partnership with Perthshire Abandoned Dogs Society (PADS), each one focusing on a different dog breed. The gins aim to capture the characteristics of each breed: Labrador (top left, left-hand bottle) is traditional and mellow, Spaniel (top left, right-hand bottle) is spicy and spirited, and Dachshund Lime Gin Liqueur (top left, second bottle from left) is sweet and sharp. For every bottle sold, £1 is donated to dog rescue charities.

McQueen Gin and Trossachs Distillery

Callander, Perthshire
Distillery

ESSENTIAL INFORMATION

Key botanicals (McQueen Super Premium Dry Gin): juniper, grains of paradise, lime, grapefruit, vanilla

Output: 250,000+ bottles a year

Location: The Barn, Upper Drumbane, Callander, FK17 8LR

Telephone: 01877 339929

Email: info@mcqueengin.co.uk

Website: www.mcqueengin.co.uk

Facebook: www.facebook.com/mcqueengin

Instagram: @mcqueengin

Twitter: @McQueenGin

Opening hours:
Monday-Friday 1000-1700

Other reasons to go: Bracklinn Falls Bridge, Loch Lubnaig, St Kessog's Church, The Trossachs National Park

Ella Carr writes: Some craft gins are 'me too', using a line-up of much the same ten botanicals, and can end up tasting pretty similar. When husband and wife Dale and Vicky McQueen (bottom left with First Minister Nicola Sturgeon) founded their brand in 2015, they wanted to stand out.

Alongside Super Premium Dry (next page, top left, left-hand bottle), their range has to date included: Sweet Citrus (next page, top left, middle bottle); Chocolate Mint; Mocha; Spiced Chocolate Orange, Forest Fruits (next page, top left, right-hand bottle) and Smokey Chilli. These flavours are pre-distilled instead of added. The result is pure and balanced rather than sickly or overbearing – belying their sweet and sticky names. Chocolate Mint leads with juniper and mint, before ending with a surprisingly savoury chocolate finish. Mocha is full bodied with notes of dark roasted coffee – almost medicinal in its richness, and very aromatic. Smokey Chilli is fiery and warm, without being too spicy. The title flavours of each gin are at once recognizable and surprising. Perfect for the adventurous gin drinker who wants to branch out from London Dry.

McQueen's gins are also useful for cocktail experiments. Try pairing Chocolate Mint with crème de menthe, or making Mocha the base for an Espresso Martini. Their strength of character means they're also excellent sipping gins.

Propelled by a flurry of awards Dale and Vicky are expanding. In 2019 they launched their new distillery (next page, middle), which they hope will increase production by more than 1,000 per cent. They also recently exchanged the original ceramic bottle for a glass one, which they

→

feel reflects the purity of their methods.

The distillery is at Callander, the gateway town to Loch Lomond, in the Trossachs National Park. They hold distillery tours every weekday at 2.30 pm, charging £15 per person, including tastings as well as the opportunity to buy bottles at a £5 discount. Weekend tours are bookable on request – see the website.

Left: bridge over the River Teith in Callander, where Trossachs Distillery is based.

Verdant Gin and Verdant Spirit Co.

Dundee

Distillery, shop and gin school

ESSENTIAL INFORMATION

Key botanicals (Verdant Gin): juniper, coriander seed, liquorice, green cardamom, cassia bark, grains of paradise, lemon peel, bitter orange

Output: not disclosed

Location: Edward Street Mill, Forest Park Place, Dundee, DD1 5NT

Telephone: 01382 220426

Email: info@verdantspirits.co.uk

Website: www.verdantspirits.co.uk

Facebook: www.facebook.com/ VerdantSpirits

Instagram: @verdantspirits

Twitter: @verdantspirits

Opening hours:

Monday-Friday 0900-1700

Other reasons to go: Broughty Castle Museum, Verdant Works, Camperdown Wildlife Centre, The McManus Dundee's Art Gallery and Museum, The V&A Dundee

*D*avid T. Smith writes: A short walk from Scotland's longest river, The Tay, is Dundee's first gin distillery: Verdant Spirits. The distillery was founded in 2014 by Andrew Mackenzie, who had previously worked in creative and educational roles at the nearby University of Dundee and the McLaren Formula One team.

The distillery is located near the heart of the city, around a 20-minute walk from Dundee railway station and takes its name from the nearby Verdant Works, which contained a jute mill during the height of the city's textile boom. Today, the mill building houses a jute museum, whilst nearby, in the engine house for an adjacent mill, sits Verdant Spirits. The Grade-A listed building was built in 1890 and, as of 2019, will also house the distillery's visitors' centre.

The visitors' centre will have a space for tutored tastings and other gin-related events, as well as a shop. It will also be home to Verdant Spirits' one-day Gin School, where attendees can learn about the history and production of gin, and explore the world of botanicals and the flavours and aromas that they impart to spirits. Sessions will culminate in participants devising their own recipe and using it to produce a bottle of their own gin to take home.

Verdant Gin (left), the core product, was launched in 2017 and designed to be a London Dry Gin with a classic, yet refreshing style. The choice of botanicals was inspired by the route used by the trading ships that sailed to and from Dundee in years gone by. In 2019, Verdant Spirits added to their spirits range when they launched their first unaged rum.

Gin Bothy Distillery and Gin

Glamis, Angus
Distillery, shop and tasting rooms

ESSENTIAL INFORMATION
Key botanicals (Gin Bothy Original):
    juniper, rosemary, heather, hawthorn
    root, milk thistle, Scots pine needle
Output: 3,000 bottles a year
Location: Kirk Wynd, Glamis, DD8 1RT
Telephone: 01575 570111
Email: info@ginbothy.co.uk
Website: www.ginbothy.co.uk
Facebook: www.facebook.com/theginbothy
Instagram: @theginbothy
Twitter: @TheGinBothy

Opening hours:
Bothy Experience, Larder Shop and
    Tasting Rooms
Thursday-Sunday 1100-1700
Tastings must be booked in advance

Other reasons to go: Glamis Castle, St
Fergus's Well, Ark Hill, Meffan Institute

Kim Cameron founded Gin Bothy on an ideal: making the most of what the land has to offer. Its location in the foothills of the Angus Glens is ideal for this endeavour, ideal for Kim and her team of foragers to find local botanicals such as pine needles, heather, milk thistle and hawthorn for use in their signature spirit, Gin Bothy Original (opposite middle, second bottle from right). The resulting taste, smell and feel reflects the freshness of Scottish woodland.

Kim started her gin journey (under her mum's instructions) by infusing the leftover berry juice from her homemade and award-winning jam with a gin she bought in from another distillery. She soon became frustrated that she had no control over the final product, so she decided to make her own.

Kim recommends serving Gin Bothy Original with ice, tonic and a slice of fresh orange to bring out the citrus in the gin, or rosemary to enhance its herby features. As a cocktail pour, try mixing Bothy Original with thyme syrup, freshly squeezed lime juice, a dash of celery bitters and a sprig of rosemary to make a refreshing summer cocktail.

She also has a gin for winter: Gin Bothy Gunshot (opposite, middle, middle bottle) which is great as a sipping gin, or mixed with ginger ale or warm apple juice and an orange stuffed with cloves to make a terrific gin-based alternative to mulled wine.

And not forgetting her origins, Kim also produces fruit-infused gins which come in a variety of flavours – strawberry, raspberry, blueberry, rhubarb and sloe.

Gin Bothy is located outside Kirriemuir, known as the 'little red town', a reference to the reddish sandstone from which the town's older properties are built. Its

history dates back to the earliest recorded times when it appears to have been a major ecclesiastical centre, and later had a reputation for witchcraft. Some older houses still feature a 'witches stane' to ward off evil. The playwright J. M. Barrie, who created *Peter Pan*, was born and buried here and a statue of the boy who never grew up stands in the town square.

As we went to press, the bothy's tasting rooms (bottom right) in the nearby village of Glamis with two rooms: one taking up to 12 guests and the other 20 at a time. They also have a Bothy Experience (opposite, bottom left) where you can learn about the founding of Gin Bothy. As we went to press, the Experience was open Thursday to Sunday from 11 am to 5 pm. Tastings can be booked via email.

They also produce cider, jam, syrups and chutney, available to buy in their Bothy Larder shop (top left and right) in Glamis.

Bothy? A Scottish term for a hut, a small cottage or a temporary shelter. Kim sees Gin Bothy both as a refuge and the embodiment of Scottish heritage – so it's not a bad name.

Arbikie Gin and Distillery

Inverkeilor, Angus
Distillery

ESSENTIAL INFORMATION
Key botanicals (Kirsty's Gin): juniper,
   blaeberry, kelp, Carline thistle
Output: not disclosed
Location: Arbikie Highland Estate,
   Inverkeilor, Arbroath, DD11 4UZ
Telephone: 01241 830770
Email: info@arbikie.com
Website: www.arbikie.com
Facebook: www.facebook.com/arbikie
Instagram: @arbikiedistillery
Twitter: @Arbikie

Opening hours: opening 2020 – check
   website for updates

Brothers Iain, John and David Stirling founded Arbikie Distillery (opposite, top left) on their family estate in 2014, and claim it to be Scotland's first farm-to-bottle distillery – their working farm grows all the ingredients used in their products. The estate has been in the Stirling family for four generations, so the brothers grew up around farming but pursued different careers.

Iain worked in branding and was involved in a number of drinks organization projects. He was discussing how to make gin with a friend and had a *eureka* moment – he realized that, with the help of his brothers and a Master Distiller, they could make their own. They renovated an old cattle barn and the distillery was opened in autumn 2014 with a focus on sustainability – they use solar power throughout the distillation process and waste is recycled as cattle feed where possible.

Kirtsy's Gin (bottom left and opposite, middle) was Arbikie's second product, released in July 2015 and named after Master Distiller Kirsty Black, who developed the recipe over two years. Aware of juniper's endangered status, Arbikie grow their own which is distilled using the one-shot method (page 68) with their own vodka (made with potatoes from the farm) and the rest of the botanicals. The product is then cut with water from their underground lagoon (fed by water from the surrounding mountains). Kirsty recommends serving the gin with a quality tonic, a handful of blueberries and a lemon twist. It also works well in a Gimlet.

Launched to celebrate Burns Night in 2017 Arbikie's second gin, AK's Gin (opposite, bottom right), was named after their father, Alexander Kirkwood Stirling. The

gin is distilled using honey from their own beehives, plus black pepper, mace, cardamom and a wheat-based spirit (rather than potato) in order to create its buttery character. Arbikie recommends serving this with ice, ginger beer and a lime or orange wedge.

The gins can be bought from the online shop. As we went to press, Arbikie were hoping to open the distillery to visitors some time in 2020, when visitors will be able to drive through the fields to the car park – getting the full farm-to-bottle experience having then had a tour of the distillery. A café/restaurant is also planned, serving local produce such as bread, cakes and coffee.

Eden Mill Gin and Distillery

St Andrews, Fife
Distillery and gin school

ESSENTIAL INFORMATION
**Key botanicals (Golf Gin): juniper, heather,
    pine needle, gorse flower, seaweed**
Output: 30,000+ bottles a year
**Location: Main Street, Guardbridge, St
    Andrews, KY16 0UU**
Telephone: 01334 834038
Email: hello@edenmill.com
Website: www.edenmill.com
**Facebook: www.facebook.com/
    edenmillstandrews**
Instagram: @edenmill
Twitter: @EdenMill

Opening hours:
Monday-Sunday 1030-1730

**Other reasons to go: St Andrews Castle, St
Andrews Cathedral, British Golf Museum,
St Andrews Aquarium**

David T. Smith writes: Eden Mill Distillery and Brewery (opposite, top left) is located in the village of Guardbridge, close to the town of St Andrews in Fife, famous as the spiritual home of golf, and Scotland's oldest university. The distillery sits alongside the River Eden, namesake for both the distillery and its brands of whisky and gin.

The history of distilling in Guardbridge began in 1810, when the Haig Family opened Seggie Distillery. This closed in 1860, becoming a paper mill that continued to operate until 2008. Two years later, the site was purchased by St Andrews University and, in 2012, Paul Miller opened Eden Brewery, before expanding into distilling in 2014. Paul had been in the wine and spirits industry for over 30 years, having previously worked at Oddbins, Diageo, and Glenmorangie.

Eden Mill Distillery launched its first gin in 2014: Hop Gin, made using Australian galaxy hops. This was followed by Eden Mill Original Gin (bottom left) in 2014. Other gins in the core range include Golf Gin, an oaked gin, and Love Gin.

The distillery periodically releases seasonal gins such as Summer Punch Gin and even Candy Cane Gin. They have also created gins in collaboration with local sports teams, as well as a range of gin liqueurs, and ready-to-drink gin cocktails.

As we went to press, Eden Mill were constructing a new distillery and visitors' centre adjacent to its current location. This will include a café and bar, tasting facilities, and a shop, as well as private function rooms.

In addition to the main distillery, Eden Mill run two satellite operations known as the Blendworks Gin Schools. One is located

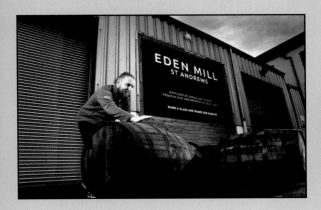

in the Rusacks Hotel, St Andrews and the other in Princes Square, Glasgow. The Glasgow site is also home to Eden Mill's JAX restaurant and bar. The Gin Schools enable visitors to find out about the flavours and aromas of gin before blending their own from a variety of botanical distillates.

Besides gin, Eden Mill produce single malt and blended Scotch whiskies and the Brewery makes a range of ales and beers.

Stirling Gin and Distillery

Stirling
Distillery, shop and visitors' centre

ESSENTIAL INFORMATION

Key botanicals (Stirling Gin): juniper, dried lemon peel, dried orange peel, Stirlingshire nettle, dried basil

Output: not disclosed

Location: The Old Smiddy, 9 Lower Castlehill, Stirling, FK8 1EN

Telephone: 01786 596496

Email: hello@stirlinggin.co.uk

Website: www.stirlinggin.co.uk

Facebook: www.facebook.com/Stirlinggin

Instagram: @stirling.gin

Twitter: @StirlingGin

Opening hours:
Monday-Sunday from 1000

Other reasons to go: Stirling Castle, The National Wallace Monument, The Stirling Smith Art Gallery and Museum, Cambuskenneth Abbey

Cameron and June McCann (opposite, middle) developed their love for gin while simultaneously running a spirit shop in the Stirling Highland Hotel and the Stirling Gin Festival. Craft gin had just taken off and Cameron wanted to make a gin that represented Central Scotland. In October 2015, on their 26th wedding anniversary, the couple celebrated by distilling their first bottle of Stirling Gin (opposite, top right) in their kitchen, on a 2.4-litre copper still called Jinty.

They started by distilling botanicals separately to get to know their individual qualities, and then blended them together until they found their recipe – after around 50 tries. The gin became so popular with the locals that they approached the Glasgow Distillery Co. (page 225) for help to increase production.

To make Stirling Gin, the nettle and basil are placed in a basket at the top of the still to be vapour infused (page 254), while the rest of the botanicals are distilled using the one-shot method (page 68). The product is then cut with water to 43%.

Stirling Gin is the base for all the products in their range including Battle Strength Gin, inspired by the battle of Stirling Bridge, at 55%. Their Folklore Collection is a range of gin liqueurs inspired by the myths surrounding Stirling Castle such as the Green Lady ghost and the Red Cap goblin (opposite, bottom left). All can be bought from the online shop.

Determined to maintain the local and artisanal spirit of their gins, on the 1st of June 2019, they expanded into a new distillery at the foot of Stirling Castle in a 19thC church temperance hall known as 'The Old Smiddy' (left). Legend has it that King

James V stabled his horses here in the 16thC.

The new distillery (above) has a visitors' centre, shop and wild flower garden and hosts tours, tastings, masterclasses, and drinks education and training. They can also be found at events such as the Gin Fayre, which runs throughout the year in various locations around Scotland – see the website for more information.

Lussa Gin

Ardlussa, Isle of Jura
Distillery

ESSENTIAL INFORMATION

Key botanicals (Lussa Gin): juniper, coriander seed, lemon balm leaf, lemon thyme, water mint, elderflower, rosehip, wild rose, lime flower, honeysuckle, Scots pine, bog-myrtle, ground elder leaf, sea lettuce

Output: 8,000 bottles a year

Location: The Stables, Ardlussa, PA60 7XW

Telephone: 01496 820196

Email: contact@lussagin.com

Website: www.lussagin.com

Facebook: www.facebook.com/lussagin

Instagram: @lussagin

Twitter: @LussaGin

Opening hours: tours by appointment only

Other reasons to go: Gulf of Corryvreckan, Paps of Jura

Ella Carr writes: The Isle of Jura, off Scotland's west coast, really is remote. Overshadowed by its mountain range, The Paps of Jura, it has a human population of 230, outnumbered by 6,000 red deer. Just 20 people live in and around Ardlussa on the northern coast, where Lussa Gin (bottom left and opposite, top right and middle) is made, reached via a 25-mile single track from Jura's ferry port. It's no wonder that George Orwell, who wrote *1984* on Jura's northern tip, called it the most 'un-get-at-able' place in the world.

Lussa's founders Alicia, Claire and Georgina (opposite, top left) were seduced by its pristine beauty and isolation. Their gin is as much a reflection of the resilience needed to live on the island as it is of Jura's unique natural setting. All 15 of Lussa's botanicals are painstakingly foraged from nearby glens, lochs, bogs and seas: the unique setting makes for a unique botanical profile, among them bog-myrtle, sea lettuce, ground elder and Scots pine.

The botanicals are distilled in Hamish, their traditional 200-litre Portuguese hand-crafted copper still (opposite, top left). Leaves, needles, cones and roots are added to the pot along with the neutral spirit and spring water from the Ardlussa hills, while the flowers and petals are vapour infused. They are suspended in a column above the pot, giving their flavour and aroma to the vapour as it passes. The mix is then warmed using a bain-marie, and the spirit is gently distilled over the course of a day.

Unusually for a British gin, even the orris root and juniper berries are locally grown. Juniper has grown in Scotland since the last ice age, but is currently under threat from disease. Jura's remoteness has spared the

juniper somewhat, and the girls are trying
to help it along by planting 500 bushes
around Lussa Glen. They should be ready
for harvest in 2022.

   The distillery (bottom) holds tours
by appointment for anyone adventurous
enough to make the journey. However,
there's plenty on Jura to make the journey
worthwhile. Aside from the thrill of visiting
one of Scotland's (perhaps even Europe's)
last true wildernesses, the island is also
scattered with relics from its Stone Age
and Mesolithic past, and host to a dizzying
array of wildlife – including golden eagles,
sea eagles, hen harriers, owls, adders, grey
seals, dolphins and porpoises.

Inshriach Gin and Distillery

Aviemore, Scottish Highlands
Distillery and bar

ESSENTIAL INFORMATION
Key botanicals (Inshriach Gin): juniper,
rosehip, fir needle
Output: 3,000 bottles a year
Location: Inshriach House, Aviemore,
    PH22 1QP
Telephone: 01540 651341
Email: walter@inshriachgin.com
Website: www.inshriachgin.com
Facebook: www.facebook.com/
    Inshriachdistillery
Instagram: @inshriach
Twitter: @Inshriach

Opening hours: open days once a month –
    see Facebook page for more information

Other reasons to go: Strathspey Steam
Railway, Rothiemurchus, Loch an Eilein

Walter Micklethwait's (opposite, top right) grandparents bought the beautiful small Highland estate of Inshriach in 1970. When they died Walter and his mother Lucy bought out a couple of aunts who had inherited, piling up debt. To make the place viable, they had to be resourceful. The main house was let and Walter built a yurt, a shepherd's hut, a bothy and converted an old army lorry into a camper, all for holiday rentals. Local TV took an interest in his imaginative building work, especially The Shed (bottom left) which later housed the distillery (opposite top left) and a gin bar (opposite, top right). Soon Inshriach was on the map.

Then someone approached Walter with a good idea for a gin brand, but no premises or access to ingredients. Juniper grew like a weed on the land (opposite, bottom right), and Walter had just started work on The Shed. They formed a partnership, produced a gin that immediately took off, winning awards, but after a couple of years the partnership didn't work out, so Walter started again, alone, as Inshriach Gin (opposite, middle). He did his homework, rooted around in the woods for botanicals and came up with a much-changed recipe and a more considered, slower, labour-intensive distilling process.

He makes about 5,000 bottles a year, of which 4,000 are standard strength and 1,000 53%. A single making is done in the 150-litre alembic still by blending two single-shot runs. Nothing is added after distilling. In 2017 he added Douglas fir to the recipe which he reckons gives it "a creamy smoothness and a hint of orange and pine." The juniper is picked fresh, then frozen, which gives more complexity than

dried juniper. He tries to pick the rosehips at the last minute: they vary dramatically year to year and only the ripest give the slightly jammy flavour he wants. On the tongue the 45% is a classic, dry juniper-led gin, but with the "edges knocked off." The 53% has more teeth.

Walter is proud that (in a business plagued with hot air and hype) his gin is genuinely local. On Inshriach "there are places where you can stand and within five paces you could pick all the ingredients... It tastes and smells like taking a walk in the woods, fresh and airy and piney... a tribute to where we live." Bottling is within 5 miles of Inshriach and "in three years we have not produced one gram of packaging or merchandising that couldn't be recycled."

Shed open days are local events. "After winning the 2015 Shed of the Year Award hundreds of people were wanting to come by for a look. The last thing I needed was a visitors' centre – we live here because it's peaceful. So rather than turning visitors away, we told them to all come back on the same day. We promised music, a bar with gin cocktails and wood-fired pizzas." On a sunny summer day they get 150 people, but as few as 20 if there's snow.

Badachro Gin and Distillery

Badachro, Gairloch
Distillery and shop

ESSENTIAL INFORMATION

Key botanicals (Badachro Gin): juniper, coriander, liquorice, cubeb, elderflower, lavender, rosehip, gorse blossom, wild myrtle

Output: 8,000-10,000 bottles a year

Location: Aird Hill, Badachro, IV21 2AB

Telephone: 01445 741282

Email: gordon@badachrodistillery.com

Website: www.badachrodistillery.com

Facebook: www.facebook.com/badachrodistillery

Instagram: @badachrodistillery

Twitter: @BadachroGin

Opening hours:
Monday-Saturday 1200-1400

Other reasons to go: Gairloch Heritage Museum, Shellfish Safaris, Gair Loch, Eilean Horrisdale

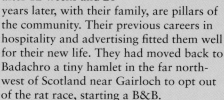

Authentically small batch (maximum 180 bottles per making), products of their environment, pure (diluted with rain and loch water), individual – Badachro gins tick all the boxes. Gordon and Vanessa (opposite, top left) met in the Badachro Inn, married after 12 weeks and 20 years later, with their family, are pillars of the community. Their previous careers in hospitality and advertising fitted them well for their new life. They had moved back to Badachro a tiny hamlet in the far north-west of Scotland near Gairloch to opt out of the rat race, starting a B&B.

They didn't set out to make gin, but noticing their guests keen interest in taking away a product that would remind them of the area, Vanessa suggested room scents. Gordon's reply was 'Why not a liqueur?'

They developed one using local botanicals, then experimentally added juniper – and the gin was born. Badachro Gin (left), their core product, is a classic London Dry but with unexpected complexity and depth, leading not just with juniper but myrtle. Gordon says that this reflects its surroundings (above) because on the face of it the local way of life is simple, but the dramatic wilderness mountain and seascape scenery strikes deep chords.

Their Gairloch Coastal Gin is very different: bright and fresh, with fennel and wild thyme dominating, and two seaweeds. Their third gin, Storm Strength (opposite, top right), is 57%.

The distillery visitor tours (right), led by Gordon, are nicely personal, reasonably priced, and entitle you to a 10 per cent discount on purchases.

Gordon wisely declined approaches from major supermarkets to stock Badachro, preferring to remain a genuine small producer. But he is selling in Denmark, Germany and the Middle East and this has benefitted the locality generally: unknown Badachro is increasingly on the map for visitors, with a distillery visit the making of a trip to the Gairloch and Shieldaig Bay neighbourhood.

Sea Glass Gin and Deerness Distillery

Deerness, Orkney
Distillery and shop

ESSENTIAL INFORMATION

Key botanicals (Sea Glass Gin): juniper, orange peel, tarragon, mint, lemon verbena, cucumber, lavender

Output: 18,000 bottles a year

Location: Newhall, Orkney, KW17 2QJ

Telephone: 01856 741264

Email: info@deernessdistillery.com

Website:
www.deernessdistillery.com

Facebook: www.facebook.com/ DeernessDistillery

Instagram: @deerness_distillery

Twitter: @deer_distillery

Opening hours:
1 April-30 September
Monday-Sunday 1000-1700
Tours 1100 and 1300
Visits by appointment only during winter

Other reasons to go: Skara Brae Prehistoric Village, Ring of Brodgar, Maeshowe

Probably the most remote distillery in the guide: the Orkney Island group off the NE tip of Scotland is two hours by ferry from Scrabster on mainland Scotland – out on a limb by any measure. You dock at Stromness on Mainland Orkney and from there you must cross the island via the main town, Kirkwall, then head out over a narrow neck of land to East Mainland Orkney where you eventually reach the rugged, windswept coastal area known as Deerness. Here there is not much except ancient legends and Deerness Distillery, which was the first to open in the Orkney Islands.

Perhaps unexpectedly, it's an unusually good place to visit. Orkney folk are not known for being good communicators, but Adelle and Stuart Brown's operation offers an above-average visitor experience with tours of the whole distillery area, tastings and a well-stocked shop (above) displaying not only the distillery's gin (left) and vodka, plus a unique collection of tonic waters from across the UK and Europe, but also unique Orkney Islands products such as locally crafted glass and thoughtfully selected Scottish home and beauty ware.

Adelle says her gin has "a beautiful aroma of juniper and citrus, with lavender undertones. On the tongue it is smooth, juniper led but with citrus elements and a fresh, clean aftertaste." The taste reflects its surroundings – "fresh and clean – like the Orkney Islands." She came up with the name Sea Glass because one of her family's favourite activities is beachcombing for sea glass in its endless variety of shapes, sizes and colours washed up on Deerness beaches.

Loch Ness Gin and Loch Ness Spirits

Dores, Inverness-shire
Distillery

ESSENTIAL INFORMATION

Key botanicals (Loch Ness Real & Rare Gin): juniper, plus other secret ingredients

Output: 2,000 bottles a year

Location: Dores, Loch Ness, Inverness, IV2 6TU

Telephone: 01463 751773

Email: info@wearelochness.com

Website: www.wearelochness.com

Facebook: www.facebook.com/ lochnessspirit

Instagram: @lochnessspirits

Twitter: @Lochnessspirits

Opening hours:
Monday-Friday 1000-1700

Other reasons to go: Loch Ness, Urquhart Castle, Loch Dochfour, Loch Duntelchaig

*D*avid T. Smith writes: Loch Ness Distillery is located in one of the most mysterious places in the UK. With many local intrigues and legends, and long-associated with the elusive Loch Ness monster, the loch is also an icon of Scottish Highlands scenery. The area has long attracted tourists, with cruises and outdoor sports on offer. It's 20 miles SW of Inverness and its international airport. Inverness can also be reached by the Caledonian Sleeper train services from London.

The distillery was founded in 2015 by husband and wife, Kevin (next page, top left) and Lorien Cameron-Ross (above), whose family have lived on the banks of the Loch for more than five centuries. Kevin and Lorien put Loch Ness at the very heart of their spirits: from the botanicals in its recipe to using locally sourced water.

Their first gin was released in 2016 and all of the botanicals, including the juniper (next page, top right), are foraged from Loch Ness. Lorien says "If it doesn't grow within 500 metres of our house, it is not in our gin." Botanicals are foraged, by hand, by the Loch Ness team, so each batch of gin represents the botanicals harvested in a particular year.

In 2018, Loch Ness Distillery released the first in their 'Legends' range (next page, bottom left, right-hand bottle). Based on the original gin recipe (left and next page, bottom left, left-hand bottle), each gin features an additional local botanical such

as hawthorn berries.

The distillery also makes cocktail bitters using local ingredients and, in 2018, they released a Blanche Absinthe. Created by Lorien, it is the first absinthe made using Scottish wormwood and won Gold at Absinthiades Festival in Pontarlier.

Thompson Bros Organic Highland Gin and Dornoch Distillery

Dornoch, Sutherland
Distillery

ESSENTIAL INFORMATION

Key botanicals (Thompson Bros Organic Highland Gin): juniper, coriander, cardamom seed, black peppercorn, orange peel, aniseed, freeze-dried raspberry, elderflower, meadowsweet, pine needle

Output: not disclosed

Location: Dornoch Castle Hotel, Castle Street, Dornoch, IV25 3SD

Telephone: 01862 810216

Email: info@dornochdistillery.com

Website: www.thompsonbrosdistillers.com

Facebook: www.facebook.com/dornochdistillery

Instagram: @dornochdistillery

Twitter: @DornochDist

Opening hours: not open to the public

The Thompson family have owned the Dornoch Castle Hotel (above) since 2000, establishing its reputation as a whisky hotel. When brothers Phil and Simon (left) were old enough, they started working behind the bar and developed a love for spirits, experimenting with their own whiskies, when it dawned on them to build a distillery (next page, top). In 2015, they secured planning permission to convert a 19thC fire station on the grounds, selling their flat and starting a crowdfunding campaign to help with financing. By Christmas 2016, they'd raised enough money to start doing test runs and, while the focus remained whisky, they released their first experimental gin in June 2017.

Most of the botanicals in Thompson Bros Organic Highland Gin (left) are distilled with 90% organic grain spirit for 36 hours before being infused with raspberries and elderflower (next page, bottom right) for a further 24 to 36 hours. The product is then blended with their own single malt new-make spirit before it's cut with water to 45.7%. The bottle, →

resembling an original 19thC fire grenade, is a nod to the building's history. Try serving the gin with Mediterranean tonic and a raspberry.

In 2018, the brothers launched a second crowdfunding campaign and, as we went to press, had recently bought new, larger premises, which they planned to open to visitors in 2020, complete with a tasting room and a shop.

Rock Rose Gin and Dunnet Bay Distillers

Dunnet, Caithness
Distillery, shop and tasting room

ESSENTIAL INFORMATION

Key botanicals (Rock Rose Gin): juniper, liquorice, cinnamon, water mint, blaeberry, hawthorn berry, rowan berry, *Rhodiola rosea*, sea buckthorn

Output: 105,000 bottles a year

Location: Dunnet Bay Distillery, Thurso, KW14 8XD

Telephone: 01847 851287

Email: hello@rockrosegin.co.uk

Website: www.dunnetbaydistillers.co.uk

Facebook: www.facebook.com/rockrosegin

Instagram: @rockrosegin

Twitter: @RockRoseGin

Opening hours:
Monday-Saturday 1000-1600 (booking advised)

Other reasons to go: Dunnet Head Lighthouse, Mary Ann's Cottage, Castlehill Heritage Centre

One of the most northerly distilleries in the guide, Dunnet Bay was established in 2014 with the aim of creating spirits that reflect Caithness. Their signature gin, Rock Rose (bottom left), is an infusion of local and traditional botanicals, five of which are hand foraged from the surrounding cliffs and forests – rowan, hawthorn berries, sea buckthorn, blaeberries, watermint and the key ingredient *Rhodiola rosea*, a rose found along the cliffs of the Pentland Firth – a 'rose in the rocks.' The rock element of the gin is also represented in its stone bottle.

The botanicals are vapour infused (page 254) with a wheat base spirit bought in from the Langley Distillery. The result is a clean, zesty, smooth tasting gin. The flavour kicks off with earthy, warm Italian juniper, which gives way to a hint of lemon sherbet from the Bulgarian juniper. Next is the berries and to finish, you're left with a combination of sweet liquorice, spicy cinnamon and the slightly bitter flavour of the *Rhodiola rosea*.

Dunnet Bay recommends serving 25 ml of Rock Rose Gin with 50 ml of Fever-Tree tonic and a curl of orange or a sprig of toasted rosemary to garnish. For a cocktail, try adding 50 ml of Rock Rose Gin to 25 ml of fresh lime juice and 12.5 ml of mint syrup, with plenty of ice and a sprig of fresh mint.

The gin can be bought from the distillery shop (next page, top left), along with a →

selection of Distiller and Garden Editions, which are only available at the distillery. They also produce Holy Grass Vodka (previous page, top right), named after its key botanical, *Anthoxanthum nitens* (Holy Grass), a sweet herb that is distilled with Highland apples and the wheat base spirit.

Dunnet Bay offers seasonal tours where you learn about the spirits, botanicals and their still, Elizabeth (top right). Tours conclude with a tutored tasting (right). Advanced booking is advised – see previous page for contact details.

Devil's Staircase Highland Spiced Gin and Pixel Spirits Distillery

North Ballachulish, Fort William
Distillery, bar and gin school

ESSENTIAL INFORMATION

Key botanicals (Devil's Staircase Highland Spiced Gin): juniper, coriander, cardamom, nutmeg, cassia bark, orange peel, lemon peel, grains of paradise

Output: 3,000 bottles a year

Location: Old Ferry Bar, Loch Leven Hotel, Onich, by Fort William, PH33 6SA

Telephone: 07443 656528

Email: info@pixelspiritsltd.co.uk

Website: www.pixelspiritsltd.co.uk

Facebook: www.facebook.com/pixelspirits

Instagram: @pixel_spirits

Twitter: @pixelspirits

Opening hours:

Old Ferry Bar

Monday-Wednesday 1200-2300

Thursday-Saturday 1200-0000

Sunday 1230-2300

Distillery tours by appointment only

Other reasons to go: Loch Leven, Glen Coe

Loch Leven Hotel is a family-run hotel, part-owned by Craig and Noru Innes. In 2015, the husband and wife team launched a separate company, Pixel Spirits, and spent two years converting a dilapidated 17thC barn in the hotel grounds into a craft gin distillery. They chose gin for its versatility.

Also in the hotel grounds is The Old Ferry Bar (bottom left), which dates from the 1700s. It stocks more than 50 gins, including their home-distilled tipple – Devil's Staircase Highland Spiced Gin (left) – and other experimental drinks which you can sample at the bar. Devil's Staircase takes its name from the most treacherous part of the West Highland Way, minutes from the distillery's doorstep, and is made with imports from sustainable sources along traditional spice routes. The juniper and coriander are steeped in neutral grain spirit overnight and then the rest of the botanicals are added just before distillation in a 100-litre stainless steel still, Orsetta (little bear), which makes batches of 75 bottles at a time.

In November 2017, Pixel made a limited edition gin, Neptune's Staircase, named after part of the Caledonian Canal in Fort William. This was a dry-style gin featuring bladderwrack seaweed and local nettles and only 240 bottles were made. As we went to press, their latest release was Drookit Piper, a citrus-led gin launched in June 2019. The gins can be bought from the online shop.

Pixel offers gin school classes in the former byre (cowshed) of the distillery where, for £89, you learn about gin's key botanicals and create your own recipe on a mini still. The class lasts four hours and can cater for groups of two to eight – group discounts are available on request. Email them for dates and availability.

Misty Isle Gin and Isle of Skye Distillers

Portree, Isle of Skye
Distillery, shop and gin school

ESSENTIAL INFORMATION

Key botanicals (Misty Isle Gin): juniper, coriander, liquorice root, cassia bark, grains of paradise, cubeb, lemon peel, lemon verbena, a secret flower picked at high altitude on the island

Output: 28,000 bottles a year

Location: The Distillery, Hillfoot, Viewfield Road, Portree, IV51 9ES

Telephone: 01478 611746

Email: info@isleofskyedistillers.com

Website: www.isleofskyedistillers.com

Facebook: www.facebook.com/ IsleOfSkyeDistillers

Instagram: @isleofskyedistillers

Twitter: @IsleSkyeDistil

Opening hours:
Shop and Gin School
Monday-Saturday 1000-1700

Other reasons to go: Portree Harbour, Scorrybreac, The Lump

The word Skye probably derives from two Norse words: *ski* meaning cloud and *ey* meaning island. Whether Skye is any more cloudy or misty than the other Western Isles is debatable – their climate is largely governed by Atlantic weather fronts and the Gulf Stream which produce more than usual low-lying cloud and mist. Still, Misty Isle is a nicely romantic and local name for the gins produced by brothers Alistair and Thomas (opposite, bottom right) who are also nothing if not locals: they were raised on the island and built their distillery with their own hands in the back garden of the family house outside Portree, the largest town on the island. Their family has lived there for four generations and their mother still does.

Alistair worked as a bar and restaurant manager on the mainland, Thomas was a soldier, builder and council employee until they started building the distillery in 2016. The first batches of their core product, Misty Isle Gin (below left, middle bottle), dripped from from their two small stills in 2017. Within four months, such was the heartwarming support for their enterprise on the island, they had to install two more. They describe the gin as "juniper heavy, with a hint of spice, earthy sweetness and a refreshing citrus aftertaste." Pure local water from the Storr Lochs is used to dilute the spirit to strength.

Tommy's Gin (left, left-hand bottle) was the second launch in August 2017 in memory of their late father. A stronger and dryer gin than Misty Isle, it's made with six botanicals including juniper, coriander, liquorice root, poppy seed, Scottish blaeberries and orange peel. Possibly it's the only gin distilled with poppy seeds. It's

a juniper-heavy gin with a dry, sweet and strong flavour. A donation from each bottle sold is given to military charities.

A third gin, Misty Isle Mulled Christmas Gin (opposite, bottom left, right-hand bottle) was launched for the Christmas season in November 2017 flavoured with juniper, cassia bark, orange peel, lemon peel, liquorice root, star anise and Tonka beans. The botanicals are soaked in Amarone red wine before distillation to give a rich Christmassy flavour.

The brothers launched a gin school at their shop (above right) in Portree before the guide went to press – the distillery being too small to accommodate visitors. They teach you to run a miniature still (top right), combining botanicals to create your own uniquely flavoured 50-cl bottle of gin, and to design your own label – nice touch.

Isle of Harris Gin and Distillery

Tarbert, Isle of Harris
Distillery, bar and shop

ESSENTIAL INFORMATION
**Key botanicals (Isle of Harris Gin): juniper,
coriander seed, liquorice root, cassia
bark, cinnamon, cubeb, bitter orange peel,
sugar kelp**
Output: not disclosed
Location: Tarbert, Isle of Harris, HS3 3DJ
Telephone: 01859 502212
Email: info@harrisdistillery.com
Website: www.harrisdistillery.com
**Facebook: www.facebook.com/
   isleofharrisdistillers**
Instagram: @isleofharrisdistillers
Twitter: @harrisdistiller

**Opening hours: scheduled tours – see
   website for details**

**Other reasons to go: beaches, Harris Tweed
shop, St Kilda archipelago**

Ella Carr writes: The Isle of Harris, off the far north-western coast of Scotland, is exposed and rocky, with rugged shores and golden sands. As with all Outer Hebridean islands, local tradition holds fast – be it through the Gaelic language and song, or the skill of local weavers in turning raw wool into Harris tweed.

US-born Anderson Bakewell fell head over heels in love with the island when he first visited in the 1960s and decided to create Isle of Harris Gin (above and bottom left) in order to provide a sustainable local product that would help the island's economy without being intrusive. In 2015, after raising £10 million, he opened Isle of Harris Distillery (opposite, top left and right), also known as The Social Distillery. So staunch are its local values that the distillery is the gin's only stockist, so every purchase is tied to the Tarbert location – and this hasn't held back sales. They now offer an immediate pick-up service from an ever-growing network of Click & Collect partners to make it easier for customers to get their hands on the gin. The gin is also available to drink in many bars and restaurants across the UK and beyond.

The distillery's team were charged with formulating a gin that celebrated the island, eventually settling on sugar kelp as the gin's star ingredient. Each summer the kelp is harvested from the isle's lochs and shoreline by local diver Lewis Mackenzie (opposite,

middle); in winter the underwater forests are left to replenish. Once dried, the gold-green fronds are distilled – along with eight other carefully chosen botanicals – in a pot still named The Dottach after a feisty local lady.

The kelp works a treat with the juniper and sweet liquorice, creating a fresh and piny gin – best enjoyed neat. However, it's the bottle that makes Isle of Harris exceptional: a ribbed swirling design with an azure base, rippled like the rough seas of Harris, while also echoing the weave of Harris tweed. Each label is hand-flecked with fragments of copper leaf (reflecting the copper still) and sugar kelp, and the cork stopper is sealed with a tag bearing the distillery's map co-ordinates.

Gin lovers prepared to make a pilgrimage to Harris will be met with a warm Hebridean welcome, in keeping with the Social Distillery ethos. They're open to visitors six days a week, and drop-ins can visit the convivial canteen and shop (right), stocked with fresh daily batches of Isle of Harris Gin. Organized seasonal tours are £10 per person for those wanting to see the distilling in action, with whisky and gin samplings included.

Shetland Reel Gin and
The Shetland Distillery Company

Unst, Shetland Islands
Distillery

ESSENTIAL INFORMATION

Key botanicals (Shetland Reel Gin):
juniper, coriander seed, cinnamon, citrus
peel, apple mint, bladderwrack seaweed

Output: 67,000 bottles a year

Location: Saxa Vord Distillery, Unst,
Haroldswick, ZE2 9EF

Telephone: 01957 711217

Email: info@shetlandreelgin.com

Website: www.shetlandreel.com

Facebook: www.facebook.com/
shetlandreel

Instagram: @shetlandreel

Twitter: @ShetlandReelGin

Opening hours:
Guided tastings
April-September – Tuesdays, Thursdays and
Saturdays at 1200

Other reasons to go: Unst Boat Haven, Unst
Heritage Centre

Ella Carr writes: The Shetland Islands
are at the very northern tip of the
British Isles, where the North Sea meets
the Atlantic Ocean, and Unst (opposite,
bottom right) – where Saxa Vord distillery
is located – is their most northerly point.
Closer, in fact, to Norway in both distance
and culture than it is to Scotland. Far-
flung places such as these – whose regional
identities are singularly hybrid – have a
knack of producing excellent craft gins.

True to form, Shetland Reel Gin (bottom
left, left-hand bottle) – which started out as
a small batch operation only available on
Shetland – has steadily grown in reputation,
and is now stocked globally. They've stayed
true to the small craft ethos however,
producing all gin on site and taste testing
each batch.

The distillery was founded by two
couples, united by their ambition to set up
the most northerly gin and whisky distillery
in Britain. Frank and Debbie Strang had
already developed Saxa Vord (formerly an
RAF base) into an award-winning tourist
resort. Stuart and Wilma Nickerson were
founders of The Malt Whisky Company.
The couples' first commercial distillation
run making Shetland Reel Gin was in
September 2014, with 55 limited edition
bottles presented in Shetland tweed bags.

The aim was to make a traditional gin
with a Shetland twist: the modest botanical
count of nine includes classics such as
coriander seeds, cinnamon and citrus
peel, plus the unique ingredient of Unst-
harvested apple mint – a member of the
mint family with a slightly fruitier aroma,
that gives the gin a subtle and refreshing
minty finish.

Shetland Reel Ocean Sent Gin (left,

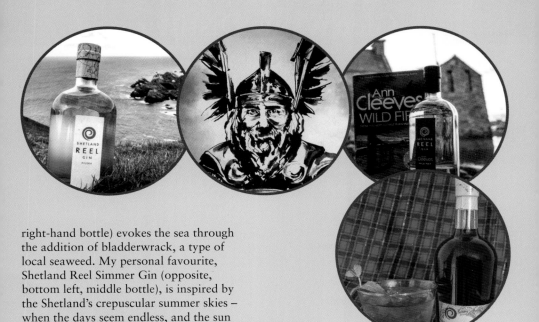

right-hand bottle) evokes the sea through the addition of bladderwrack, a type of local seaweed. My personal favourite, Shetland Reel Simmer Gin (opposite, bottom left, middle bottle), is inspired by the Shetland's crepuscular summer skies – when the days seem endless, and the sun barely falls below the horizon, known to Shetlanders as Simmer Dim.

They also produce Shetland Reel Filska Gin (top left), made with red grapefruit, Wildfire Gin (top right), a limited edition collaboration with Ann Cleeves, author of the BBC drama *Shetland*, and a Rhubarb and Bramble Gin Liqueur (above right).

Each January they produce a new cask aged gin, bottled at navy strength, as a nod to Shetland's seafaring history. It celebrates the annual fire festival, Up Helly Aa, held in Lerwick on the last Tuesday of January, which sees more than a thousand Shetlanders dressed as Vikings (top middle) in procession through the streets with flaming torches and setting fire to a longship.

GoodWill Gin and GlenWyvis Distillery

Upper Dochcarty, Dingwall
Distillery

ESSENTIAL INFORMATION

Key botanicals (GoodWill Gin): juniper, coriander, cinnamon, almond powder, lemon peel, orange peel, hawthorn berry

Output: 20,000 bottles a year

Location: 1 Upper Dochcarty, Dingwall, IV15 9UF

Telephone: 01349 862005

Email: info@glenwyvis.com

Website: www.glenwyvis.com

Facebook: www.facebook.com/GlenWyvis

Instagram: @glenwyvis

Twitter: @glenwyvis

Opening hours: not open to the public

This distillery is mainly about whisky – producing 1,200 litres a week whereas gin was around 200 litres a week as we went to press – nonetheless making GoodWill gin (bottom left) a genuine, small-batch craft spirit. Whisky production started in January 2018 and GoodWill Gin followed six months later.

GlenWyvis (opposite, top left) can claim to be the world's first 100 per cent community-owned whisky and gin producer, its cash raised from more than 3,500 people in some 36 countries investing more than £3.3 million. Of course many of the shareholders are local, so it's a true community project. John Mckenzie (founder/managing director) and Duncan Tait (Distillery Manager – opposite, middle) have strong local connections.

They are proud that the plant is powered 100 per cent by renewable energy – wind, solar and hydro. Surplus electricity is exported to the National Grid and a Biomass Woodchip Boiler produces all the steam used on site. The distillery's own borehole water is condensed through the gin still the day before distillation to make exceptionally pure water for diluting the spirit down to regular strength.

The gin botanicals (hawthorn berries foraged locally) are soaked for 24 hours in the pot still with 400 litres of spirit at a strength of 55%. This is then distilled in the traditional sequence: the first 60 litres are collected as foreshots (the head), the next 200 litres collected as spirit (the heart) with the remainder of the liquid collected as feints (the tail). The foreshots and feints are mixed with new spirit to make part of the next distillation.

The still (opposite, bottom right) is a

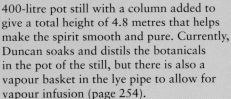

400-litre pot still with a column added to give a total height of 4.8 metres that helps make the spirit smooth and pure. Currently, Duncan soaks and distils the botanicals in the pot of the still, but there is also a vapour basket in the lye pipe to allow for vapour infusion (page 254).

On the nose, GoodWill is strong in juniper, with lighter orange and lemon elements. On the tongue you get orange and lemon, then spices. The finish is smooth and clean with a warming spicy finish.

Duncan Tait ran Scotch whisky distilleries for nearly 30 years and was one of the original investors when fundraising started in 2016, as of course was John Mckenzie, who used to be an army helicopter pilot, farmer and green energy advocate.

GlenWyvis gets its name from Ben Wyvis, an isolated, whale of a mountain of more than 2,000 m which rises NW of Dingwall, where the distillery is located near the Firth of Cromarty (top right). Check the website to find out when the planned visitors' centre and shop opens.

Colonsay Gin and Wild Thyme Spirits

Upper Kilchattan, Isle of Colonsay
Distillery and retreat

ESSENTIAL INFORMATION

Key botanicals (Colonsay Gin): juniper, coriander seed, liquorice root, orange peel, calamus root

Output: 10,000 bottles a year

Location: Tigh na Uruisg, Upper Kilchattan, Isle of Colonsay, PA61 7YR

Telephone: 01951 200082

Email: wildthymespirits@btinternet.com

Website: www.wildthymespirits.com

Facebook: www.facebook.com/ WildThymeSpirits

Instagram: @colonsaygin

Twitter: @ColonsayGin

Opening hours:
Tuesday-Thursday 1200-1600
Saturday 1200-1600

Other reasons to go: Kiloran Bay, Balnahard Beach

Husband and wife team Finlay and Eileen Geekie founded Wild Thyme Spirits in August 2016, after moving from Oxfordshire to Colonsay to pursue their dream of island living. The couple had spent many a family holiday in the Western Isles and always fancied living and working there. In 2015 at Junipalooza, the international gin festival, they met Martin and Claire Murray of Dunnet Bay Distillery (page 265) and, inspired by the couple's success, decided to go for it themselves. After a year of researching the industry and developing their traditional London Dry-style recipe with the help of Strathearn Distiller Tony Reeman-Clarke, Colonsay Gin (bottom left, middle bottle) was launched in March 2017. Strathearn continued to distil the gin until spring 2018, when the Geekies brought it home to the island.

The juniper berries (opposite, middle) are bruised and steeped for 30 minutes in a 48% solution of neutral grain spirit along with the rest of the botanicals (opposite, top left) before they are distilled for around six hours in a 100-litre copper still. The spirit is then rested in a holding tank for four to five days before it's cut with water to 47% and rested again for a further 24 hours before bottling. The result is a smooth, sweet gin with a kick of spice and lemon sherbet. Finlay and Eileen recommend serving the gin with Fever-Tree tonic and a twist of orange peel or, for the adventurous, with a slice of green chilli.

In Autumn 2018 they released Colonsay Bramble Liqueur (left, second bottle from right), made partly from locally foraged, and partly commercially sourced blackberries, which are added to Colonsay Gin along with sugar and water before being pressed

and left to steep in the holding tank for a week. The liqueur is then quadruple filtered before being bottled at 20%.

As we went to press, Fin and Eileen had just released a limited edition bottle of Colonsay Gin – Colonsay Wild Thyme 909 (909 indicating the number of bottles produced – bottom right and opposite bottom left, left-hand bottle) – to celebrate the first batch to be distilled on the island. Check the online shop for availability.

The couple offer a Gin Lover's Retreat for four people. You get two nights (from Friday to Sunday) full board accommodation in their house, two pre-dinner cocktails on Friday, a five-gin tasting on Saturday, and transport to and from the ferry port.

As we went to press, Wild Thyme had just been granted planning permission to build their own distillery. They were also working on several new products, including new gins and collaborations with other award-winning artisan producers.

Isle of Arran Gin and Distillery

Whiting Bay, Isle of Arran
Distillery

ESSENTIAL INFORMATION

Key botanicals (Isle of Arran Gin): juniper, coriander, lemon balm, hogweed seed, meadowsweet, fuchsia, noble fir, sea lettuce

Output: 10,000 bottles a year

Location: Shore Road, Whiting Bay, Isle of Arran, KA27 8HJ

Telephone: 01770 700229

Email: info@isleofarrangin.com

Website: www.isleofarrangin.com

Facebook: www.facebook.com/isleofarrangin

Instagram: @isleofarrangin

Twitter: @isleofarrangin

Opening hours:
Monday-Saturday 1000-1700

Other reasons to go: Arran Whisky Distillery tours, Lochranza

When local Arran shopkeeper, Stuart Fraser, thought about making gin a few years ago, there were two people that came to mind that would help make his dream a reality: old pals Ross Hamilton and George Laird, who he'd known since primary school. Together, the three of them had all the skills needed to set up their own brand, except one – they were missing a recipe-maker. Enter George Grassie.

Stuart knew that George's artisan bakery, Blackwaterfoot Bakehouse, was one of the most exciting foodie hotspots on Arran and during many conversations about their mutual passion for locally sourced food and drink, they mused over the lack of an Arran gin. The four cronies (opposite, top left) put their heads together and, in 2017, Isle of Arran Gin (below left) was launched. Stuart describes the gin as Arran in miniature: its bottle is inspired by the island's sea and mountains and its botanicals (opposite, right and bottom left) take advantage of Arran's rich coastal plant scene to create their signature London Dry-style gin.

As we went to press, the owners had just bought a building in Brodick which would become their new distillery. Visitor experiences including foraging trips and a gin school were being planned, plus a bar, shop and café.

Until the new distillery is ready, the foraging team takes the botanicals to Glenshee Craft Distillery, where they are distilled by Persie Distiller Simon Fairclough (page 241). The result is a floral and herbaceous aroma with an oceanic and vegetal dimension, a creamy feel in the mouth with a floral, sweet and spicy flavour. Stuart recommends serving Isle of Arran with Fever-Tree Mediterranean tonic

water and a grapefruit and mint garnish.

The gin can be bought at Stuart's shop, The Bay Kitchen & Stores, and George's bakery, Blackwaterfoot Bakehouse, as well as various bars and restaurants around the island and, more recently, mainland Scotland. They also have an online shop and were hoping to make Isle of Arran Gin available across the whole of the UK sometime in 2019.

Porter's Gin Microdistillery and Orchid bar

Aberdeen, Aberdeenshire
Distillery and bar

ESSENTIAL INFORMATION

Key botanicals (Porter's Gin): juniper, coriander, liquorice, cassia bark, cinnamon, almond, lemon peel, orange peel, pink peppercorn, Buddha's hand citron

Output: 30,000 bottles a year

Location: 51 Langstane Place, Aberdeen, AB11 6EN

Telephone: 01224 516126

Email: info@orchidaberdeen.com

Website: www.orchidaberdeen.com

Facebook: www.facebook.com/ OrchidLovesYou

Instagram: @orchidaberdeen

Twitter: @Orchid_Aberdeen

Opening hours:
Sunday-Thursday 1800-0200
Friday 1700-0300
Saturday 1800-0300

Other reasons to go: Cathedral of St Mary of the Assumption, Aberdeen Music Hall

Ella Carr writes: Dour, largely granite-built Aberdeen has a surprisingly good bar scene, in which Orchid is a relaxed, stylish oasis. They do classic and contemporary cocktails, and aim to 'raise standards' of mixed drinks and cocktails in Scotland. See Orchid's website for details of its mixology classes where you learn the history of cocktails and get behind the bar to make your own (opposite, bottom right).

In 2016 founders Ben, Josh and Alex (opposite, top left) decided to start a gin distillery in the basement, assembling the components of an unusual still that would enable 'cold' distilling (opposite, top right). The technique, pioneered in the USA and also known as the vacuum distillation method, is used by only a few UK gin distillers and creates especially bright, fresh flavours. A pump attached to the still draws off vapour inducing a partial vacuum. This in turn means vapourization at a relatively low temperature, well below boiling point: the ingredients aren't 'cooked' as in conventional distillation, instead their 'raw' essence is gently drawn off.

Not every botanical responds well to this treatment, but after experimenting they found that Buddha's hand citron did, so it is a major element in the refreshing taste of Porter's, which is designed to be drunk neat, or used in terrific highballs and G&Ts. Dr Andrew Porter of Aberdeen University helped them put together the still and experiment with the botanicals, and the first edition of Porter's, launched in 2015, was named after him.

Buddha's hand (opposite, middle) originates like all citrus from China and gets its name from the finger-like segments of its fruit. It contains no pulp, only aromatic 'skin'.

Porter's was followed by Tropical Old Tom Gin (opposite, bottom left), a twist on the classic Old Tom, flavoured with cold-distilled passionfruit, guava and white tea.

Ben, Josh and Alex's output has increased, but the still remains in the basement and they've also stuck to their roots by using classic gin recipes, though adding refinement by using cold distillation. They're now offering 'behind the scenes' visits combined with gin tastings.

Caorunn Gin and Balmenach Distillery

Cromdale, Strathspey
Distillery and tasting room

ESSENTIAL INFORMATION
Key botanicals (Caorunn Gin): juniper, coriander seed, cassia bark, lemon peel, orange peel, rowan berry, Coul Blush apple, heather, dandelion leaf, bog-myrtle
Output: not disclosed
Location: Balmenach Road, Cromdale, Granton-on-Spey, PH26 3PF
Telephone: 01479 874933
Email: contact@caorunngin.com
Website: www.caorunngin.com
Facebook: www.facebook.com/caorunngin
Instagram: @caorunngin
Twitter: @CaorunnGin

Opening hours:
Monday-Thursday 1000-1600
Friday 1000-1200

Other reasons to go: Cairngorms National Park, Cairngorm Reindeer Centre, Loch Garten Osprey Centre, CairnGorm Mountain

Founded by James MacGregor in 1824, Balmenach Distillery (bottom left) became one of the first in Scotland to produce Scotch whisky legally. The distillery has been producing whisky ever since and in 2009 it released Caorunn Gin, named after one of its botanicals – *caorunn* is Gaelic for rowan berries.

The distillery's location in the Cairngorms National Park makes it ideal for foraging botanicals, which are hand picked by Master Distiller Simon Buley. He wanted to combine traditional spirit-making methods with Celtic botanicals found in the Cairngorms. He uses five in Caorunn Gin: Coul Blush apple, dandelion leaf, heather, bog-myrtle and rowan berries. These are vapour infused (page 254) with the rest of the botanicals, a pure grain-based spirit and Scottish Highland water in the world's only working Copper Berry Chamber – the botanicals are spread over four perforated trays while the spirit vaporizes, becoming infused with the aromas and flavours of the botanicals as it rises through the chamber.

Caorunn Gin is produced in 1,000-litre batches to create a triple-distilled London Dry Gin at 41.8%. The bottle has a five-sided base, representing the five Celtic botanicals. Balmenach recommends serving the gin with a quality tonic and a slice of red apple. It also works well in an Alexander cocktail: mix 37.5 ml of Caorunn Gin with 12.5 ml of Creme de Cacao White, 25 ml cream and 12.5 ml of milk, with some grated nutmeg to garnish.

For £10, Balmenach offers distillery tours, including a tutored deconstructed nosing and tasting session in their bothy, a neat sample of Caorunn Gin as well as a Caorunn G&T served with red apple.

Avva Scottish Gin and Moray Distillery Ltd

Elgin, Moray
Distillery

ESSENTIAL INFORMATION

Key botanicals (Avva Scottish Gin): juniper, coriander, lemon, orange, mint, nettle, dandelion, rowan, red clover

Output: 8,000 bottles a year

Location: 10 Chanonry Road North, Elgin, IV30 6NB

Telephone: 01343 548700

Email: info@avvascottishgin.co.uk

Website: www.moraydistilleryltd.co.uk/

Facebook: www.facebook.com/ avvascottishgin

Instagram: @avvascottishgin

Twitter: @AvvaScottishGin

Opening hours: tours held in May and by pre-booking with six weeks' notice through selected tour operators between May and September

Other reasons to go: Elgin Cathedral, Spynie Palace, Moray Motor Museum, Duffus Castle

Moray is Scotland's historic home of distilling, containing Speyside, where many of the world's most famous single malt whisky brands are produced. Gin is the newcomer, with small distilleries springing up rapidly – approaching ten by the end of 2018. Single malt whisky tours are a key draw for visitors and as part of the Spirit of Speyside Whisky Festival, Moray Distillery Ltd (bottom left) hosts open days, where visitors get a behind-the-scenes experience, plus a tasting of their signature product, Avva Scottish Gin.

Jill Brown's is a genuine small batch operation, launched in 2016, making 220 bottles of Avva Gin from the heart of each run. She produces from what can claim to be the UK's first Scottish-made gin still named 'JJ' after Jill's two grandmothers, Jessie and Jean. The aroma is juniper led, followed by herbaceous, floral and citrus elements. On the tongue it's smooth juniper combined with balanced herbaceous flavours and the finish is fresh citrus and mint. Besides Avva, Jill produces a navy strength gin, a cask-matured gin and some liqueurs.

After one sip of Avva you naturally want to Avvanother, but the name is far from being a droll joke. In Dravidian, one of the ancient languages of India, *avva* is a respected mother, grandmother or older woman; and in Hebrew the same word means ruin. So the name deftly nods not just to Jill's grandmothers, but to gin's old reputation as Mother's Ruin.

Visiting the Elgin area is also great for Elgin's cathedral, which features on Avva Gin's label. The cathedral opened in 1224 and is known as the Lantern of the North because it shines out as one of Scotland's most impressive and numinous buildings.

LoneWolf Gin and BrewDog Distilling Co.

Ellon, Aberdeenshire
Distillery

ESSENTIAL INFORMATION
Key botanicals (LoneWolf Gin): juniper, coriander seed, cardamom, almond, lemon peel, grapefruit peel, pink peppercorn, mace, kaffir lime leaf, Thai lemongrass, lavender, Scots pine needle
Output: 54,600 bottles a year
Location: Balmacassie Industrial Estate, Balmacasse Dr, Ellon, AB41 8BX
Telephone: 01358 287138
Email: hello@brewdogdistilling.com
Website: www.brewdog.com/brewdog-distilling-co
Facebook: www.facebook.com/lonewolfgin; www.facebook.com/brewdogdistillingco
Instagram: @lonewolfgin
Twitter: @LoneWolfGin

Opening hours:
Monday-Friday 0900-1700

Other reasons to go: Pitmedden Garden, Haddo House, Tolquhon Castle, Forvie National Nature Reserve

BrewDog bosses Martin Dickie and James Watt launched BrewDog Distilling Co., their grain-to-bottle operation, under the name LoneWolf Spirits in 2016 after a number of crowdfunding campaigns enabled them to build a distillery (bottom left) in their Aberdeenshire brewery. The duo brought in Master Distiller Steven Kersley in 2014 to help build the recipe and after two years of experimenting with more than 80 different botanicals and over 192 different distillations, LoneWolf Gin (opposite, bottom right) was born.

To make the gin, Steven starts with a mix of 50% wheat and 50% barley spirit (pumped directly from the brewery), which is distilled in what claims to be the world's only triple bubble still (opposite, top left). This allows for maximum copper contact with the spirit, raising the strength to 91% before it passes through an 18 m rectification column for further purification to 96.4%. Steven uses only the heart of the neutral spirit, which is then cut with water to 40% before it's re-distilled with 14 botanicals (see list, above left). Steven recommends serving it with a quality tonic and a pink grapefruit slice. It also works well in a Negroni.

Sustainability plays a big role in the BrewDog Distilling Co. ethos and every few weeks members of the team forage for pine needles across Aberdeenshire and the Cairngorms in denser patches of woodland so they can collect smaller amounts from a number of trees.

Steven's second gin is LoneWolf Gunpowder Gin, made at a strength of 57% with dill seed, bitter orange peel, green cardamom, star anise and Szechuan peppercorn for a kick of oriental spice. He

also produces Cloudy Lemon Gin, made with the same botanicals as LoneWolf Gin, with the addition of Sicilian lemon peel. The gins are available from the online shop, where you can also buy ready-mixed cans of LoneWolf G&T.

Future plans include the launch of a new gin, Zealot's Heart, as well as branching out into rum and whisky.

Gordon Castle Gin

Fochabers, Moray
Distillery

ESSENTIAL INFORMATION
Key botanicals (Gordon Castle Gin):
juniper, coriander seed, liquorice,
cinnamon, cassia bark, lemon peel, orange
peel, nutmeg, mint, lavender
Output: 10,000 bottles a year
Location: Gordon Castle Estate, Fochabers,
IV32 7PQ
Telephone: 01343 612317
Email: info@gordoncastlescotland.com
Website: www.gordoncastlescotland.com
Facebook: www.facebook.com/
GordonCastleScotland
Instagram: @gordoncastlescotland
Twitter: @gordoncastlegin

Opening hours:
Monday-Sunday 1000-1600

Other reasons to go: Moray Monster
Trails, Fochabers Folk Museum & Heritage
Centre, Loch Oire

The history of Gordon Castle Gin goes back to the late 18thC when the castle after which it's named was enlarged by the fourth Duke of Gordon to become one of Scotland's most palatial seats. Located in Speyside, the castle had links with the spirits industry and in 1823 the Duke put legislation through Parliament which first legalized whisky distilling. The castle was used as an auxiliary hospital for soldiers wounded in the First World War and a barracks in the Second. When it was sold in the 1930s to pay punitive death duties it fell into disrepair until rescued by Lieutenant General Sir George Gordon Lennox, a direct descendant of the fourth Duke of Gordon. In 2008 his grandson, Angus, and his wife Zara took over the running of the estate and transformed it into a visitor attraction offering accommodation, self-catering holiday cottages and salmon fishing. In 2014, they launched their craft gin, Gordon Castle; a luxury beauty and bath range; and a collection of tweed and bone china products.

Gordon Castle Gin (below left, middle bottle and opposite, bottom right) is made from botanicals picked in the estate's Scottish Walled Garden by head gardener Ed (opposite, bottom left). As we went to press, the garden was being renovated – possibly to be completed by 2020. Try serving 50 ml of Gordon Castle Gin with lemon, lime, fresh mint and a premium tonic with plenty of ice.

You could also try Gordon Castle Raspberry Gin Liqueur (left, left-hand bottle) and Gordon Castle Plum Gin Liqueur (left, right-hand bottle). All the gins can be bought from the online shop, starting at £5.49 for the Gordon Castle Miniature bottle and

reaching £44.25 for a personalized, engraved bottle of Gordon Castle Gin. They also sell Winter Spice Infusion Bags for Gin at £12.50, a Gordon Castle Gin Trio Set and a Gin Connoisseurs Gift Set, which includes a 50-cl bottle each of Gordon Castle Plum Gin and Raspberry Gin Liqueurs, plus two crystal liqueur glasses.

Duncan Taylor's Indian Summer Gin

Huntly, Aberdeenshire
Distillery

ESSENTIAL INFORMATION
Key botanicals (Indian Summer Gin):
juniper, coriander seed, liquorice root, cassia
bark, almond, lemon peel, orange peel, saffron
Output: not disclosed
Location: Duncan Taylor Scotch Whisky Ltd,
   King Street, Huntly, AB54 8HP
Telephone: 01466 794055
Email: info@duncantaylor.com
Website: www.duncantaylor.com
Facebook: www.facebook.com/Duncan-
   Taylor-Scotch-Whisky-Ltd
Instagram: @indian_summer_gin
Twitter: @IndianSummerGin

Opening hours: not open to the public

This claims to be the only British gin flavoured with saffron (right), giving it a unique summery taste and colour. Because the spice is so delicate – and expensive – it's added after distilling in order not to compromise the subtle taste.

The result, at a little higher than average alcoholic strength, is a top sipping gin with a rich aftertaste, but it is also good in cocktails – try watermelon as a garnish. If you want to use it in a G&T, prefer a premium quality, low-sugar tonic that does not compete too strongly with the saffron and add a twist of lemon peel rather than a slice. The price is above average.

Duncan Taylor is mainly a bottling and whisky business, with quite a long history. Founded in 1938, it was a cask-broker and whisky trading company. Euan Shand, who acquired it in 2001, grew up around whisky – his father, the late Albert Shand, was a manager of the Glendronach Distillery. While whisky remained Duncan Taylor's core business, in around 2008 Euan launched Indian Summer (left) as a sideline, relaunching in 2015. The makers won't tell us how much gin they make compared with whisky, so it's unclear whether this a genuine small-batch craft gin.

As we went to press, Duncan Taylor, based at Huntly on the edge of Speyside single malt country, wasn't offering visitor tours.

House of Elrick Gin

Newmachar, Aberdeenshire
Distillery

ESSENTIAL INFORMATION

Key botanicals (House of Elrick Gin):
  juniper, coriander seed, citrus peel,
  pink peppercorn, sweet fennel, heather,
  rose petal
Output: 17,000 bottles a year
Location: Elrick House, Newmachar,
  Aberdeen, AB21 7PY
Telephone: 01651 862141
Email: info@houseofelrick.com
Website: www.houseofelrick.co.uk
Facebook: www.facebook.com/
  houseofelrick
Instagram: @houseofelrick
Twitter: @HouseOfElrick

Opening hours: not open to the public

Fans of the TV show *Dragon's Den* might remember Stuart Ingram, (next page, top left) who appeared on the show in 2018 with his House of Elrick Gin (bottom left). Stuart won an £80,000 investment deal but later turned it down as he and Peter Jones couldn't agree on a percentage stake for the whole company. However, this hasn't hindered the success of House of Elrick Gin – quite the contrary. In the same year, Stuart launched a crowd-funding campaign to secure £350,000 to expand the business, including the regeneration of a walled garden, and the construction of a sustainable garden restaurant and distillery. As we went to press, the redevelopment was still in progress.

The business really took off in 2018, but Stuart had submitted his plans to redevelop his Elrick House estate into a gin distillery in 2015. Its location in the lowlands of Aberdeenshire make it ideal for hand picking local botanicals and, as we went to press, House of Elrick was the only craft gin to use water from Loch Ness, giving the gin a fresh, earthy, bold flavour. One of the key botanicals, rose petals, might add more than just flavour to the gin – it is also historically interesting. Bonnie Prince Charlie visited House of Elrick and gave it the Jacobite rose that still grows in its gardens. The gin is produced in batches of 600 bottles per run, which makes it genuinely small batch.

House of Elrick also produce an Old Tom Gin (next page, bottom right, left-hand bottle) made from the same botanicals as the Original Gin but sweetened with syrup. In 2018, they released Old Tom Coconut (next page, bottom left, right-hand bottle), which is made of the same botanicals as Old Tom but is sweetened

→

with syrup and infused with coconut flavouring. Their Navy Strength Gin also contains the same botanicals as the Original, but it contains less water to produce a higher strength of 57%.

The distillery recommends adding ice and the zest of an orange to an orange-rimmed glass of House of Elrick Gin to enhance the citrus, rose and peppercorn flavours. For a refreshing summer cocktail, try mixing 35 ml of the Original Gin to 15 ml of rose liqueur, 12.5 ml of coquelicot liqueur, 12.5 ml of sauvignon blanc, 20 ml of fresh lemon juice, a dash of rose water, with Fever-Tree tonic water and rose petals, juniper berries and a sprig of mint to garnish. The distillery calls this Elrick's Summer Night Dream.

The spirits can be bought from the House of Elrick website along with a Botanical Box, priced at £22.50. This includes cardamom, cassia, hibiscus, juniper, liquorice, pink pepper, rose petals and star anise so you can experiment with different garnishes. They also sell their own embossed gin glasses for £12 and for £75 you can buy a 'Professional Set' comprising a 70-cl bottle of the Original Gin, two House of Elrick gin glasses, a botanicals box and a cocktails book containing 12 cocktail recipes.

The Crown Liquor Saloon

Belfast, County Antrim
Bar

ESSENTIAL INFORMATION

Location: 46 Great Victoria Street, Belfast,
    BT2 7BA

Telephone: 028 9024 3187

Email:
crownliquorsaloon@nicholsonpubs.com

Website: www.nicholsonspubs.co.uk/
    thecrownliquorsaloonbelfast

Facebook: www.facebook.com/
    crownbarbelfast

Instagram: @crownliquorsaloon

Twitter: @CrownBarBelfast

Opening hours:

Monday-Saturday 0900-0000

Sunday 1100-0000

Other reasons to go: Grand Opera House

Run by Nicholson's pubs and owned by the National Trust, this well-preserved Victorian gin palace (bottom left) was opened in 1885, and has been renovated several times to restore its original features. These include an altar-style red granite-topped bar, gas lamps on the red and gold carved ceiling and a mosaic floor – classic Victorian grandeur.

The bar has also retained the nine snugs (booths) that, while now used for comfort, were originally installed for privacy and feature the original gun metal plates used for striking matches – ornamental since the smoking ban, of course.

Now to the gin – the bar serves 40 different brands including Shortcross (page 294), which is their house gin. Their recommended serve uses elderflower tonic, an orange wedge and a sprig of mint. The Saloon's annual summer Gin Festival (see below) sees them collaborate with distillers from around the world, including Tarquin's Gin (page 44) and Chase Distillery. As we went to press, they had just added limited releases of Tarquin's Strawberry and Lime Gin and Chase Rhubarb and Bramley Apple to their menu.

The bar has been hosting its Gin Festival each year since 2017. Some 40 different gins from the UK and Ireland are showcased from the end of July to the end of August.

Muriel's Cafe Bar

Belfast, County Antrim
Bar

ESSENTIAL INFORMATION
Location: 12-14 Church Lane, Belfast, BT1 4QN
Telephone: 028 9033 2445
Email: murielsbelfast@gmail.com
Website: N/A
Facebook: www.facebook.com/ muriels.cafebar
Instagram: @murielsbelfast
Twitter: @MurielsCafeBar

Opening hours:
Monday-Friday 1130-0100
Saturday 1130-0100
Sunday 1000-0000

Other reasons to go: Albert Memorial Clock, Titanic Belfast Museum, Belfast City Hall, St George's Market, Ulster Museum

It's rumoured that Muriel, the eponymous former resident here, was a 17thC hat-maker who moonlighted as a madam. Re-opened as a bar (left and bottom left) and deli in 2008, owner Janine Kane wanted to reflect the bar's history as a hat-shop-cum-brothel: underwear hanging from the ceiling, damask drapes and velvety, boudoir-style interiors alongside mannequins (below right) wearing various hats capture this rather well.

The focus is gin: it stocks 92 brands, one of which is used as their gin of the month. As we went to press, this was Hendrick's Midsummer Solstice served with Fever-Tree tonic and an orange slice.

She also operates her Juniper Club – 'Around the World in 80 Gins'. You're given a card on which 80 different gins are listed and you then reach into a suitcase to retrieve a luggage tag bearing the name of one of the gins. You work your way through the selection of gins, not all in one session, ticking them off on the card.

As we went to press, Muriel's was hoping to expand to double the size and was working on a rooftop terrace.

Rita's

Belfast, County Antrim

Bar

ESSENTIAL INFORMATION
Location: 44 Franklin Street, Belfast,
   BT2 7GE
Telephone: 028 9024 8000
Email: rita@ritasbelfast.com
Website: www.ritasbelfast.com
Facebook: www.facebook.com/ritasbelfast
Instagram: @ritasbelfast
Twitter: @RitasBelfast

Opening hours:
Monday 1700-0100
Tuesday 1700-0000
Wednesday-Thursday 1700-0100
Friday-Saturday 1300-0100
Sunday 1700-0000

Other reasons to go: Ulster Hall, The Titanic
Memorial Garden, St Malachy's Church

In the 19thC Belfast was the world's main producer of linen – to the S of Belfast City Hall is The Linen Quarter where old linen mills now house offices, restaurants and bars, including Rita's (bottom left). Don't be put off by the pink neon sign on the door – it's not a strip club. Nicknamed 'the Den', Rita's opened on the 6th December 2014 and is modelled on an Asian-style brothel – 'Rita' being the madam of the house. The interior reflects this, resembling a boudoir with velvet drapes and booths (top), fringed lamps and an open fire.

The bar stocks around 70 gins including Star of Bombay (page 115), Jensen's Old Tom (page 58) and Portobello Road (page 89). Try their recommended Clip Joint cocktail: Tanqueray No.10 mixed with Chambord, lemon juice, peach, and rhubarb bitters topped with Prosecco. For a G&T, ask for Whitley Neill Rhubarb Gin (page 176) with elderflower tonic, fresh ginger and a couple of raspberries.

The bar is run by the Linen House Group who also own The Perch Rooftop Bar, Sweet Afton bar and Tutti Frutti nightclub, which can also be found on Franklin Street.

Shortcross Gin and Rademon Estate Distillery

Crossgar, County Down
Distillery and visitors' centre

ESSENTIAL INFORMATION

Key botanicals (Shortcross Gin): juniper, coriander, cassia bark, orange, elderberry, green apple, elderflower, wild clover

Output: not disclosed

Location: 62 Ballynahinch Road, Crossgar, Downpatrick, BT30 9HS

Telephone: 02844 830001

Email: hello@shortcrossgin.com

Website: www.shortcrossgin.com

Facebook: www.facebook.com/ SHORTCROSSGIN

Instagram: @shortcrossgin

Twitter: @ShortcrossGin

Opening hours:
Monday-Friday 0915-1700
Saturday 1215-1700

Other reasons to go: National Trust Rowallane Garden, Inch Abbey, Delamont Country Park, Clea Lough

*D*avid T. Smith writes: Rademon Estate Distillery is in the picturesque grounds of the Rademon Estate, around 20 miles SE of Belfast. The nearest village is Crossgar, which takes its name from *An Chrois Ghearr*; which in Gaelic means 'the short cross', and is the origin of both the name and logo of the distillery's gin, Shortcross (right).

The distillery was founded in 2012 by husband and wife team, Fiona and David Boyd-Armstrong. David had previously worked as an engineer in the defence industry and Fiona was a property surveyor.

The Rademon Estate may be familiar as a film location for productions such as Game of Thrones. It has its own hydroelectric dam, and fruits and flowers are grown in the hedgerows and gardens, some of which find their way into Shortcross gins.

The first gin was launched in 2014, followed in 2016 by an aged gin and Estate Foraged Gin, a collaboration with That Boutique-y Gin Company. Shortcross currently have two gins in their core product range: Classic, and Bartender Series One.

In 2018, the distillery's visitors' centre (left) opened following a £2.5 million investment. It aims to provide guests with a comprehensive experience: they discover the world of botanicals and the process of gin and whisky distillation, and can undertake a gin and botanical tasting and a Gin & Tonic Masterclass. The distillery also hosts one-off events and activities.

Beyond gin, The Rademon Estate Distillery also produces single malt and single pot still Irish whisky.

Boatyard Gin and Distillery

Enniskillen, County Fermanagh
Distillery and visitors' centre

ESSENTIAL INFORMATION

Key botanicals (Boatyard Double Gin):
juniper, coriander, liquorice, grains of
paradise, unwaxed lemon peel, bog-myrtle

Output: 120,000 bottles a year

Location: 346 Lough Shore Road,
Drumcrow East, Enniskillen, BT93 7DX

Telephone: 07757 219431

Email: teresa@boatyarddistillery.com

Website: www.boatyarddistillery.com

Facebook: www.facebook.com/
theboatyarddistillery

Instagram: @boatyarddistillery

Twitter: @BoatyardDistill

Opening hours:
Monday-Saturday 0900-1700 (booking
required)

Other reasons to go: Enniskillen Castle
Museum, Castle Coole National Trust,
Devenish Island

Sweet gale is one of the most unusual
botanicals you'll come across in this
guide, possibly the most unusual. It's also
known as bog-myrtle, scientific name
Myrica gale, a shrub typical of acid peat
bogs, growing 1-2 m high. For centuries it's
been useful to man as an insect repellant;
as a remedy for stomach complaints; as a
flavouring for beer; and in Denmark and
Sweden for schnaps. It has a slightly sweet,
resinous taste.

Joe McGirr (next page, bottom left),
founder of Boatyard Distillery (bottom left),
collects it from a bog on his family's farm and
uses it to flavour his Boatyard Double Gin
(next page, bottom right). Double gin? The
distilling process is somewhat similar to that
used in The Netherlands to make genever
– the spirit is exposed to the juniper berries
twice for an extra juniper blast. (A handful
of other distillers in the guide use bog-myrtle,
for example Dyfi Distillery on page 118.)

Joe is a wine and spirits industry
professional who worked at Glenmorangie
in Scotland and at Moet Hennessy before
founding Boatyard. In common with a few of
the most dedicated craft gin makers, he and
two colleagues, Orlaith and Teresa, make their
own base spirit from local grain – however,
it is blended with a bought-in organic spirit
before introducing the botanicals.

The result, according to The Gin
Foundry's taster, is extreme when sipped
neat. The grains of paradise and lemon peel
whack your tongue and throat, but when
mixed it becomes soft and sippable, with
the complex flavours shining through. Joe's
recommended garnish is a slice of grapefruit.

The distillery is in a lovely waterside
location on Lough Erne, Northern Ireland's
second biggest lake. The lough, with its

many attractive islands and islets, is in fact a widened section of the River Erne and divides into two parts – Upper and Lower. The new visitors' centre and renovated distillery (top left and right) completed 2019 are in the pleasant Tullybay neighbourhood of the Lower Lough and make a top gin tourism experience, with tours and talks held regularly.

Boatyard makes a second gin, Old Tom (£48), aged in Pedro Ximenez barrels, sweetened with local honey. It also produces a vodka and, as the guide went to press, was planning a whisky, too.

Blackwater Gin and Distillery

Ballyduff Upper, County Waterford
Distillery, bar and visitors' centre

ESSENTIAL INFORMATION

Key botanicals (Blackwater No.5 Irish Gin): juniper, coriander, liquorice root, green cardamom, cinnamon quills, bitter almond, lemon, bitter orange, allspice, lemongrass

Output: 150,000 bottles a year

Location: Church Road, Ballinlevane East, Ballyduff, P51 C5C6

Telephone: 058 60732

Email: hello@blackwaterdistillery.ie

Website: www.blackwaterdistillery.ie

Facebook: www.facebook.com/Blackwaterdistillery

Instagram: @blackwaterdistillery

Twitter: @BlackDistillery

Opening hours:
Monday-Friday 0900-1700

Other reasons to go: Lismore Castle, Cappoquin House and Gardens, Tourin House, Mount Melleray Abbey

*D*avid T. Smith writes: Blackwater Distillery is located in a 1950s hardware store a stone's throw from the Blackwater River in the village of Ballyduff Upper in County Waterford which is about 30 miles NE of Cork and about 45 miles W of Waterford on Ireland's southern coast.

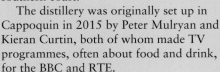

The distillery was originally set up in Cappoquin in 2015 by Peter Mulryan and Kieran Curtin, both of whom made TV programmes, often about food and drink, for the BBC and RTE.

The distillery and visitors' centre covers two floors. The central part of the ground floor houses the distilling equipment (above), which is clearly visible to visitors via a mezzanine gallery that surrounds the building on three sides. The mezzanine is made up of a number of distinct areas: an apothecary area, where botanicals are weighed out for the gins and where visitors can learn more about botanicals' aromas and flavours; a bar (next page, top left), where patrons can sample the distillery's spirits and mixed drinks; and a library that is used for tutored tastings (next page, bottom left).

After exploring upstairs, you can visit the working distillery floor, accompanied by a member of the Blackwater team, to see gin and whisky production first-hand.

Blackwater launched their first gin, Blackwater No.5 Irish Gin (left), in 2015. This was followed by Juniper Cask Gin

(right, top bottle), which is aged in a 50-litre cask made of juniper wood; and Wexford Strawberry Irish Gin (top left), which is made with local strawberries and is notably less sweet than many other fruit gins.

In 2016, Blackwater joined forces with That Boutique-y Gin Company to create Monastic Gin, inspired by the plants that would have grown in an 11thC Irish monastic garden.

Bertha's Revenge Gin and Ballyvolane House Spirits Co.

Castlelyons, County Cork
Distillery

ESSENTIAL INFORMATION

Key botanicals (Bertha's Revenge):
    juniper, coriander, cardamom, cumin,
    Alexander's seed
Output: 27,000 bottles a year
Location: Castlelyons, P61 FP70
Telephone: 025 36349
Email: info@ballyvolanespirits.ie
Website: www.ballyvolanespirits.ie
**Facebook: hwww.facebook.com/
    berthasrevenge**
Instagram: @berthasrevenge
Twitter: @berthasrevenge

Opening hours: tours by appointment only

**Other reasons to go: Lismore Castle
Gardens and Art Gallery, Kinsale town,
Crawford Gallery, English Market in
Cork City**

Ballyvolane House – a charming country house hotel – and its distillery's main product, Bertha's Revenge (bottom left and next page, bottom left), are synonymous and sum up everything this guide wants of a craft gin.

Distillers Justin Green and Antony Jackson (next page, top left) have known each other since school, where they started drinking gin at 15, "possibly younger". Together they founded their distillery in 2015 and were the first to make gin using spirit distilled from whey – the clear fluid that arises when milk goes sour and the solids are separated from liquid. One or two others have copied their idea, but Bertha's Revenge remains the gin produced from this base and its fame is spreading.

Why use whey? First, it makes a rich, silky spirit compared with grain, that isn't dwarfed by big botanical flavours. Second, it is produced by local cows (next page, middle), connecting the gin umbillically with the land.

Third, it allowed them to name their gin after Bertha, Co. Kerry's most famous cow. Bertha was a local celebrity, possibly the world's oldest cow who died in 1993 aged 48 after giving birth to 39 calves. She was fêted even in her lifetime, once leading the local St Patrick's Day Parade. A wake was held at a local pub after she died which lasted three days – well, this is Ireland.

Moreover: in Gaelic Ballyvolane means 'place of the springing heifers'; they use water from their own well on the farm to dilute the spirit; Justin and Antony's distillery started in a (very cold) cowshed; and the whey is produced in a local cheesery.

The dominant flavour is cumin – Bertha's Revenge carries much more of

the spice than other craft gins. The other botanicals are listed on the previous page. The Alexander's seeds, which contribute a peppery punch, are foraged locally, of course. They also produce a sloe gin.

Output was 500-600 bottles a week in 2018 – genuinely small batch, which with the arrival of a new still was set to triple – but keeping this admirably local enterprise firmly in the genuine microdistillery league.

Future plans include a Navy Strength gin (57%) to be released in early 2020.

Beara Gin and Distillery

Derrymihin West, County Cork
Distillery and bar

ESSENTIAL INFORMATION

Key botanicals (Beara Ocean Gin): juniper, coriander seed, cardamom, citrus peel, celery seed, fuchsia, sugar kelp seaweed, Atlantic salt water

Output: 20,000 bottles a year

Location: Castletownbere Commercial Park, Derrymihan, Castletownbere, P75 AX79

Telephone: 027 70861

Email: sales@thebearadistillery.ie

Website: www.thebearadistillery.ie

Facebook: www.facebook.com/bearadistillery

Instagram: @bearadistillery

Twitter: @BearaDistillery

Opening hours: not open to the public

'The cure to everything is sea air and salt water' is Beara Distillery's motto – to which distiller John Power (top, far right) might add that he is the only man in the British Isles who has managed to bottle them.

The Beara Peninsula on Ireland's SW coast, an unspoiled area with dramatic ocean views, sticks out into the Atlantic – sourcing the sea water is the easy part. John has to distil the brine as a separate process, purifying it, then reintroduce the salt. He then has just one of the five components needed to make his core gin (bottom left, left-hand bottle) – the others being the base spirit, the pre-prepared citrus zest (next page, bottom right), sugar kelp gathered locally and fuschia (next page, middle).

Fuschia is the symbol of the Beara Peninsula and in summer the hedgerows are red with its blossom. They pick in bulk and then distil enough, again as a separate process, to last until the next season. It gives the gin a light floral flavour.

The five components are blended according to the recipe, then distilled. The resulting spirit (80%) is diluted to standard strength with water from the Cork and Kerry Mountains.

John's family were local fisherfolk for generations, so salt water is not only in their

gin but in their blood. He and his sister Eileen (previous page, top middle) launched the new venture in 2017, having done due diligence by visiting many a trade show and microdistillery.

Does it really taste of the sea? According to the critics yes: Beara gins have an undeniably salty taste, not overpowering, which gave them a savoury edge that's an interesting contrast to the fruit gins.

John runs distillery visits in association with the local tourist board (email restaurant@berehavenlodge.com for details) – while you're there you'll want to stop for a few in the friendly gin bar (top).

Garnish Island Gin and West Cork Distillers

Skibbereen, County Cork
Distillery

ESSENTIAL INFORMATION

Key botanicals (Garnish Island Gin):
juniper, coriander, liquorice, cardamom,
bitter orange, cocoa nibs, rosemary,
thyme, strawberry, lavender, hibiscus,
rose petal, Iris

Output: not disclosed

Location: Marsh Road, Skibbereen,
West Cork

Telephone: 028 22815

Email: info@westcorkdistillers.com

Website: www.westcorkdistillers.com

Facebook: www.facebook.com/
WestCorkDistillers

Instagram: @westcorkdistillers

Twitter: @WestCorkDistill

Opening hours:
Tours (booking required)
Saturday 1000-1400

Other reasons to go: Lough Hyne, Drombeg
stone circle, Heir Island, Whale Watch
West Cork

County Cork has a history of artisan food and drink, so it was only a matter of time before it produced its own take on the juniper-based spirit. Founded in 2003 by John O'Connell and his lifelong friends, cousins Denis McCarthy and Ger McCarthy, West Cork Distillers set about making premium quality spirits, as well as providing sustainable employment in this southern corner of Ireland.

The signature gin, a London Dry variety called Garnish Island Gin (above right and bottom left) takes its inspiration from the almost sub-tropical woodland gardens of Garnish Island, located in Bantry Bay. Here, the sheltered harbour of Glengarriff and the influence of the Gulf Stream provide the right conditions for warm-climate plants, some of which are exclusive to south-western Ireland and northern parts of Spain and Portugal. A range of botanicals that reflect the essence of the gardens, such as hibiscus, rose, rosemary, and iris are infused to release their essential oils and then slowly distilled in small batches to create the gin.

For the perfect G&T, West Cork recommends serving the gin with plenty of ice, fresh lime zest, slices of strawberry and premium tonic water (next page, middle). The gin is also delicious when paired with floral mixers such as hibiscus or elderflower, or simply sip it on its own to savour its unique flavours.

West Cork produces another London Dry variety called Two Trees Gin, which has the citrus aroma and sweet aftertaste that you would expect of a London Dry. They have also added coriander leaves, creating a

unique twist on this age-old classic.

As we went to press, they were in the process of building a new distillery and visitors' centre, due to open at the end of 2019. The visitors' centre will be attached to the distillery (top), allowing guests to get a first-hand experience of the working distillery. Most of the equipment here (right) was handcrafted on site, so the team have intimate knowledge on how to use their machinery to create the perfect balance of flavours in their gin. The Master Distiller, Deirdre Bohane, has much experience in crafting true artisan gins, having developed around 30 to date. While the new distillery and visitors' centre are under construction, the current distillery is open for unofficial tours on Saturday mornings.

Conncullin Irish Gin and Connacht Distillery

Ballina, County Mayo
Distillery

ESSENTIAL INFORMATION
Key botanicals (Conncullin Irish Gin):
   juniper, hawthorn berry, elderberry
Output: not disclosed
Location: Belleek, Ballina
Telephone: +353 96 74902
Email: hello@connachtwhiskey.com
Website: www.connachtwhiskey.com
Facebook: www.facebook.com/
   connachtwhiskey
Instagram: @conncullin_gin
Twitter: @connachtwhiskey

Opening hours:
Wednesday-Friday 1030-1800
Saturday 1200-1700

Other reasons to go: St Muredach's
Cathedral, Belleek Wood and Park

This is the brainchild of Americans Robert Cassell, Tom Jensen, and PJ Stapleton and his cousin, Irishman David Stapleton. Their initial aim was to bring single malt pot still Irish whisky back to western Ireland as, at the time, no Irish companies were making it. They also wanted to create Irish spirits which could be exported to the US – they'd had difficulty finding real Irish spirits in the States. The distillery opened in 2015 on the banks of the River Moy, which joins the Atlantic Ocean.

Conncullin Irish Gin (below left) gets its name from two lakes in County Mayo – Lough Conn and Lough Cullin – whose water is used to dilute the spirit. The gin was originally launched in spring 2017 at 47% but was re-released in April 2019 at a lower strength of 42.3%. Head distiller John Parks uses the traditional pot distillation method to create a berry-forward gin with a juniper and citrus finish. As we went to press, the gin could be bought from the Celtic Whiskey Shop website (page 323). Connacht also produce limited edition gins, such as their Conncullin Cask Aged Irish Gin. Released in April 2018, this was sold exclusively from the distillery.

Although most of their tours concentrate on whisky, Connacht offer the chance to taste Conncullin Irish Gin on their Ultimate Craft Experience. For 22.50 euros you get a guided tour followed by a sampling of their whisky, vodka, *poitín* and gin – see the website for booking information.

Drumshanbo Gunpowder Irish Gin & The Shed Distillery of PJ Rigney

Drumshanbo, County Leitrim
Distillery

ESSENTIAL INFORMATION

Key botanicals (Drumshanbo Gunpowder Irish Gin): juniper, coriander seed, cardamom, lemon, grapefruit, star anise, caraway seed, kaffir lime, meadowsweet, Gunpowder Tea

Output: 100,000 cases a year

Location: Carrick on Shannon Road, Drumshanbo

Telephone: +353 1507 9170

Email: prigney@thesheddistillery.com

Website: www.thesheddistillery.com

Facebook: www.facebook.com/ theshedrumshanbo.ie

Instagram: @thesheddistillery

Twitter: @SHEDDISTILLERY

Opening hours: not open to the public

Patrick Rigney had been in the drinks industry for more than 30 years when he launched the Shed Distillery in 2014, which he claims is the first distillery in Connacht for 101 years. Pat's first project was a whisky, but with a three-year ageing process, he worked on other spirits while it matured and in 2016 launched Drumshanbo Gunpowder Irish Gin (bottom left).

Gunpowder fuses traditional recipes with local ingredients such as meadowsweet, plus botanicals Pat collected on his travels. He came across Gunpowder Tea on a trip to Morocco, where he took part in a traditional tea ceremony. Intrigued by the pellet-shaped leaves and their slightly spicy flavour, he journeyed to their source in Zejiang, China, where he also discovered the oriental grapefruit, known locally as 'the forbidden fruit', a cross between Indonesian pomelo and Jamaican sweet orange.

Shed Distillery uses a combination of distillation methods: juniper, coriander seed, cardamom, angelica, orris root, star anise, caraway seed and meadowsweet are distilled on the pot still, while the Gunpowder Tea, lemon, oriental grapefruit and kaffir lime are vapour infused (page 254). For the perfect serve, add 40 ml of Drumshanbo Gunpowder Irish Gin to 140 ml of quality tonic with a wedge of fresh grapefruit and cubed ice. For a cocktail, try serving the gin with fresh lime and grapefruit juice, sugar syrup, fresh mint and grapefruit to make a Curious Jackalope.

As we went to press, Shed Distillery was not open for tours but were planning to open a visitors' centre in early 2020. This will include tours, tastings, a café, herb garden and shop.

HYDE Bar and Gin Parlour at The Forster Court Hotel

Galway

Bar

ESSENTIAL INFORMATION
Location: Forster Street, Galway, H91 PY7E
Telephone: +353 91 564111
Email: info@hydebargalway.ie
Website: www.hydebargalway.ie
Facebook: www.facebook.com/
    HydeBarGalway
Instagram: @hydebargalway
Twitter: @HydeGinBar

Opening hours:
Monday-Thursday 0700-2330
Friday-Saturday 0700-0030
Sunday 1100-2300

Other reasons to go: Galway Cathedral,
Galway City Museum, Eyre Square

With brightly coloured murals and sunhat fairy lights hanging from the ceiling, HYDE bar and Gin Parlour is like a Mad Hatter's tea party come to life. The bar claims to hold the largest collection of gins in Ireland, and with more than 500 gins to choose from, it's probably right. It opened in May 2018 after the Connacht Hospitality Group (who run several bars and hotels around Galway) spent 12 months collecting the gins from around the world. They worked closely with the Celtic Whiskey Shop (page 323), who helped them to source some of the gins. Marketing manager Eveanna Ryan says the most unusual gin in stock is Unicorn Tears Gin Liqueur, a bittersweet concoction with an iridescent shimmer. The house gin is Bombay Sapphire (page 115) which they recommend serving with Fever-Tree tonic.

The entire bar screams to be Instagrammed, but its most striking focal point is the flower wall (left), designed by local team Third Mind, and containing more than 7,500 flowers. They also have custom-made Gunpowder Irish Gin table lamps (page 306), Bloom London Dry Gin vases and a Greenhouse room which can be closed off for special occasions or meetings.

HYDE also offers brunch and dinner. It's a short walk from Eyre Square, Galway's popular city centre park (also known as John F. Kennedy Memorial Park), so combining a stroll in the park with a visit to HYDE makes a gin day out.

Micil Gin and Distillery

Galway
Distillery and visitors' centre

ESSENTIAL INFORMATION

Key botanicals (Micil Gin): juniper, heather, bog-myrtle, hawberry, Connemara bogbean

Output: not disclosed

Location: Oslo Bar, 226 Upper Salthill, Salthill, Galway, H91 N9WK

Telephone: +353 91 456 572

Email: info@micil.ie

Website: www.micildistillery.com

Facebook: www.facebook.com/ micildistillery

Instagram: @micildistillery

Twitter: @micildistillery

Opening hours:
Monday-Sunday 1200-2000

Other reasons to go: Galway Cathedral, Galway City Museum, Eyre Square

Pádraic Ó'Griallais (above) developed a love for spirits from his grandfather, a fourth-generation distiller who began teaching him the craft from the age of 14. Pádraic's family specialized in *poitín*, a grain-based spirit similar to whisky which he calls the original Irish spirit. After a career in teaching, Pádraic decided to go back to his roots and opened Galway's first legal distillery for more than a hundred years, naming it after his great-great-great-grandfather Micil Mac Chearra, who began distilling in Connemara in 1848.

Pádraic saw there was a shared heritage between *poitín* and gin – they were both originally distilled from wine and botanicals – and wanted to create a uniquely West of Ireland gin. In July 2018, Micil Irish Gin (left) was launched in tandem with the opening of the distillery's visitors' centre. Pádraic distils Micil with a combination of classic and wild Connemara botanicals (see list, top left) and classifies the gin as a contemporary style gin that's best served with a wedge of citrus and a quality tonic. For a cocktail, try it in a Connemara Collins or Micil Gin Sour.

Micil Distillery offers tours and tastings, where you learn about the history of *poitín* and gin, and how they're made, and get to sample their spirits – see website for booking information.

Nora's Irish Dry Gin and Tigh Nora bar

Galway

Bar

ESSENTIAL INFORMATION

Key botanicals (Nora's Irish Dry Gin): juniper, bitter orange peel, peach, rose petal
Output: not disclosed
Location: 8 Cross Street Lower, Galway
Telephone: +353 91 563 757
Email: info@frontdoorpub.com
Website: www.tighnoragalway.com
Facebook: www.facebook.com/ TighNoraGalway
Instagram: @tighnoragalway
Twitter: @TighNoraGalway

Opening hours:
Monday-Thursday 1600-0200
Friday-Saturday 1100-0200
Sunday 1200-0200

Other reasons to go: Galway Cathedral, Galway City Museum, Eyre Square

In the heart of Galway's Latin Quarter, Tigh Nora (above), named after James Joyce's wife Nora Barnacle, stocks around 200 different gins including Drumshanbo Gunpowder Irish Gin (page 306), Micil Irish Gin (page 308), Beara (page 301) plus their own recipe – Nora's Irish Dry Gin (bottom left). Launched in April 2019, it's a floral-led London Dry sold exclusively through Tigh Nora, its adjoining pub The Front Door, and a selection of local bars and shops, including McCambridge's of Galway. Manager Fiachra McKenna recommends serving Nora's Gin with a quality tonic, a grapefruit slice, a sprig of mint and some cracked black pepper.

Tigh Nora also offers gin tasting classes, plus gin masterclasses where you learn about the history and distillation of gin, as well as garnishes and tonics. Classes are for a minimum of six people and can be booked over the phone. Also bookable by phone is their Hendrick's High Tea, where G&Ts are served in teapots and china cups alongside scones, sandwiches and cakes.

They also offer a Gin Passport (above middle) which gets a stamp every time you try a new gin. You get a free Tanqueray G&T once you've collected ten stamps.

Listoke Gin, Distillery and Gin School

Drogheda, County Louth
Distillery and gin school

ESSENTIAL INFORMATION

Key botanicals (Listoke 1777 Gin): juniper, coriander seed, cardamom, cassia bark, orange, rowan berry, jasmine

Output: 40,000 bottles a year

Location: Unit 9 Tenure Business Park, Tenure, A92 XP70

Telephone: 041 2145044

Email: hello@listokedistillery.ie

Website: www.listokedistillery.ie

Facebook: www.facebook.com/ listokedistillery

Instagram: @listokedistillery

Twitter: @listokedistill

Opening hours:
Tuesday-Friday 1000-1600
Saturday 1100-1600

Other reasons to go: Boyne Viaduct, Millmount Fort

Blanaid O'Hare and her fiancée James McKenna were visiting their native Ireland in 2015 after hectic years working in and owning New York bars, on the lookout for a new business and a less frantic lifestyle. They met Bronagh Conlon, who had been involved in a couple of distillery start-ups and who had visited Burleigh's distillery and gin school (page 142) in England. Recognizing there was nothing like the gin school in Ireland, they took the punt, installing two mini stills in their kitchen sinks, where they started to develop their recipe. Soon they had moved to a barn on the Listoke House estate and bought a 500-litre still, in 2016 launching Listoke 1777 (1777 being the year Listoke first appeared on a map of Ireland – left and above right). That year they also opened their gin school (opposite, top), which, with the gin, expanded so rapidly that now they occupy a custom-built space. "Game on" says Blanaid – "and it has been ever since." In 2018 Listoke was launched in the USA.

Listoke's flavour was achieved collaboratively: "Bronagh wanted elderflower, it was super trendy and there was plenty of it locally. I wanted something more subtle, honeysuckle or the like. We eventually agreed on jasmine. I also wanted orange in the recipe. Bronagh had once been a commercial jam maker and my grandmother used to make rowan berry jam when I was a child, so we threw that in

the mix, and it really worked well with the other ingredients, bringing the total to nine. We use well balanced amounts of each."

The resulting taste is multi-dimensional. Juniper emerges immediately and dances through to the end. Sweet orange adds to the juniper's bitterness and the rowan berries tartness, giving way to a pleasant floral interlude. The finish has an unexpected, spicy kick from the cardamom.

You can enjoy Listoke 1777 neat, or as a Martini. The flavours open up nicely with the addition of an ice cube and a twist of orange peel, and of course it makes a terrific G&T.

The gin school can claim to be one of the best gintourism experiences in Ireland, perhaps the best. They do it properly: on arrival, a Listoke 1777 and tonic plus distiller-quality juniper berries and a twist of orange peel. Then a tour of the distillery, where you learn the brand's story. Then back to the school where you are given three classic gin styles to taste – and are asked to work out which you prefer. Next, serious classwork: you explore botanicals in depth (right). Next you distil your own bottle of gin in your chosen style (above right). While waiting for distillation to complete, you try some local food specialities and get "more ginformation."

No.57 Irish Gin and The Headline Bar

Dublin

Bar

ESSENTIAL INFORMATION

Key botanicals (No.57 Irish Gin): juniper, coriander, liquorice, cinnamon, lemon, orange, grapefruit, ginger

Output: 250-300 bottles a year

Location: 57 The Headline, 56-57 Clanbrassil Street Lower, Dublin 8

Telephone: +353 1 532 0279

Email: hello@57theheadline.ie

Website: www.57theheadline.com

Facebook: www.facebook.com/57-The-Headline

Instagram: @57theheadline

Twitter: @57theheadline

Opening hours:
Monday-Thursday 1500-2330
Friday-Saturday 1500-0030
Sunday 1300-2300

Other reasons to go: Dublin Castle, St Patrick's Cathedral, Guinness Storehouse

No.57 Gin Bar stocks more than a hundred different gins, and aims to source every Irish one. As we went to press, these included Arbikie Kirsty's Gin (page 248), An Dúlamán (page 319), Beara (page 301), plus their own recipe, which they sell exclusively from the bar: No.57 Irish Gin (bottom left), a smooth gin with a kick of ginger. They also create limited edition infusions, the most recent example (as we went to press) being No.57 Irish Gin with cranberries, barberries and hibiscus.

The focal point of the bar is their Gin and Tonic station, a wall covered by shelves of different gin bottles and an assortment of botanicals and garnishes, which form their 'Gin of the Week', made in a perfect serve.

The bar is only open on Fridays and Saturdays (though it can be booked for private events throughout the week) but downstairs they have a Gin Parlour (top), which can be booked seven days a week. This is a semi-private area of the bar where there's space for groups of around six people.

No.57 sells gin hampers on the online shop, ranging in price from 66 to 99 euros. These include a bottle of gin (picked from a list of 22), four bottles of quality tonic, two large glasses, and three different garnishes.

Street 66

Dublin
Bar

ESSENTIAL INFORMATION

Location: 33-34 Parliament Street, Temple
   Bar, Dublin 2
Telephone: +353 (0) 874 216759
Email: info@street66dublin.com
Website: www.street66.bar
Facebook: www.facebook.com/
   street66Dublin
Instagram: @street66dublin
Twitter: @st66dublin

Opening hours:
Monday-Thursday 1230-0000
Friday-Saturday 1230-0230
Sunday 1200-0000

Other reasons to go: City Hall, Dublin
Castle, Christ Church Cathedral

Street 66 (bottom left) is located on Parliament Street, just a two-minute walk from Temple Bar. Formerly an LGBT hotspot known as The Front Lounge, the bar was taken over by Cris Llarena and Siobhan Conmy in December 2016, who gave it a live music dimension focusing on disco, reggae, funk, soul and jazz. Despite initial concerns that the bar would 'go straight' under the new management, its Pride parties, drag-themed events and LGBT game nights, combined with its Pop Art decoration, have kept the LGBT spirit alive.

Gin is unquestionably the star of the show here, and the bar (above) boasts more than 150 craft gins from around the world, including Shortcross (page 294), Bertha's Revenge (page 299) and Caorunn (page 282). For cocktails, they recommend a classic Negroni, using Beefeater 24 Gin (page 86) or a Dry Martini, using Boatyard Gin (page 295), Glendalough Winter Edition Gin (page 315) or Plymouth Navy Strength Gin (page 45).

The knowledgeable bar staff help you discover which one will suit you. The menu not only gives a brief history and taste profile of each gin, but describes which garnishes work best. For example, they recommend serving Plymouth Gin with strawberries and rosemary, and Sipsmiths (page 71) with a slice of orange, cardamom and a lemon twist.

Sling Shot Gin and Lough Ree Distillery

Lanesborough, County Longford
Distillery

ESSENTIAL INFORMATION

Key botanicals (Sling Shot Gin): juniper, coriander seed, cardamom, citrus fruits, celery seed, mint, lemon balm, peat
Output: not disclosed
Location: Main Street, Lanesborough
Telephone: +35343 332 1542
Email: info@lrd.ie
Website: www.lrd.ie
Facebook: www.facebook.com/LoughReeDistillery
Instagram: @loughreedistill
Twitter: @LoughReeDistill

Opening hours: visitors' centre opening 2020

Other reasons to go: Rathcline Castle, St Mel's Cathedral, Inchcleraun Island

Three siblings are behind this operation – Peter and Michael Clancy and Sheila Mullen. Sheila worked in finance and hospitality while Peter was an engineer and Michael a brewing consultant. Ally Alpine of the Celtic Whiskey Shop (page 323) and Alan Wolstenholme, of the Scottish Distillers Association, are non-executive directors.

Slingshot Gin (bottom left) is Lough Ree's first product, possibly the first gin made in Co. Longford, launched in 2018 at their microdistillery. Long term, the plan is to make a range of spirits including whisky in their main plant opposite the microdistillery, which (as we went to press) was due to be completed in summer 2020, and claims to be Co. Longford's first modern distillery.

Sling Shot's most original feature (apart from the bright blue bottle) is its peat flavour. To achieve this, peat is distilled separately, as are citrus fruits (orange, pink grapefruit, lemon and lime) and fresh mint. The three distillates are then blended and added to the base gin spirit which is flavoured with the key botanicals listed above left.

The result is a complex flavour, starting with a fresh citrus aroma, developing into a spicy boldness on the tongue and finishing with an earthy roundedness from the peat, plus a fresh waft of mint. As we went to press it had won several international awards.

Current gin production is genuinely small batch, with about 1,450 bottles being finished each fortnight.

Sling Shot? The legendary Queen Maeve of Connaught was killed by a slingshot strike while bathing in Lough Ree. Lanesborough is on Lough Ree's northern tip.

The new distillery, after a substantial investment, will have a visitors' centre offering a variety of gin and whisky experiences.

Glendalough Gin and Distillery

Newtonmountkennedy, County Wicklow
Distillery

ESSENTIAL INFORMATION

**Key botanicals (Glendalough Wild
Botanical Gin):** juniper, coriander,
liquorice, lemon, water mint, lemon
balm, lady's bedstraw, red clover, sweet
cicely, wild raspberry, sloe berry, bilberry,
elderflower, bell heather, wild rose petal,
pine, blackberry leaf, yarrow, oxeye daisy,
sheep's sorrel, woodruff, wood sorrel

Output: not disclosed

Location: N/A

Telephone: N/A

Email: info@glendaloughdistillery.com

Website: www.glendaloughdistillery.com

Facebook: www.facebook.com/
GlendaloughDistillery

Instagram: @glendaloughdistillery

Twitter: @GlendaloughDist

Opening hours: tours by appointment only

**Other reasons to go: Great Sugar Loaf,
Lough Tay, Coillte, Vartry Reservoir**

The beautiful and remote
valley of Glendalough,
with its monastic settlement
founded in the 6thC by
St Kevin, is one of Co.
Wicklow's top tourist sites
and this distillery located
a few miles away clearly
benefits from the association
– perhaps fair enough since
monks often distilled and
sold spirits in order to
fund their communities.
A logo image of St Kevin
(see below for more about
him) appears on the bottles
and botanicals are foraged
(next page, middle) in the Wicklow hills and
mountains of which Glendalough is a gem.

They have a big product range: three
whiskies, a *poitín* and no less than nine gins.

The core gin is Glendalough Wild
Botanical Gin (above and next page,
top left), made with an amazing list of
botanicals (see list, above left) collected
around Glendalough by a full-time forager
who respects the plants by cutting with
scissors, never uprooting, and leaving
behind enough to ensure a healthy new crop
next season. She treads carefully, aiming to
leave no trace that she was there. The bulky
ones are macerated in a copper still (left),
the lighter ones hung in baskets in the still
to allow gentle extraction of flavour.

On the nose you get juniper, citrus and
pine – and, claims the distiller (next page,
bottom right), rain; the taste on the tongue
is summer flowers, autumn fruit and spice;
the aftertaste is long and spicy.

Alongside Wild Botanical there are four
seasonal gins: Glendalough Spring, Summer,

founders, from left to right: Brian Fagan, Kevin
enan, Barry Gallagher, Gary McLoughlin

Autumn and Winter Gin. And lastly the 'Ginteresting' series led by Glendalough Sloe Gin and joined by Dillisk, Beech Leaf and Wild Blackberry & Mountain Heather. Dillisk is another name for dulse – an Irish seaweed.

The distillery welcomes visitors as part of a Meet the Makers Tour – details from the Glendalough website or local tourist office. The Wicklow Heather Restaurant (with rooms) and The Glendalough Hotel are both close to Glendalough and sell the distillery's products.

As for St Kevin: his name is a translation of the Gaelic *Coemgen* which means fair begotten or of noble birth. There's a legend that he was descended, like St Columba, from early Irish royalty. He was an ascetic, divorced from worldly pleasures, eating and drinking the bare minimum and at one time living in a cave which can still be seen in the hillside above Glendalough's upper lake (Glendalough means valley of two lakes). Beside the lower lake are the remains of his monastic settlement, including a church dating from the 9th to 12thC but with much earlier elements, possibly from St Kevin's time – he was born in AD 498. There's a song about Kevin's asceticism performed by The Dubliners, describing how he drowned a woman who tried to seduce him.

Mór Irish Gin and Arderin Distillery

Tullamore, County Offaly
Distillery

ESSENTIAL INFORMATION

Key botanicals (Mór Irish Gin): juniper, coriander, rosemary, blackberry, raspberry, cranberry

Output: 60,000 bottles a year

Location: Unit 12 Cloncollig Industrial Estate, Church Road, Tullamore

Telephone: N/A

Email: info@arderindistillery.com

Website: www.moririshgin.com

Facebook: www.facebook.com/Moririshgin

Instagram: @moririshgin

Twitter: @MorIrishgin

Opening hours:
Monday-Sunday 0900-1600

Other reasons to go: Tullamore Dew Visitors' Centre, Clonmacnoise Abbey, The Slieve Bloom Mountains

Eoin Bara, Arderin's founder and distiller, has an engagingly Irish attitude to life – and gin. He is a believer in the power of mantras, of good stories – and of bad decisions. The first two don't need explanation, but the last? In fact he doesn't mean real bad decisions, simply decisions that aren't entirely safe, such as when he decided to leave his steady job in a design agency and go into craft gin. A friend asked him after one too many gins "What do you love?" "I love gin" was his reply, only partly in jest.

Eoin gave in his notice and spent four months travelling the world learning how to make gin. Back in Ireland he started building the distillery in Tullamore, named after Arderin, the highest peak in the Slieve Bloom Mountains (next page, bottom right) that rise from Ireland's central plain.

Mór (left) is made in four stages: juniper, coriander, angelica and rosemary (next page, bottom left) are distilled together; then the berries (next page, top left and middle) separately. Next all are blended together to achieve consistency and refine the taste and lastly the blend is distilled. The number of bottles produced varies. Eoin used to go to great lengths finding the purest water, driving into the mountains in a pickup truck and pumping fresh sandstone filtered mountain water into a tank, but gave up after the legality was questioned.

The first thing you notice about Mór is its beautiful berry-aroma on the nose. The taste on the tongue is earthy at first,

with coriander and rosemary making a big impression. Then it becomes sweet and juicy with bundles of fresh berry flavour at the core. The finish has a hint of pepper. He also produces Pineapple Edition Gin (previous page, top right).

In 2019 he opened a gin school in Donabate, North Dublin, leaving Arderin very much a working distillery.

An Dúlamán Irish Maritime Gin and Sliabh Liag Distillers

Carrick, County Donegal
Distillery

ESSENTIAL INFORMATION

Key botanicals (An Dúlamán Irish Maritime Gin): juniper, coriander, cassia bark, lemon, orange, carrageen moss, sugar kelp, channel wrack, dulse, pepper dulse

Output: 14,352 bottles a year

Location: Line Road, Carrick, F94 X9DX

Telephone: +353 74 973 9875

Email: info@sliabhliagdistillers.com

Website: www.sliabhlagdistillers.com

Facebook: www.facebook.com/AnDulamanGin

Instagram: @andulamangin

Twitter: @andulamangin

Opening hours:
Monday-Friday 0900-1700
Saturday 1200-1700

Other reasons to go: Sliabh Liag Cliffs, Slieve League Cultural Centre, Silver Strand Beach, Sliabh Liag boat tours

James and Moira Doherty were picking dulse on Muckross Head in Donegal one day in 2010 when Moira (below right) asked if it could be used to flavour gin. After much experimenting, they found that it gave a light, salty flavour with a peppery undertone. This discovery evolved into their mission to capture the essence of the Donegal coast in a 'gin of the sea', using five different types of seaweed. The result, An Dúlamán Irish Maritime Gin (bottom left), was launched in October 2017.

Besides dulse, they use sugar kelp to give the gin a natural sweetness and enhance the flavours of the other botanicals. Channel wrack (or Dúlamán seaweed) gives the gin its name and balances the spice of the pepper dulse with bitter hints of tannin.

James and Moira use the London Dry method to distil the botanicals, except for the fifth seaweed, carrageen moss, which is vapour infused (page 254) – it turns to jelly if boiled. The moss gives a roast chestnut flavour. The resulting taste is a complex mix of floral, citrus and spicy. They recommend serving the gin with a quality lemon tonic, plenty of ice and a lemon slice. It also works well in a Negroni.

Their distillery, Sliabh Liag, can claim to be the first in Donegal for 175 years, reviving Donegal's distilling heritage – there were thought to be more illicit stills here in the 1850s than in the rest of the country put together.

319

Old Carrick Mill Gin and Distillery

Derrylavan, County Monaghan
Distillery

ESSENTIAL INFORMATION

Key botanicals (Old Carrick Mill Gin):
juniper, cucumber, pear, black tea

Output: 10,000 bottles a year

Location: Derrylavan, Carrickmacross

Telephone: 0871 034890

Email: oldcarrickmill@gmail.com

Website: www.oldcarrickmill.ie

Facebook: www.facebook.com/
   oldcarrickmill

Instagram: @old_carrick_mill

Twitter: @OldCarrickMill

Opening hours: not open to the public

Other reasons to go: Riverwatch Aquarium,
Guildhall, Tower Museum, Peace Bridge

"I have a long love of the magic of the spirits industry," says Old Carrick's founder Steven Murphy. "It's the way distillers turn a simple grain into something with such depth and flavour."

He watched the rise of the craft beer movement for several years, wondering if craft gin would have the same popularity. By 2014, he reckoned it would, and booked into a distilling course in Seattle, on the NW coast of the USA. He got his distilling licence in 2016 and, using a still designed by himself, became the first new distiller in Co. Monaghan for 157 years.

He operates from the site of a former flour mill outside Carrickmacross, whose once-owners are now wine growers of some repute near Bordeaux. He has visited their vineyard, Chateau Magnol, with happy results – see below.

Steven's aim was a gin with depth and smoothness that could stand out from the many citrus and spice-led craft gins crowding the market. He played down the most common citrus botanicals – lemon, lime and grapefruit – replacing them with pear, cucumber and black tea. The resulting aroma is well balanced, making it hard to pick out a single flavour; the taste opens with juniper and finishes with pear, cucumber and black tea. Steven lets the gin (left) rest before bottling, believing it's better the next day "like a good stew."

Chateau Magnol? The former mill owners, happy to see their mill in safe hands, and put to creative use, gave Steven 50 barrels they'd been using to age their best wines. The barrels are now at Old Carrick Mill, used for maturing the whisky Steven also distils.

OTHER CRAFT GIN BARS AND DISTILLERIES

These bars and distilleries weren't quite right for the main section. Either they don't currently welcome visitors, they opened too close to publication, or we were unsure of their quality.

Esker Spirits Gin and Distillery, Aboyne
Kincardine Estate, Kincardine O'Neil, Aboyne, Aberdeenshire, AB34 5AD
Founded in October 2015 by husband and wife team Steven and Lynne Duthie, Esker claims to be the first gin distillery in Royal Deeside, Aberdeenshire. Their main product, Esker Gin, is produced in copper stills, using more than 12 botanicals including silver birch sap. In 2017, Esker launched their second product, Honey Spiced Gin, and as we went to press their latest release was a minty gin, Silverglas.

Brennan's Old House Irish Gin, Ballinakill
Brennan's Old House, Aughnactoss, Ballinakill, County Laois, Ireland
Named after the thatched Irish farmhouse in which it's made, Brennan's Old House Gin was created by Brian Brennan and Carla Taylor. The team met in 2011 through Carla's daughter who was working for Brian in a fish pedicure business in Kilkenny. They started discussing business ideas and landed on spirit production. Old Brennan's Gin was launched in late 2016, using botanicals from the cottage grounds including heather, corn and bilberries.

The Gin Vault, Birmingham
16 Gas Street, Birmingham, West Midlands, B1 2DS
This bar can be found in Birmingham's canal area and offers more than 350 gins, plus gin experiences. The Gin Experience includes a gin cocktail, a three-gin paddle (sample) board, plus tapas and dessert. They also offer a Gin Cocktail Masterclass, Afternoon G&T, and The Gin Journey, where they provide a selection of five different gins: floral, spice, botanical, dry, and sweet.

The Escape Gin Bar, Brockenhurst
Thatched Cottage Hotel, 16 Brookley Road, Brockenhurst, SO42 7RR
Escape claims to be the New Forest's only specialist gin bar, offering more than 300 different gins, including locally made Conker (page 35), Pothecary (page 40) and Twisted Nose (page 52) gins. They offer Tasting Flights where you get three different gins to compare.

Continued on next page

OTHER CRAFT GIN BARS AND DISTILLERIES

Johnsmas Gin and Orkney Gin Company, Burray
Burray, Orkney, KW17 2SS
This is a family-run operation which started with Gary and Andrea Watt making Christmas presents for friends and family. Their main product is Johnsmas Gin, made with local botanicals distilled using the bathtub method (page 168). As we went to press, their latest edition was Johannistag Navy Strength Old Tom, released in June 2019 to mark the centenary of the Scuttling of the German High Seas Fleet in Orkney's Scapa Flow. Only 1,000 bottles were produced.

Cambridge Gin Laboratory, Cambridge
10 Green Street, Cambridge, CB2 3JU
The sister establishment of Cambridge Distillery (page 161), the Gin Laboratory, has four rooms: the Classroom offers tastings and a history of gin production and you can also create your own gin recipe, if booked in advance; the Study is available for private hire; The Tasting Room offers a range of Cambridge Distillery Gins for sampling; and the Shop, where you can buy Cambridge Distillery products, and blend your own gin with no appointment necessary.

Kintyre Gin and Beinn an Tuirc Distillers, Campbeltown
Lephincorrach Farm, Torrisdale, Carradale, Campbeltown, Argyll, PA28 6QT
Kintyre Gin is made here, using 12 botanicals including Icelandic moss and sheep sorrel which grow on the estate. The gin is distilled using both maceration and the vapour infusion method (page 254) before it's cut with water from Beinn an Tuirc – the hill after which the distillery is named. Directors and brothers Niall and Kenny Macalister Hall use a hydro-electric scheme to power their copper still, Big Don, and plant a tree for every case of gin sold. They hold distillery tours which must be booked in advance (see their website – www.kintyregin.com) and future plans include a visitors' centre.

Gin with a Hint of Ginger Gin and Brennan and Brown, Cheltenham
2C Bramery Business Park, Alstone Lane, Cheltenham, GL51 8HE
Brennan and Brown was founded by Richard Bamber in 2012 after

becoming the first in a hundred years to produce a ginger flavoured gin – Gin with a Hint of Ginger. After experimenting on his still, Una, Richard took the recipe to Master of Malt who made the finishing touches to the recipe and introduced him to rotary evaporation (page 72), which is now the chosen distillation method. At first, production took place in a rotary evaporator called Gin-Of-Eve, but demand meant they had to buy two more – Heidi and Flo-Mo. The distillery has a Ginsperational Tasting Room where you can learn how gin is made and blend your own recipe. They also host tasting events.

The Wrecking Coast Gin and Distillery, Delabole
Pentire Workshops, Unit 2, High Street, Delabole, PL33 9BA
Avian Sandercock, Daniel Claughton, Steve Wharton and Craig Penn launched this distillery in 2014 after struggling to find a gin that ticked all their boxes. They wanted to capture Cornwall in a bottle and were determined to make a recipe using clotted cream. Avian steeps 12 of the botanicals in neutral grain spirit for two weeks before they are added to the still and rested for seven days. He uses the vacuum distillation method (page 53) to make a clotted cream and spirit mix, allowing it to stay cool so it isn't cooked and caramelized. This is then added to the still with the rest of the distillates before it's cut with Cornish natural spring water to 44%. They recommend serving the gin with a quality tonic, ice and a strawberry.

Celtic Whiskey Shop, Dublin
27-28 Dawson Street, Dublin 2
Don't be distracted by the name. This is Ireland's most important craft gin retail outlet – it stocks all of them, numbering more than 70 as we went to press alongside a similarly comprehensive Irish whisky selection. For enthusiasts, a must to visit when in Dublin.

It's a well-organized, nicely presented shop, an Aladdin's cave for spirit nuts, opened by Ally Alpine in 2003. It hosts regular tastings. It also incorporates Wines on the Green, Dublin's specialist wine merchants. As we went to press the most expensive item on sale was Telling 30 Year Old whisky at 1,500 euros/£1,350 a bottle but with such a large stock there are items for all pockets. Another Ally Alpine venture is the Celtic Bar & Larder which he opened in Killarney in 2016.

Continued on next page

OTHER CRAFT GIN BARS
AND DISTILLERIES

Bimber Gin and Distillery, Ealing
56 Sunbeam Road, London NW10 6JQ; info@bimber.co.uk
Darius Plazewski founded Bimber Distillery in 2015 with a focus on whisky. However, in 2016 they released Bimber Original Gin, which is dry with an earthy finish and notes of citrus and floral. They also produce London Classics, a sweeter gin, and in June 2019 they launched Da Hong Pao Tea Gin, made from organic oolong tea from China's Wuyi Mountain. All their gins are made with four times-distilled vodka infused with botanicals for 24 hours.

Mews Gin, East Horsley
East Horsley, Surrey, KT24 5DL
Father and son team Richard and Daniel Mew launched Mews Gin after two years of research and experimenting with different distillation methods and recipes. Their deadline was a family wedding in 2014, but they officially launched in 2015 after buying a 100-litre copper still called Betty. They use the vapour infusion method (page 254) to distil 11 different botanicals, including lavender and pink peppercorns as the most prominent flavours. They recommend serving the gin with a quality tonic and a wedge of lime or cucumber slice.

Silver Spear Gin, Fenagh
Smyth & O'Reilly Artisan Irish Distillers, Ballydarton House, Fenagh, Bagenalstown, County Carlow, Ireland
The microdistillery at Ballydarton House was founded by Smyth & O'Reilly Distillers in 2015 with the aim of producing artisan gin products. The building was home to John Henry Watson in the 1830s and the distillery's first product, Silver Spear Gin, was named after the award he received for skills in horsemanship against local militia in Colonial India. The gin is made with 13 different botanicals with a strong citrus and coriander flavour. Works well in a Gimlet.

Foxhole Gin, Haywards Heath
Bolney, Haywards Heath, RH17 5NB
Foxhole Spirits released their first gin, Foxhole Gin, in 2014. It's made using by-products of the English grape harvest, with which they make their

own wine before it's distilled for two days to make a grape spirit (page 69). The result is then blended with neutral spirit and the botanicals: juniper, coriander, lemon zest, liquorice root, bitter orange, and grapefruit zest. The result is a smooth, aromatic gin which works well in a Dry Martini.

They also produce Hyke Gin, flavoured with botanicals inspired by the origins of the grapes used in the gin – Africa and South America – including coriander, myrrh, and rooibos. The gins are presented in Burgundy-style wine bottles.

Brighton Gin, Hove
c/o The Urchin, 15-17 Belfast Street, Hove, BN3 3YS
This gin encapsulates all things Brighton, from the wax seal reflecting the blue-green seafront railings to the label, featuring one of the pier's arcade tickets. Brighton Gin is produced by Kathy Caton and Helen Chesshire in the city's first legal distillery, using a wheat grain spirit distilled with juniper, orange and lime peel, coriander seed and milk thistle from the South Downs. It's best served neat or with Fever-Tree tonic and a slice of orange.

Caithness Gin and Ice and Fire Distillery, Latheron
Newblack Croft, Smerral, Latheron, KW5 6DU
Iain Black was diagnosed with cancer in 2016 and wanted to work from home. He liked the town's history of spirit making and in 2018 he opened the distillery with his sister, Jacqueline. For Caithness Highland Gin, he distils a wheat grain spirit with eight botanicals including locally grown rhubarb and salmonberries. He uses pure Highland water to cut the gin to a bottle strength of 40%. He also produces Crofter's Tears, a nod to the family's crofting background, made with local purple heather.

Lilliput Gin, Lilliput
Lilliput, Dorset
Andy Woodfield founded Lilliput Dorset Gin in 2017 hoping to capture the spirit of his hometown, Lilliput in Poole. The gin is based on the classic (and traditionally sweet) London Dry formula but rosemary, basil, thyme and olive give it a savoury dimension and a Mediterranean twist which Andy claims is in keeping with the nearby Jurassic coast. These botanicals are infused separately in a grain spirit before being blended with the rest,

Continued on next page

including hand-picked juniper from Bosnia. The mixture is then distilled in a copper still in small batches. Serve the gin with plenty of ice, a premium light tonic, rosemary, a wedge of lime and a Kalamata olive.

Dancing Cows Gin, Lymington
Sadlers Farm Workshops, Lower Pennington Lane, Lymington, SO1 8AL
Head distiller Richard Barker ran a brewery in Lancashire for 11 years before deciding to move to Lymington in 2014. There, he opened a distillery in a shed and started to produce Dancing Cows Gin using botanicals from the New Forest including juniper, coriander seeds, cardamom, orange peel, sweet almonds, rowan berries, nutmeg and East Boldre blueberries. The blueberries give the gin a slightly blue tint when held to the light. He also produces New Forest Oak Aged Gin, aged in a combination of sherry cask and American oak wood chinks, and Myristica Gin, which is infused with nutmeg. The gins can be bought directly from the distillery, open Monday to Saturday from 9 am to 4.30 pm. Richard also holds distillery tours, bookable on the website (www.dancingcows.co.uk).

Sussex Hop Gin, Mayfield
Mayfield, East Sussex
James Rackham, founder of Emporia Brands and Mayfield Distilling Co., distils Sussex Hop Gin using seven botanicals plus Sussex hops. The botanicals are individually distilled then blended together in a 150-year-old copper pot still. The label depicts the local folklore of St Dunstan and the Devil: in the 10thC, Dunstan pulled the Devil by nose with blacksmith's tongs, after which the Devil flew off to cool down in the springs of Tunbridge Wells, giving them a reddish hue. James also produces two gin liqueurs, both made with Sussex Hop Gin: Lucky Horseshoe Elderflower and Peach, made with fresh elderflower, peach, quince, lemongrass, and blackcurrant; and Cuckoo Line Rhubarb and Ginger, made with fresh rhubarb and ginger.

Elemental Cornish Gin, St Columb
Trewenna Barn, Tregonetha, Cornwall TR9 6EL
Husband and wife team Jonathan and Jilly Meyer founded the Elemental Cornish Gin Distillery in 2012. Having been inspired by the popularity

of microdistilleries in London, they decided that Cornwall needed its own premium gin and Elemental Cornish Gin was launched a year later. Produced in batches of 200 bottles, it's made using the one-shot method (page 68) in a traditional copper still. Twelve botanicals including juniper, coriander seed and cassia bark are steeped in organic neutral grain spirit overnight before distillation. The heads and tails are removed before the spirit is cut with Cornish spring water from Bodin Moor to 42%. They also produce Elemental Raspberry Gin, and Apple Gin.

In 2018, Jon and Jilly received planning permission to build a larger distillery with a visitors' centre, offering distillery tours, tastings and other events. Everything would be run by solar power. To raise funds for the project, they launched a limited edition gin, Elemental Rising Tide, which they were offering as rewards to those who donated to the cause. This gin is cut to a higher than standard strength of 47%.

Teasmith Gin, Udny
Udny, Aberdeenshire, info@teasmithspirits.com
Nick and Emma Smalley had always loved gin and were encouraged by the gin craze to make their own. They spent two years researching the industry, and developing their recipe before launching Teasmith Gin in 2015.

It was inspired by the story of James Taylor, a 19thC tea planter from Aberdeenshire, who planted the first tea plantation in Sri Lanka – Teasmith Original centres around a Sri Lankan tea, Golden Tippy Orange Pekoe. They took it to Strathearn Distillery to perfect the recipe, which also includes juniper, coriander, liquorice root, grains of paradise, orange peel, and honeyberry.

All the botanicals, except the tea, are vapour infused (page 254). The tea is steeped in neutral grain spirit separately before it's blended with the rest of the botanicals, and left to rest for several days. It's then cut with water to 43%, producing around 600 bottles per batch. Nick and Emma recommend serving the gin with a quality tonic, plenty of ice and a sprig of mint.

INDEX

In this index, craft gin bars and distilleries are arranged in alpha order by name.

INDEX

See the maps on pages 18-27 for locations

INDEX

OTHER DUNCAN PETERSEN GUIDES

Charming Small Hotel Guides

Austria, Switzerland & The Alps

Britain & Ireland

France

Germany

Italy

Spain

On Foot Guides

Paris Walks

New York Walks

Venice Walks

Prague Walks

Rome Walks

Florence Walks

Boxed walking guides

Great Pub, Great Walk

Weekend Walks

Lake District Walks

London and the South East

Walker's Britain

Cycle Escapes London

Cyclist's Britain

Walker's Scotland

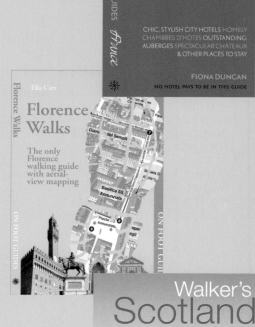

PICTURE CREDITS